Especially for

....

From

....

Date

....

Daily Wisdom for Women

2021

Devotional Collection

BARBOUR BOOKS
An Imprint of Barbour Publishing, Inc.

Our mission is to inspire the world with the life-changing message of the Bible.

Member of the
Evangelical Christian
Publishers Association

Printed in China.

Introduction

N o matter what your problem or what your circumstances, you, a woman of faith, can always count on God and His Word to give you the upside of the situation. When you are too tired to stand, Jesus invites you to rest in Him (Matthew 11:28). When a mountain is blocking your way, Jesus tells you to move it (Matthew 17:20). When you're worried about lack in your life or the lives of loved ones, Jesus tells you God will provide (Matthew 6:25–34).

To keep you looking at and for that positive side of life, you need to "fix your thoughts on what is true, and honorable, and right, and pure, and lovely, and admirable. Think about things that are excellent and worthy of praise. Keep putting into practice all you learned and received" from those who have gone before. "Then the God of peace will be with you" (Philippians 4:8–9 NLT). Day by day, you must "set your minds and keep them set on what is above (the higher things), not on the things that are on the earth" (Colossians 3:2 AMPC).

To aid you in that endeavor, *Daily Wisdom for Women 2021* contains 365 devotions that present the positive sides of life. By attentively reading these focused-on-the-upside devotions each day, you'll be training your mind to look at and for the blessings and to find things to praise about, not rage about, in both good times and bad.

Woman of faith, welcome to 2021 and a year of fixing your mind on the Light and the brighter side of life.

The Seed of Doubt

*Now the serpent was more subtle and crafty than any
living creature of the field which the Lord God had made.
And he [Satan] said to the woman, Can it really be that God
has said, You shall not eat from every tree of the garden?*

GENESIS 3:1 AMPC*

❦

And just like that, doubt entered the world. The enemy slithered in search of mankind, hoping to undo all that God had done. Eve was his first victim as he crafted confusion in her heart and mind with one question, *Can it really be?*

That question continues to haunt us today, still creating uncertainty and breeding reservation. It conditions you to mistrust others, destroying relationships in your life. It causes you to be skeptical of motives, building an impenetrable wall of suspicion and skepticism. And at the end of the day, it leaves you without joy or peace.

You have an enemy who's always looking for opportunities to ask those doubt-provoking questions. But you also have an all-powerful God who can silence them with His love, wisdom, confidence, and courage. All you have to do is ask for His help.

The Lord always wins. Doubt may be something you grapple with from time to time, but it doesn't have to have the last word.

> *Lord, thank You for being a voice of truth in my life.
> Help me remember to ask You for help when doubt
> creeps in. With You, I know I can live in confidence!*

A 365-Day Genesis to Revelation Bible Reading Plan that follows each devotion can be found at the back of this book.

Choose to Be Different

But Noah was different. GOD liked what he saw in Noah.
GENESIS 6:8 MSG

M uch like today, earth in Noah's time was a hot mess. It was full of every wicked thing, and humankind chose evil on a regular basis. As a matter of fact, the world was so out of control the Word says God *regretted* its creation (Genesis 6:6–7).

Knowing God's patience and love, imagine how terrible things must have been for Him to see no other choice but to destroy the very creation He found to be *very good* just a few chapters earlier.

Yet in the midst of the terrible, wicked world. . .there was Noah. He stood out from everyone else, and God saw things in him that made Him smile. And because of Noah's character and morality, his life was protected.

What if you decided to follow in Noah's footsteps, choosing to live in such a way that God sees you as a bright spot in your family and community? What if you decided to take a hard stand for what you know is right even if it's the unpopular stance? What if you lived each day for the Lord, spending time in His Word and walking it out?

Be different, brave one. The world needs to know there's a better way.

Lord, I am choosing to stand up for truth in a world that has its own version. Give me the courage to make smart choices and encourage others to do the same.

No Room for Guilt

They came to Noah and to the ship in pairs—everything and anything that had the breath of life in it, male and female of every creature came just as God had commanded Noah. Then GOD shut the door behind him.

GENESIS 7:16 MSG

Can you imagine the weight that must have immediately lifted off Noah's shoulders when it was God who closed the ark's door behind him? There was no opportunity for him to second guess himself, wondering if he should have done more. He didn't have to worry about offering space to his neighbors or others as the waters began to rise. Noah didn't have to battle any anxiety about closing the door too early, wondering if others would have been saved too had he given it five more minutes.

There was room for every kind of male and female animal. There was room for Noah and his family. But God made sure there was no room for guilt.

What role does guilt play in your life? Sometimes guilt is the Holy Spirit's conviction to help us make better choices, but other times guilt is nothing more than condemnation from the enemy. It's the kind of guilt that leaves you feeling horrible, and it isn't from God.

You don't have to live in guilt any longer. With God's help, you can live in freedom with a God-given grace to embrace your imperfections.

Lord, help me remember there's no room for condemnation in my life. What a gift!

You Are Who You Hang With

*Abram settled in the land of Canaan, while Lot settled among
the cities of the valley and moved his tent as far as Sodom.*
GENESIS 13:12 ESV

L ot was playing with fire. He left the company of his God-fearing uncle and chose to pitch a tent right next to one of the most blatantly sinful cities. The people in Sodom had turned away from God and were living for themselves, steeped in wickedness and every kind of evil. And by choosing to spend time right next door to them and their ways of living, Lot was setting himself up for a huge moral compromise.

The truth is that you often pick up the good and bad characteristics of those you spend the most time with.

Who are your people? Think about those you hang out with the most. Maybe it's your small group from church or your running group. It could be a group you graduated with or your neighbors. These are the ones who have the most influence over what you do and how you live. Do they motivate you to live and love well or compromise what you know is right?

You are brave and brilliant. Be sure to choose your tribe using both those attributes. Doing so could make all the difference.

*Lord, do I need to make changes in who I spend time with?
Are there negative influences I'm not seeing? Help me surround
myself with those who live with love and wisdom.*

God Sees You

*She answered GOD by name, praying to the God
who spoke to her, "You're the God who sees me!
Yes! He saw me; and then I saw him!"*

GENESIS 16:13 MSG

As women, we have an innate need to be seen. There's a deep desire inside where we want others to know us—to know those things that help us and hurt us. Even more, we want others to *want* to know! It's about being pursued and appreciated. It's about being worth the time and effort of others. It's about being important enough for someone to want to learn us—learn what matters most to our heart.

While you may crave that from those around you, it's important to remember that God already knows you better than you know yourself. He's your Creator, and He has firsthand knowledge of what makes you tick. He understands what delights your heart and has knowledge of what hurts it. God knows everything there is to know about you.

That means you are fully known and fully seen right now. Your heart's desire for that kind of intimacy has been met. And even more, your heavenly Father is crazy about you.

The next time you feel unloved or unwanted, remember that God sees you and loves you willingly and completely.

*Lord, thank You for caring enough to not only know
my deep desires to be seen and known, but to do so
fully. No one could do it any better.*

Don't Look Back

But Lot's wife looked back and turned into a pillar of salt.
GENESIS 19:26 MSG

As they fled the city, she turned back to see it one last time. Lot's wife knew the command to keep their eyes facing the direction they were going—away from the sinful city of Sodom—but something made her turn around. Maybe she longed for her friends or her home. Maybe she was curious about what was happening. Or maybe she realized she'd left something behind.

While it may be easy to decide it's time to walk away from your own sinful places, actually *doing* it is another thing altogether. Talk is often cheap, and chances are you've grown accustomed to compromise. Turning away from it can feel like abandoning an old friend or leaving a place of comfort and security.

When God asks you to let go of something—be it a bad relationship, a dangerous addiction, the hold of unforgiveness, a negative influence, or some other unhealthy person, posture, or place—what's your reaction? God loves you so much, and He wants you to experience freedom in Him—something that can't happen when you're continually glancing back.

Choose to keep your eyes on God, willing to follow wherever He leads.

Lord, I don't want to settle for the wrong things. I don't want to compromise what I know is Your will. Instead, help me find contentment in a relationship with You that meets my every need.

Obedience on Steroids

*When they reached the place God had told him
about, Abraham built an altar there and arranged
the wood on it. He bound his son Isaac and laid him
on the altar, on top of the wood.*

GENESIS 22:9 NIV

A braham agreed to sacrifice the son he had waited for years to have—the one God promised to him. He was willing to give up his child, his own flesh and blood. This pillar of the faith knew the anger and disappointment he'd inevitably face from his wife, Sarah, yet he chose to follow God's command.

Abraham made the hard decision to say yes to God, even though His plan made no sense in the natural. Truth is, he didn't care. God asked it and that was all that mattered to Abraham.

Can you remember a time God asked something of you that felt overwhelming? Maybe it was volunteering or taking a new job. Maybe it was following a strict budget or diet. Maybe it was speaking up or stepping out. Maybe it was giving up something unhealthy.

Saying yes matters to God. His magnificent plan for your life requires your radical obedience not your full comprehension. What is He asking of you right now?

*Lord, help me be like Abraham, willing to do what You
ask without questions or tantrums. I trust You, and I
know everything You do is for my benefit and Your glory.
Give me the guts and grit to always say yes—to You!*

The Manipulation Game

*Isaac said, "Come close, son; let me
touch you—are you really my son Esau?"*
Genesis 27:21 MSG

While his mother, Rebekah, suggested the deceitful scheme. . .it was Isaac who agreed to the manipulation game and walked it out. He'd already taken the birthright away from his brother, Esau. Now, Isaac wanted Esau's blessing. So, in a devious plan, Isaac and his mother fooled his father, Jacob, into believing he was Esau. And the blessing was given to the wrong son.

As women, we're very influential in the lives of those around us. Some of it just comes naturally. We find creative ways to make our kids obey and act extra-loving to our husband when we want him to agree to something. We try to sway friends to side with us by sharing our version of the story and hope to win others over by using our charm or flexing our competent, can-do attitude. But at the end of the day, it's manipulation.

What are some ways you try to control the outcomes, endings, and responses of those around you? Are your motives pure? Ask God to help you be a lover of others, and always treat them with respect and honor.

Lord, I don't want to misuse my influence and ideas. I don't want to be the kind of woman who manipulates others for my benefit. Would You give me the wisdom and discernment to know when I am mishandling my hopes through insincerity?

Work for What You Love

And Jacob loved Rachel; so he said, I will work for you
for seven years for Rachel your younger daughter.
GENESIS 29:18 AMPC

Isaac was smitten with Rachel. He knew exactly what he wanted! And it was that love for her and desire for marriage that gave him motivation to work for seven years to earn the privilege of being her husband. Isaac wasn't afraid of putting forth the effort to get what his heart desired.

In the same vein, there's something sweet to be said about working toward your own goals. There's no doubt hard work pays off. And when you've given it all you've got and end up getting the prize, it's such a satisfying feeling.

Even more, God knows your heart's desire. And if you ask and it's in His will for you, He'll give you everything you need as you work toward it. You don't have to go it alone, friend. You don't have to muster your own strength or find your own wisdom. You don't have to make everything come together perfectly. All you have to do is bathe your heart's desire in prayer, take the next right step, and invite God into the journey with you.

Lord, I don't want to be afraid to work for what I
love. And I don't want to take it all on myself, feeling
pressure to be my own savior of sorts. I know You'll
give me what I need to reach my goals.

God Sees It All

"And He said, 'Look up and see: all the males that are
mating with the flocks are streaked, spotted, and speckled,
for I have seen all that Laban has been doing to you.'"

GENESIS 31:12 HCSB

How refreshing to know God sees everything others have done and are doing to you. You may be suffering in silence—afraid to tell others—but nothing misses God's eye. That means He sees the mean-spiritedness and gossip. He sees the rejection and abandonment. God sees it when people try to lead you astray or lie to your face. He sees the betrayal you're walking through as well as the hurtful words spoken to you.

He is a safe place to hide. God is your tower and refuge, a place where you can be protected. He always cares about and for you, and He is the One who will give you the courage and confidence needed to take the next right step.

Think about who or what is challenging you today. Where are you suffering alone? Who is taking advantage of you? Where are you feeling overwhelmed? Trust that God sees every second of these moments and that He's ready, willing, and able to help.

Lord, it's so comforting to know You're always with me. Sometimes
I forget, and I try to endure the hard moments and seasons all
by myself. Would You remind me that You see everything and
that You love me enough to engage when I need You?

Radical Forgiveness

*But Esau ran up and embraced him, held him
tight and kissed him. And they both wept.*
GENESIS 33:4 MSG

❧❧❧

J acob had every reason to be afraid for his life and the life of his family. He was a real stinker to his only brother—the brother whose blessing he stole right out from under him. His manipulation and greed forever changed the trajectory of Esau's life, so being terrified of his wrath was completely justified. But it never materialized.

Can you think of someone who has hurt you so deeply, and you're holding on to unforgiveness? Maybe she betrayed you or rejected you. Maybe she walked away when you needed her help the most, deciding you weren't worth her time or effort. Maybe he sat in judgment of you. Maybe he has been found untrustworthy. While you may have every good reason to stay offended, maybe God included the story of Esau's radical forgiveness in the Bible for a time such as this.

This brother ran up to, embraced, helped, kissed, and wept with the one who probably hurt him the most in life. And his choice allowed him to live free from the prison of unforgiveness—a place that only hurts its residents. Choose to forgive, knowing it will usher in freedom!

*Lord, I don't want to let unforgiveness keep me from living
with joy and peace. Instead, I want to be a radical forgiver
because I know it will make for a more fulfilling life.*

The God Who Answers

Then let us arise and go up to Bethel, and I will make
there an altar to God Who answered me in the day
of my distress and was with me wherever I went.

GENESIS 35:3 AMPC

God promises to answer your prayers. But here's where that promise gets tricky. He doesn't always answer them the way you may want them answered, and He rarely answers them in the same timeframe you want them answered. God's ways are not your ways, and His thoughts are not yours either.

That means, when you pray and ask God for answers, you must surrender your ideas and trust the provision He's made for your life. You have to let God be God. Hard to do? Yes! But the Word says His plans for you are filled with hope for a future that will help you become more like Christ. And at the end of the day, isn't that the goal of your life anyway?

Friend, you can confidently and fully trust that God's responses to your prayer requests are always for the very best. Even more, His timing will always be perfect. Remember this especially in those moments when God answers in ways you never expected or planned for.

Lord, thank You for being a God who answers me.
Help me trust Your will and ways and Your timing.
You've never let me down, and I know You won't start now!

The Nasty Beast of Jealousy

But when his brothers saw that their father loved [Joseph]
more than all of his brothers, they hated him and could not say,
Peace [in friendly greeting] to him or speak peaceably to him.
GENESIS 37:4 AMPC

J ealousy is a nasty beast that relentlessly hunts you down. It hides around every corner, lurks in the shadows, and is ready to pounce when you least expect it. It points out all the things you don't have. Jealousy tells you you're not good enough. And it whispers ways life could be better *if* you had what others had.

When you're jealous, it brings out the worst in you and bleeds into your relationships. It steals your joy and peace and creates disharmony in your heart.

If you read Genesis 37, you'll see the story of envy unfold, and you'll see how it unraveled a family. Joseph's brothers were so envious of the coat their father gave him, it got the best of them. From your own experience, what do you think that lavish gift spoke into the hearts of his siblings?

Think about it. Is jealousy something you struggle with? We all have those pangs of covetousness from time to time. Everyone feels greed and bitterness in life. But if jealousy is robbing you of living and loving well, talk to God about it. He'll help you get the right perspective—His!

Lord, I don't want jealousy to have any control
in my life. Help me see my blessings!

Keep Asking

*You shall have charge over my house, and all my
people shall be governed according to your word [with
reverence, submission, and obedience]. Only in matters
of the throne will I be greater than you are.*

Genesis 41:40 ampc

And just like that, Joseph went from a prisoner to second in command in Egypt. Talk about an immediate promotion! One minute he was in jail for a crime he didn't commit, and the next Joseph is interpreting a dream for the king and is elevated to Pharaoh's number two. For years Joseph had been praying and hoping for his situation to change, and when God's plan called for a move. . .a move happened.

Let this encourage you! Sometimes it's hard to continue praying for God's intervention over and over and over again. Our perseverance peters out. We worry He may grow tired of our request, or we give up altogether because we think His answer is a firm *no*. But the truth is that it's not yet time for the next right step.

It's hard to understand God's timing, so we have to choose to trust it because God is God and we are not. Yet we need not grow weary of asking, for we won't wear God out. And we'll have peace if we live our lives knowing that when it *is* the right time, God's answers *will* come.

*Lord, I want Your timing over mine any day.
Please give me perseverance to keep asking and
patience to wait for Your perfectly timed answer!*

The Prison of Paranoia

But Benjamin, Joseph's [full] brother,
Jacob did not send with his brothers; for he said,
Lest perhaps some harm or injury should befall him.

GENESIS 42:4 AMPC

D ad was scared to send his youngest to Egypt with the older brother. Benjamin was the baby of the family and loved by all. And after the supposed death of his favorite son, Joseph, Jacob was too paranoid something might happen to Benjamin as well. He knew his aging heart just couldn't handle the loss of his beloved Rachel's second son, so he kept Ben home safe with him.

Too often, we live our lives like this—afraid that bad events will happen. That mind-set keeps us from branching out and trying new things. It makes us second-guess our plans or cancel them altogether. It breeds distrust in relationships, prompting us to obsess over all that could go wrong. Fear traps us and robs us of joy and peace.

While it's wise to be aware, it's foolish to let worry take control, because it will always point to horrible outcomes and endings. It will point to the worst-case scenario. And if you choose to live here, your life will be wasted on *what ifs*.

Give your fears to God. Ask Him to replace them with faith.

Lord, living in a place of fear is a dead-end street and one
road I don't want to travel. Will You give me courage and
confidence to trust You instead? Help me be brave!

An Anointed Assessment

But now, do not be distressed and disheartened or vexed
and angry with yourselves because you sold me here,
for God sent me ahead of you to preserve life.

GENESIS 45:5 AMPC

Joseph saw the big picture. After all the heartache and betrayal, after every up and down, in spite of every tumultuous twist and turn throughout his life, this man was able to see his Creator's hand in it all.

Perspective is a beautiful gift from above. It allows you to make sense of the crazy. It has the ability to answer your *why me* questions. It gives you a peek into God's plan for your life. And it helps to settle your heart, which has been struggling to understand.

Where do you need divine perspective right now? Maybe it's in a relationship that's falling apart or finances that are failing. It could be a child who's making horrible choices or a career that feels like a dead-end. Maybe you're just tired of trying to hold everyone and everything together, wrestling with discouragement as you wait for a response from God.

Friend, we all have seasons and moments that need an anointed assessment from time to time. Ask God for perspective, then ask for an extra measure of faith to trust Him through it.

Lord, sometimes I just need a peek deeper into my situation
to help settle my heart. If it's Your will, would You give
me that? If not, would You help me trust Your plan?

The Beauty of Restoration

Joseph had his chariot made ready and went to Goshen to meet his father Israel. As soon as Joseph appeared before him, he threw his arms around his father and wept for a long time.

Genesis 46:29 NIV

W hat a beautiful picture of a father and son reconnecting after so many years apart. Regardless of the circumstances surrounding how they got there, no matter what factors kept them apart, they found one another, and the reunion was breathtaking.

There are many reasons we disconnect from family or friends. Sometimes it's what needs to happen because a relationship is unhealthy. Other times we walk away offended and want to make a statement. There are people who exhaust us by inviting drama into our lives or throwing pity parties. And sometimes it's the miles apart that become the biggest factor for a severed or strained relationship. Yes, there are many reasons that can make doing life with someone difficult or impossible.

Yet when God brings restoration, it's magical. He softens hearts, shortens distances, heals hurts, and changes attitudes so we're able to embrace one another again.

Is there someone you're wanting to reconnect with? Are you hoping for a reunion with someone once dear to you? Pray for God to make it possible.

Lord, my heart aches for reconciliation. I want to work through the issues and have a relationship with that person. I know this is something only You can make happen. Would You do that for me?

Plans for Good

> *"Don't you see, you planned evil against me but God
> used those same plans for my good, as you see all
> around you right now—life for many people."*
>
> GENESIS 50:20 MSG

Joseph made a powerful statement in today's scripture reading. It takes great maturity to see his life through spiritual eyes, able to see God's plan through his messy life. It reveals his complete surrender to God's will above his own desires. And it's a great example for us today.

Think about tough situations you've walked through. Maybe you're in one right now. Take inventory of the spine-weakening and spirit-breaking situations and how they've challenged your peace and joy. Are those what you focus on the most? Do they determine your mood and attitude? Are you angry? Are you trying to control and manipulate these circumstances to your favor?

If you responded like Joseph, you'd choose to trust that God allowed these trials only for your benefit and His glory. You would choose to believe He is always in the driver's seat. You'd adopt a position of surrender and activate your faith in God's will and ways. And at the end of the day, no matter how messy it was, you'd embrace the truth that He will use everything planned for evil. . .for good.

God has you, sister. He sees you. He loves you. And He's protective of His girl.

*Lord, please give me spiritual eyes to
see Your good over the world's evil every time.*

Blessing for Obedience

And because the midwives honored God,
God gave them families of their own.
EXODUS 1:21 MSG

᪥

The Egyptian king asked the midwives to do the impossible. He wanted every son born to an Israelite woman to be killed at birth. The girls could live, but the boys couldn't. His scheme was hatched from the fear of the growing number of Israelites. He was afraid they'd rise up with Egypt's enemies or walk away and abandon his people if war broke out.

These midwives—Israelites themselves—didn't follow orders. No baby boys were killed. They risked their lives to protect their countrymen. And God saw it all.

It's not always easy to stand up for what's right, especially when a threat's involved. From losing your job to compromising a friendship to risking your reputation, taking a hard stand for true and right isn't often convenient or simple. It takes guts and grit to hold the line so many others cross without consideration. But when you do the hard thing and follow God's way, He will not only see it but promises to bless your obedience.

What keeps you from doing the things you know will please God?

Ask God for courage. Ask Him to make you brave. Ask for wisdom. And rest knowing that if God is asking something from you, He'll give you everything you need to walk it out.

Lord, give me confidence to stand for what's true and
pleasing to You rather than take the easy way out.

The Tangle of Insecurity

*Moses objected, "They won't trust me. They won't listen to a word
I say. They're going to say, 'GOD? Appear to him? Hardly!'"*
EXODUS 4:1 MSG

M oses is one of the most insecure characters in the Bible. He lacked confidence in himself and his abilities, which makes him one of the most relatable characters as well. The truth is that insecurity is something that knits us together as women.

We all struggle to feel good enough in a world with impossibly high standards. Every day, we're bombarded with messages through social media that remind us we're *less than* others. Be it someone's epic vacation, flawless family picture, career promotion, holiday party, or diet success, we're left feeling unsuccessful, unwanted, and insignificant.

So, when amazing opportunities come along, we just don't have the self-confidence needed to embrace them. Like Moses, we come up with excuses as to why we can't.

Woman, God didn't make a mistake when He made you. He knew exactly what He was doing. He created you with specific gifts and talents that would bless others and benefit your community. He put you together with intentionality from head to toe. He decided details like where you'd live, the jobs you'd have, the money you'd make, and the friends you'd have. And in God's eyes, you are complete and perfect.

There is nothing *less than* about you.

*Lord, please untangle me from insecurity and
remind me of who I am because of You.*

The Hardened Heart

But the Lord hardened the heart of Pharaoh,
making it strong and obstinate, and he did not listen
to them or heed them, just as the Lord had told Moses.

EXODUS 9:12 AMPC

D id you notice it was God who hardened Pharaoh's heart? So often, we're the ones to harden our own heart because we hold on to bitterness. We cling to unforgiveness. We choose to live offended, refusing to embrace peace. Even more, we proudly wear it as a badge of honor. We justify our hard heart by listing all the ways we've been wronged.

Yet other times, it's God who hardens hearts. Why do you think He'd do that? Since it always does, how could God's hardening of hearts benefit us and glorify Him?

Maybe it's because it provides an opportunity for His magnificence to be highlighted. Think about it. Have you ever seen a 180-degree positive turnaround in someone's attitude and thought *That had to be God*? Maybe He hardens hearts—be it ours or someone we love—because it forces us to learn patience and grace. It teaches us perseverance and how to love like Christ loves. And while we may not understand why He does what He does, having faith means we choose to trust Him regardless.

A hard heart has purpose, and so does the moment it becomes fleshy again. Trust God through them both.

Lord, please give me perspective so I can understand the
condition of my heart and the hearts of those I love.

And Then Some

The LORD had made the Egyptians favorably
disposed toward the people, and they gave them
what they asked for; so they plundered the Egyptians.
EXODUS 12:36 NIV

The Plague of the Firstborn was the last straw for Pharaoh. It broke him, and he finally conceded. He summoned Moses and Aaron, telling them to take the Israelites and leave Egypt. But they didn't go empty-handed.

God's instruction to His children was simple: *Ask the Egyptians to hand over their gold, silver, and clothing to take away with you.* So, they did. And because God's favor rested on them, the Egyptians—once their harsh and cruel bosses—generously handed over their riches. The Israelites' freedom wasn't enough. The Lord had more in store for His people!

Isn't that just like God? His love is lavish! Can you think of a time when His favor shined brightly on you? Maybe money showed up when you needed it most or a new job offer came out of nowhere. Maybe someone offered to fix your car for free or your child's school tuition was covered anonymously. Maybe groceries were on your doorstep after a long day of work or you walked into a spotless house, courtesy of your teenagers.

You serve a generous Father who will make sure your needs are met. . .*and then some.*

Lord, thank You for being a God of "and then some."
I am so thankful for Your kindness and generosity
toward me! I'm so grateful for Your favor!

Letting God Fight for You

*The Lord will fight for you, and you shall
hold your peace and remain at rest.*
EXODUS 14:14 AMPC

L etting God fight for us can be a tall order because we're capable women, ready and able to handle what comes our way. It may not be pretty, but we get the job done. We are moms and wives, company owners and shift managers, coaches and teachers, and everything in between. And when we're standing in God's strength and wisdom, we're a force to be reckoned with. Amen?

Yet there are times we're to let God fight for us. We're to take a step back and trust as He handles the situation. We're to wait on His timing and plan, even when it seems there's no movement whatsoever. And instead of jumping in and trying to make everything come together, we're to take a seat. We're to let God be God.

What makes that hard for you? Are you more comfortable in the driver's seat? Do you feel better when you're calling the shots? Is it easiest when you get to control all interactions and outcomes?

God is asking you to trust Him enough to surrender your game plan to His. And when you do, you'll find peace.

*Lord, I'll admit this is hard for me. I like being in control.
But I know that You are God and I am not. Will You grow
my faith so I can surrender to Your will and way?*

Just Stop Complaining

The Israelites said to them, "If only we had died by the LORD's hand in Egypt! There we sat around pots of meat and ate all the food we wanted, but you have brought us out into this desert to starve this entire assembly to death."

EXODUS 16:3 NIV

L et's put this in perspective. The Israelites, the ones enslaved to the Egyptians for four hundred years, the ones battered, beaten, and bloodied on a regular basis, were complaining about *food*. Somehow, they'd forgotten the reality of their Egypt and were whining about their grumbling tummies.

Rather than stand in gratitude for all God had done for them, they complained. They fixed their attention on what they didn't have instead of what they did. And because of that, they became self-focused and not God-focused.

Complaining is so easy to fall into, isn't it? And honestly, there's so much to complain about! Life isn't easy or fair, and we often pick up offenses and talk about them to anyone who will listen.

When you're critical and condemning, it keeps you from living in the peace of Jesus. It keeps you stirred up and unhappy, and it makes you ungrateful and difficult to be around. Although there may be times you may need to vent with someone you trust, just be careful you don't focus on the negative.

Lord, life isn't perfect, but it's good! Help me see that when my perspective is locked on the wrong things.

Who or What Is Your God?

You shall have no other gods before or besides Me.
EXODUS 20:3 AMPC

This is the first command God gave His people. It was numero uno, top of the list. And its position on the Ten Commandments wasn't by mistake. We serve a jealous God who is unmatched.

They say that whatever gets the majority of your time is your god. Think about it. Who are the gods in your own life? Netflix? Your workout routine? Instagram? Maybe you focus most on being a mom or wife, both vital and valuable pursuits but not to be placed above God. Maybe it's food or fun or friends.

God wants that number one place in your heart. He wants no one or nothing to be above Him. He wants you to include Him in your day, your struggles, your challenges, as well as your joys. God desires a robust relationship with *you*.

What are some things you can change today that will help you keep priorities in the right order? How can you reorder your to-do lists? What needs to shift on your calendar? God is eager to be your God above all else.

Lord, I am sorry that I've not always put You first. Forgive me for having other gods in my life. Sometimes my values get turned upside down, and I put my time and effort in all the wrong people, places, and practices. You are my only God. Help me live that way.

Go Ahead, Take a Break

Six days you shall do your work, but the seventh day you shall
rest and keep Sabbath, that your ox and your donkey may rest,
and the son of your bondwoman, and the alien, may be refreshed.

EXODUS 23:12 AMPC

L ife moves at ninety miles an hour. Our calendars are maxed out with everything from sports practices to work schedules to doctor visits to volunteer hours. Too often, we have to be in four places at the same time, and the pace is killing us. No wonder we're exhausted, overwhelmed, and cranky.

God created Sabbath with great intentionality. He knew we must have much-needed downtime on a regular basis to stay at our best. Even God—when creating the heavens and earth—took a break. The truth is we are not God. We simply don't have endless energy and focus. We need to be deliberate to schedule our own Sabbath because He will use it to restore us.

You may curl up and read a good book or take a hike to enjoy nature. You might sleep and make it a pajama day. You might even rock on the porch, listen to your favorite music, or get a massage.

There may be every excuse to not do it, but what if you did? And how might God bless you through it?

Lord, thank You for knowing how important it is
to take a break. It's hard to make that kind of time
for me, so I'll need Your help to make it happen.

A Standing Invitation

The LORD said to Moses, "Come up to me on the mountain and stay here, and I will give you the tablets of stone with the law and commandments I have written for their instruction."

EXODUS 24:12 NIV

God wants to spend time with you. Just like a human parent yearns to have a connection with her own child, the Lord craves a relationship with you. You may feel rejection here on earth from friends and family, but you will never experience that from your heavenly Daddy. People may make you feel unwanted, but God never will. And although you may have experienced abandonment, times when no one would stand with you, God will never forsake you.

God's invitation is a standing one. Whether it be one o'clock in the afternoon or one o'clock in the wee hours of the morning, God is available. No matter how many times you've shared your thoughts and feelings with Him before, He'll listen again for He welcomes you into His presence whenever you want and wherever you are.

What keeps you from reaching out to God? Is it a busy schedule? Do you feel like an annoyance? Is it pride? Do you think He has bigger fish to fry? Well, friend, just like He did for Moses, God is inviting you to come and spend time with Him. Will you?

Lord, You make me feel wanted and seen. Thank You for the standing invitation to spend time with You. In a world where many are too busy for me, I'm grateful You never are.

From Personal Experience

*And they shall know [from personal experience] that I am
the Lord their God, Who brought them forth out of the land of
Egypt that I might dwell among them; I am the Lord their God.*

EXODUS 29:46 AMPC

W e all have personal experiences that point to our Creator—times when we know God intervened. Take a moment to recall those moments when you knew He was the reason for your bravery, strength, wisdom, peace, or joy. Seasons you knew there was Divine intervention on your behalf. Maybe you had the motivation to forgive someone you thought was unforgivable. Or you found the ability to love someone many considered unlovable. Maybe a broken marriage was fixed or an unexplained illness healed. Or maybe your heart was filled with confidence and courage at just the right moment. Chances are you have a storehouse full of personal experiences, courtesy of your heavenly Father.

It's important to remember God has a perfect track record in your life. You need to know He is real, alive, and active today. And it's vital that you can look back and recall those times He showed up, because it reminds you that if He's done it once, He will do it again. It's called hope.

Lord, thank You for the gift of personal experiences. They are perfect reminders that You are working in my life every day. And it's those memories that help to encourage me to trust You even more.

Divine Directions

And He gave to Moses, when He had ceased communing
with him on Mount Sinai, the two tables of the Testimony,
tables of stone, written with the finger of God.
EXODUS 31:18 AMPC

God has plans for you. Before He even set out to create, He put time and effort into thinking up your life and how it would impact the world for good. He's always had a planned-out direction for your time on earth. And the best way you can discover that plan so you can walk it out well is to spend time with God.

It's in those moments reading the Bible, spending time in worship, or on your knees in prayer that God speaks. Think for a moment. Have you ever read a certain scripture and it seemed to jump off the page? Or listened to a worship song that seems to be written with you in mind? Or have you ever felt God's presence so thick while in prayer that you were overcome with emotion? That could be the Lord talking, sharing the plans He has thought up just for you.

Relationships take two beings, and a healthy one thrives when both parties talk and listen to one another. That same truth applies to your relationship with the Lord.

God does speak. Don't become too engrossed in life that you don't take the time to listen.

Lord, help me become a better listener. I want to
hear the things You have to share with me.

Have a Little Patience

When the people saw that Moses delayed to come down from the mountain, [they] gathered together to Aaron, and said to him, Up, make us gods to go before us; as for this Moses, the man who brought us up out of the land of Egypt, we do not know what has become of him.

EXODUS 32:1 AMPC

It's hard to have patience in a world that wants (and expects) everything immediately. We live in a microwave society that caters to our impatience. We hate waiting in line for coffee, can't handle a slow-loading website, and are frustrated when traffic threatens to make us late.

And while we're sometimes critical of the Israelites for their lack of trust, short memory span, and ridiculous decisions, too often we're the exact same way.

The Israelites' frustration with Moses isn't too hard to understand. They grew bored and aggravated with the amount of time he was taking, so they took matters into their own hands. Even after the divine signs and wonders they'd seen under Moses, it didn't take much for God's people to toss him aside. Being forced to wait and no longer able to handle delay, they angered the Lord.

When the answers seem to be taking longer than expected, choose to activate your faith and trust God's timing. Trust Him no matter what.

Lord, forgive my impatience. You are never late. Help me remember You are working all things for my good—in Your timing.

Your Time with God Shows

When Moses came down from Mount Sinai carrying the
two Tablets of The Testimony, he didn't know that the skin
of his face glowed because he had been speaking with GOD.

EXODUS 34:29 MSG

M oses' face literally glowed from his time with God. He was visibly marked from that experience, enough so that others could literally see it. What a powerful visual it must have been for the Israelites to look on his face and understand the profound effects spending time with the Father had.

Your face may not sparkle and shimmer after being with God; but make no mistake, your life does reflect it. It will make you a more loving wife and patient mom. You'll be a more faithful friend and trustworthy confidant. It will give you wisdom to share with others and courage to do the hard things. Investing your time with the Lord will help you become kinder, willing to extend grace and forgive others faster.

How could this investment benefit your life and relationships? What would need to change in your schedule to allow for it? And what would happen if you decided not to make room for time with God?

If your goal is to be more like Jesus and point others to Him, then be sure to make spending time with the Lord a priority.

Lord, I am sorry for not giving You the time You deserve.
Forgive my mixed-up priorities. I am committed to spending
time with You every day because I want my life to reflect it.

More Than Enough

After Moses gave an order, they sent a proclamation
throughout the camp: "Let no man or woman make anything
else as an offering for the sanctuary." So the people stopped.
The materials were sufficient for them to do all the work.
There was more than enough.

EXODUS 36:6–7 HCSB

❧

I magine what it must have been like to witness Moses leading the Israelites to build the tabernacle. He heard loud and clear from God how to construct it, who to appoint to tend it, and how to best direct His people. Exodus 36–38 contains detailed accounts of how everything was to be pieced together.

One by one the Israelites continued to bring freewill offerings to supply what was needed for tabernacle construction. At one point the craftsman for the sanctuary told Moses the people were bringing more than enough.

Sometimes the world might make you feel insignificant or less than you really are. You just might not feel like you're enough. The truth is you are more than enough to God. Instead of focusing on how to be the very best at something, focus on how to be the very best version of who God created you to be. A holy, set apart, redeemed, and secure woman of God!

Jesus, I confess I can get caught up doing more than necessary
when You just want me to let Your grace be sufficient. Help me
accept that, in Your eyes and plans, I am more than enough.

Receive the Blessing

*The Israelites had done all the work just as the LORD
had commanded Moses. Moses inspected the work
and saw that they had done it just as the LORD had
commanded. So Moses blessed them.*

EXODUS 39:42–43 NIV

❧

The Israelites and their leaders worked at completing the task God set before them. They recognized the construction of the tabernacle as a great endeavor, one they took seriously. Because of their and Moses' obedience, the Lord blessed them. And Moses' inspection and approval of the people's work provided great support and encouragement to them as well.

When you, daughter of the King, do as God commands, it might often feel laborious. Sometimes your work will be very detailed and time-consuming. Other times, it might require you to make some sacrifices. But as you keep your mind fixed and focused on your Creator, there will be blessings in store. Consider what it will feel like to finish the task or meet the goal. It might be nice to hear praises from those closest to you, those who've shown their support and affection. But most importantly, it will be wonderful to sense the Lord saying to you, "Well done!"

So, go ahead, do your work as commanded, and receive your blessing!

Abba Father, I want to receive all of the blessings that You have in store for me this side of heaven. I look forward to one day seeing You and hearing You say, "Well done, good and faithful servant!"

A Worship Offering

*Then he must remove all the sheep's fat, just as he does with the
fat of a sheep presented as a peace offering. He will burn the
fat on the altar on top of the special gifts presented to the LORD.
Through this process, the priest will purify the people from their sin,
making them right with the LORD, and they will be forgiven.*

LEVITICUS 4:35 NLT

Burnt offering. Grain offering. Peace offering. Sin offering. So many details to remember.

Perhaps the laundry list of instructions found in Leviticus 1–4 seems a bit overwhelming, daunting, and rather confusing. But if you look upward and ask God for His perspective, you'll realize that many of the Levitical rules and rituals can be translated into worship offerings. Those people in the Old Testament who cared enough to follow all of God's laws and decrees obviously loved God enough, wanted to obey Him, and took Him at His word.

Thankfully, because of what Jesus did on the cross, you don't have to follow a thousand different rules! You don't have to walk through a series of steps just to make your sins right with God. That means you can enjoy reading the book of Leviticus and worship Him with gratitude as you do so.

*Lord, I thank You that I don't have to go through a bunch of
rituals in order to be purified from my sins. Instead, I can
go to You and ask for Your forgiveness, and I do so now. . . .*

Cleansed and Rejuvenated

These are the instructions for the Whole-Burnt-Offering,
the Grain-Offering, the Absolution-Offering, the Compensation-
Offering, the Ordination-Offering, and the Peace-Offering which
GOD gave Moses at Mount Sinai on the day he commanded the People
of Israel to present their offerings to GOD in the wilderness of Sinai.
LEVITICUS 7:37–38 MSG

G od spoke to Moses so clearly, giving him very specific instructions on how each offering was to be conducted. A cleansing process that would hopefully provide peace and security for a person on the inside—mentally, emotionally, and spiritually—and on the outside, physically.

When you have made a mistake and know you need to apologize or ask for forgiveness, have you ever felt unclean figuratively? If so, imagine what it would have been like living during Old Testament times and having to follow through on these instructions to feel better.

Just like taking a shower after sweating from a hard day's work outside or other physical activity, you too can feel the cleansing of God's goodness on the inside. You too can feel as though God is showering His love over you and through you when you go to Him and confess your mistakes. Go, dear sister, and be cleansed and rejuvenated once more!

God, I'm so grateful I don't have to do anything to earn
Your forgiveness and love. Help me not look inward or
downward on my own sins. Instead, help me to look upward,
toward the freedom You provide through forgiveness.

Presence Process

*And Moses and Aaron went into the tent of meeting, and
when they came out they blessed the people, and the glory
of the LORD appeared to all the people. And fire came out
from before the LORD and consumed the burnt offering
and the pieces of fat on the altar, and when all the people
saw it, they shouted and fell on their faces.*

Leviticus 9:23–24 esv

God wanted His presence to be made known among His people,
the Israelites. But for His presence to be fully realized among His
chosen, there was a long process they had to go through.

First, Moses would hear a word (or two) from God. Then, in conjunction with Aaron's leadership, Moses and his brother carried out the
Lord's detailed plan. They communicated God's messages for building
the tabernacle and His instructions for the offering and atonement of
sins. They helped their fellow people obey and follow God so that they
might experience His forgiving presence.

Sister in Christ, continue to follow God's path. Keep looking up
and leaning into His Word, reading the Bible every day. As you remain
faithful and obedient on this straight and narrow path He has called
you to, you *will* experience His awesome presence.

*Father God, I want more of You in my life. Help me to not focus on
the sometime arduous aspects of getting closer to You. Instead,
help me remain encouraged so I can witness Your glory.*

Set Apart, Holy

I am the Lord your God; so consecrate yourselves and be holy, for I am holy; neither defile yourselves with any manner of thing that multiplies in large numbers or swarms. For I am the Lord Who brought you up out of the land of Egypt to be your God; therefore you shall be holy, for I am holy.

LEVITICUS 11:44–45 AMPC

G od once again spoke to Moses and Aaron about how He wanted the people of Israel to conduct themselves. This time the rules were around the foods they ate and how they handled themselves after childbirth.

As a woman of God, you might read these lists and find yourself expressing gratitude for the fact that you *aren't* living in Old Testament times. For you were born *after* Jesus, whose final sacrifice on the cross—an act that tore down the curtain between man and God—brought forth a new covenant, providing immediate access to your Creator.

Yet even though God doesn't require for you to live legalistically, He *still* wants you to be set apart, holy. To do so, you must be cognizant of your thoughts and your resulting actions. To start, keep your mind fixed and focused on the One who made you. Meditating on God's Word, then serving others accordingly, is a good place to start.

Lord Jesus, help me to stay focused on what You did for me on the cross. May my life reflect Yours so that others will come to know You.

A Glimpse of Grace

*And the rest of the oil that is in the priest's hand he shall put
upon the head of him that is to be cleansed, to make an atonement
for him before the LORD. And he shall offer the one of the turtledoves,
or of the young pigeons, such as he can get; even such as he is able
to get, the one for a sin offering, and the other for a burnt offering,
with the meat offering: and the priest shall make an atonement
for him that is to be cleansed before the LORD.*

LEVITICUS 14:29–31 KJV

Think back on a time you felt physically or relationally distant from God. How did you feel?

Consider those living during Old Testament times who had a disease known as leprosy. By society's standards, lepers were looked down upon, outcast, and considered unclean.

In today's reading of Leviticus 13:1–14:31, you'll get a glimpse of grace. Look closely to read words that convey that a priest was willing to look upon lepers and help make them right with God.

No matter what physical or relational ailment may be plaguing you, causing discord and division in your life, remember God loves and accepts you just as you are! His grace is ready and waiting. Simply go to Him and ask for it.

*Lord, keep my eyes and mind open to the reality that Your grace is all
around me. Thank You for loving and accepting me just as I am.*

Upside Down or Downside Up?

*" 'You must keep the Israelites separate from things that make
them unclean, so they will not die in their uncleanness for
defiling my dwelling place, which is among them.' "*

LEVITICUS 15:31 NIV

~~~

Today, it might be challenging to find the good in reading about cleansing from defiling molds and discharges that cause uncleanliness. You might think it a very upside-down approach to your daily faith walk. But, let's turn it downside up for a moment.

This topsy-turvy text has a bottom line. A big idea that God wants His daughters to be aware of. The more you entertain sin and feed temptation, the more they grow and become moldy. The more you allow yourself to live in denial of your habits, the more you become unclean. This creates separation between you and God. In turn, your ability to witness to others weakens. *And* your less-than-desirable actions shed a bad light on the church and body of believers in your community of faith.

By continuing to do what you are already doing—reading God's Word daily, praying, meditating on scripture, seeking Him more than earthly things—the more your mind will become in step with the Holy Spirit's gentle conviction and promptings.

*Holy Spirit, I invite You to fill my mind and body with Your
goodness and will for my life. Show me the things I need to
clean up and declutter so I can be pure before You and others.*

Sabbath Rest

*On that day offerings of purification will be made for you,
and you will be purified in the LORD's presence from all your
sins. It will be a Sabbath day of complete rest for you, and you
must deny yourselves. This is a permanent law for you.*

Leviticus 16:30–31 nlt

The day of atonement bore much significance and put much weight on Moses' and Aaron's shoulders, as well as on the Israelite community. Afterward, after being purified in the Lord's presence from all sins, there would be a time of rest.

As a woman of God, you too might feel like you carry a lot of weight on your shoulders. Family, work, and church responsibilities can be a lot to manage. Then there's trying to eat well, getting in daily exercise, and the list goes on and on. A woman might wonder *Where is the rest in all of that?*

The most important thing you will ever do throughout your daily routine is spend time with your heavenly Father and Creator. Without staying in line with the One who knitted you together and knows your every thought and feeling, how can you keep a good attitude through it all? You can't. But with God's help, you can.

So, take five minutes to breathe deeply and talk to God. He wants to hear from you.

*God, I come before You in need of some rest.
From the top of my head to the bottom of my
feet, please relax my body and renew me today.*

The Straight and Narrow

GOD spoke to Moses: "Speak to the congregation of Israel.
Tell them, Be holy because I, GOD, your God, am holy. Every
one of you must respect his mother and father. Keep my
Sabbaths. I am GOD, your God. Don't take up with no-god
idols. Don't make gods of cast metal. I am GOD, your God."
LEVITICUS 19:1–4 MSG

M oses continued to hear from God about how to conduct his life and how God wanted the Israelites to also conduct theirs. In essence, God was calling them to be a peculiar people. People of noble character and integrity. People defined by their identity in a God they loved, obeyed, and honored.

Throughout much of Leviticus 19 there are words that mirror the Ten Commandments. These words are sandwiched in between two other books of the Bible that communicated the original Ten Commandments (found in Exodus 20 and Deuteronomy 10). Leviticus 19 appears to be a reminder to heed God's instructions.

This straight and narrow path with God is one of sacrifice but also significance. Take an inventory of your relationship and walk with God. Where do you feel a gentle tug to get back on track and continue down the road with the Lord?

God, I want more of You in my life and less of the things
that trip me up on this straight and narrow path of faith.
In all that I say and do, in public and in private, may my
words and actions be pleasing to You.

Appointed Times

The LORD spoke to Moses: "Speak to the Israelites and tell them: These are My appointed times, the times of the LORD that you will proclaim as sacred assemblies."

LEVITICUS 23:1–2 HCSB

There are many times throughout the calendar year that may involve time off from work for vacations with family or friends, celebrating traditions, and taking time to reflect on the goodness of God in your life. These days might also be a way to honor a special person in your life, showing him or her just how much he or she means to you.

In Leviticus 23, we read about several appointed times throughout the year during which the Israelites were commanded to remember the Lord their God. For example, Passover and the festival of unleavened bread, celebration of the first harvest, the festival of the harvest, the festival of the trumpets, the day of atonement, and the day of shelters. All of these were opportunities to not do more ritualistic things but to remember God's faithfulness.

In today's culture, you too might get caught up in some special appointed times. But what is meant to be a time of joy can often seem ritualistic. Consider how to take on a different approach and perspective so that you can remember God's faithfulness to you.

Father, I can get so caught up in what needs to get done for special days during the year instead of really enjoying them. Help me take a different approach and perspective so I can truly acknowledge Your faithfulness.

Sufficient Grace

"Therefore you shall do my statutes and keep my rules and
perform them, and then you will dwell in the land securely.
The land will yield its fruit, and you will eat your fill and
dwell in it securely. And if you say, 'What shall we eat in
the seventh year, if we may not sow or gather in our crop?'
I will command my blessing on you in the sixth year, so that
it will produce a crop sufficient for three years."
LEVITICUS 25:18–21 ESV

A Sabbath year and a year of Jubilee required a lot of faith from the Israelites. While they already knew how to obey God, today's commandments (in Leviticus 25:18–21 above) meant trusting God at His word to provide the right amount of crop. For God didn't want them to sow anything, which seemed audacious. Yet He promised He would provide more than enough for His chosen people.

These words are a reminder that God's grace is sufficient enough for all of your needs. You love, serve, and obey a God who cares about your deepest needs and desires. When you worry about the things of this world, you sink into despair and rage. Yet, when you look up at God and recount His goodness, you can rest assured that everything—including you and His plans for your life—is under His control.

Heavenly Daddy, please show me You are truly in control of my life.
I want to witness more and more of Your sufficient grace.

Heads Held High

" 'I will look on you with favor and make you fruitful and
increase your numbers, and I will keep my covenant with you.
You will still be eating last year's harvest when you will have
to move it out to makeroom for the new. I will put my dwelling
place among you, and I will not abhor you. I will walk among
you and be your God, and you will be my people. I am the LORD
your God, who brought you out of Egypt so that you would no
longer be slaves to the Egyptians; I broke the bars of your yoke
and enabled you to walk with heads held high.' "

LEVITICUS 26:9–13 NIV

G od was communicating to His children their reward for being
obedient, as well as what their punishment would be for
disobedience. He reminded the Israelites of how He brought them out
of Egypt and, by doing so, freed them from the bondage of slavery. Like
an ox wearing a heavy, burdensome yoke, God broke the figurative and
literal bars of yoke right off of His people's shoulders so that they could
hold their heads high.

Precious daughter of the King, God has broken a yoke in your life
as well. Hold your head high with humility and thanksgiving for the
God who has freed you.

Jesus, what You did for me on the cross and
for my sins has freed me to be Your child.
Thank You for loving me as You do.

The Love of God

*The LORD said to Moses and Aaron: "The Israelites are to camp
around the tent of meeting some distance from it, each of them under
their standard and holding the banners of their family. . . ." So the
Israelites did everything the LORD commanded Moses; that is the
way they encamped under their standards, and that is the way
they set out, each of them with their clan and family.*

NUMBERS 2:1–2, 34 NIV

A year after the Israelites came out of Egypt, God wanted them to take a census, a count of the people He loved—the entire Israelite community. After that, He wanted the people to arrange themselves into tribal camps.

Just as God took the time to note the people He'd chosen to love, you can do the same today. On Valentine's Day, singletons, families (tribes), and communities (clans) can celebrate the love of God and their deep appreciation and affection for one another.

So, woman of God, look past the red and pink decorations, pretty cupcakes, and fanfare. Look beyond the candy hearts and long-stemmed roses. Look deep within the souls of those you care about, and consider ways you can show them the love of God today and always.

*Lord, on this day and throughout the calendar year, may I remember
Your love for me and those I care about. Help me celebrate Your love.
Then give me the ability to consistently express it, to allow Your
love to flow through me and overflow onto others.*

Work of Serving and Carrying

*So Moses and Aaron and the leaders of Israel counted all the
Levites by clan and family. All the men from thirty to fifty years
of age who came to do the work of serving and carrying the Tent
of Meeting numbered 8,580. At GOD's command through Moses,
each man was assigned his work and told what to carry. And
that's the story of their numbering, as GOD commanded Moses.*

NUMBERS 4:46–49 MSG

The duties of the Levites, Kohathites, Gershonites, and Merarites were clearly defined by God. And Moses, Aaron, and the leaders of Israel remained accountable to His commands.

Today, on Presidents' Day, the leaders who have served us in the past, those who currently serve our country, and those who will carry out responsibilities in the future are also held in high regard. They too are held accountable to the United States citizens as well as to God. Throughout the ages, there have been many examples of servant leadership, people working to carry out proper principles and regulations.

As a woman of God, you too are called into service, into leadership that involves the work of carrying out responsibilities for the greater good.

Today, pray and give thanks for all people in leadership, including those our country benefited from and for future commanders in chief.

*God, You rule and reign over all. I thank You for those who served
our nation in the past, and I pray for those of tomorrow.*

Blessed to Be a Blessing

And the Lord said to Moses, Say to Aaron and his sons, This is the
way you shall bless the Israelites. Say to them, the Lord bless you and
watch, guard, and keep you; the Lord make His face to shine upon and
enlighten you and be gracious (kind, merciful, and giving favor) to
you; the Lord lift up His [approving] countenance upon you and give
you peace (tranquility of heart and life continually). And they shall
put My name upon the Israelites, and I will bless them.
NUMBERS 6:22–27 AMPC

This priestly blessing is often recited as a benediction, a prayer used to bless others.

In Numbers, this special prayer comes right after the instructions the Lord gave Moses for purity in Israel's camp, protecting marital faithfulness, and Nazarite laws. Like many of the commands that Moses receives from the Lord, those followed through on brought blessings upon God's people.

While you don't need to perform the tasks that God gave to Moses, He does care about your heart and mind the same way He cared for those of His people long ago. God cares about your physical body and spiritual soul too. Your job is to remain obedient to His leading and purpose for service.

Jesus, keep my mind fixed and focused on You at all times
so I may be a blessing to others. In return, show me
just how blessed I am to be Your daughter.

Sacrifice to Resurrection

And all the oxen for the sacrifice of the peace offerings
were twenty and four bullocks, the rams sixty, the he
goats sixty, the lambs of the first year sixty. This was the
dedication of the altar, after that it was anointed.

NUMBERS 7:88 KJV

T he first day of Lent is today, Ash Wednesday. This begins the annual tradition of observing the forty days leading up to Easter, a time during which people might refrain from indulging in certain temptations or luxuries.

It seems appropriate to be reading Numbers 7 today, a chapter about offerings of dedication, because Lent itself carries with it a theme of offerings and dedication. When you choose to give an offering to God, such as a tithe or special gift, you are giving something back to God. And when you dedicate yourself to God, you are choosing to be in it for the long haul, even if there is a certain amount of sacrifice associated with such a decision.

Rest assured though that on the other side of giving something back to God or of dedicating your time and energy to a goal or cause, there is always an Easter. What might feel like a sacrifice or burden now will become a blessing in your life.

God, give me Your mind-set when it comes to sacrificing
something in my life. Help me to have the eyes of faith to
see that in just a little while there will be a resurrection.

Let Your Light Shine

The Lord said to Moses, "Give Aaron the following instructions:
When you set up the seven lamps in the lampstand, place
them so their light shines forward in front of the lampstand."
So Aaron did this. He set up the seven lamps so they reflected
their light forward, just as the Lord had commanded Moses.
The entire lampstand, from its base to its decorative blossoms,
was made of beaten gold. It was built according to the exact
design the Lord had shown Moses.

NUMBERS 8:1–4 NLT

From preparing the lamps, to dedicating the Levites to be set apart from the rest of the people of Israel, to the second Passover, to the fiery cloud, to the silver trumpets, to the Israelites leaving Sinai, there's a common theme: the Lord wants His people to let their light shine. Underneath all of the rules, rituals, and change, God's love for His people springs forth.

God wants you, dear precious daughter, to be set apart. He wants you to let your light shine. Like the seven lamps in the lampstand, He wants you to be unique, one of a kind. He wants to place you in situations so that your light shines forward in front of everyone to see. He wants you to blossom in your own beautiful way.

Lord, use me to be Your conduit of love. May others
not be turned away by religion but turn to You
because of what they see flowing through me.

Provisional Power

*So Moses went out and told the people what the LORD
had said. He brought together seventy of their elders and
had them stand around the tent. Then the LORD came
down in the cloud and spoke with him, and he took some
of the power of the Spirit that was on him and put it on
the seventy elders. When the Spirit rested on them, they
prophesied—but did not do so again.*

NUMBERS 11:24–25 NIV

Moses was feeling the weight on his shoulders pressing down
upon him like a ton of bricks. The people he was trying to lead
were complaining. The Israelites even started wailing over the fish they
had gotten to eat in Egypt! The complaints of the people angered God
and troubled Moses. So he went before God, not knowing what to do.
Then God told Moses to tell the people to prepare for a miracle. The
following day, the Israelites were given a provision of meat that lasted
a whole month.

This miracle wasn't the result of anyone else's power, might, or
strength. This amazing provision occurred through the power of God
alone, giving you a glimpse of what the Holy Spirit can do.

Daughter, what do you find yourself grumbling about today? Go
to God with all of your cares and concerns. He can handle them. Ask
Him to turn your mundane messes into amazing miracle moments.

*Abba Father, I need You! I need to witness more
and more of Your provisional power in my life.*

Great Grumbling

Then all the congregation raised a loud cry, and the people
wept that night. And all the people of Israel grumbled
against Moses and Aaron. The whole congregation said to
them, "Would that we had died in the land of Egypt!
Or would that we had died in this wilderness!"

NUMBERS 14:1–2 ESV

God had done great and awesome things through Moses and Aaron to benefit those they were called to lead. Unfortunately, many still wanted to go back to Egypt, where God had freed them from slavery. But, after spying, leaders Joshua and Caleb assured the people the promised land was a good place for them. Numbers 14:7–9 says:

"The land, which we passed through to spy it out, is an
exceedingly good land. If the LORD delights in us, he will bring us
into this land and give it to us, a land that flows with milk and
honey. Only do not rebel against the LORD. And do not fear the
people of the land, for they are bread for us. Their protection is
removed from them, and the LORD is with us; do not fear them."

If you find yourself grumbling at God when He is really trying to bless you, push the PAUSE button on your anger and pray with hope.

God, instead of looking down with despair, I want to look up
with hope at You. Fill me with Your divine wisdom and
perspective. Help me to walk uprightly in You.

Holy Reminders

"When you see the tassels, you will remember and obey all the commands of the LORD instead of following your own desires and defiling yourselves, as you are prone to do. The tassels will help you remember that you must obey all my commands and be holy to your God. I am the LORD your God who brought you out of the land of Egypt that I might be your God. I am the LORD your God!"

Numbers 15:39–41 NLT

God gave Moses instructions for the people of Israel to create tassels for the hems of clothing and to attach them with blue cords. These tassels were to help the people remember and obey God and His commands instead of following their own ways and desires. God wanted them to remember His ways and to be holy.

Today, you too might have holy reminders throughout your house, in your office, or wherever you spend a lot of time. These items might be the symbol of the cross, an ichthys or ichthus (a symbol that represents the profile of a fish, aka, a Jesus fish), your Bible, this devotional, a coffee cup or magnet with a scripture verse, to name a few. These items are reminders of your faith in Jesus. Instead of looking inward or downward at yourself, they will help you stay focused on a holy and awesome heavenly Father.

Jesus, thank You for holy reminders prompting me to recall all You are and do in my life.

Stop Signs

GOD said to Moses, "Return Aaron's staff to the front of
The Testimony. Keep it there as a sign to rebels. This will
put a stop to the grumbling against me and save their
lives." Moses did just as GOD commanded him.

NUMBERS 17:10–11 MSG

G od wanted to put a stop to the seemingly unceasing grumbling by His chosen people. So, He commanded Moses to get a staff, twelve in all, one from each tribe leader. And Aaron's name was to be written on the thirteenth staff, representing the tribe of Levi. The staff that sprouted—which turned out to be Aaron's—would signify the one God had chosen to minister to His people. Yet even then, despite God's clear choice in naming Aaron as the priestly leader, the people continued grumbling.

Reflect on a time when you knew God was trying to get you to change your behavior. Did you put a stop to your ungodly behavior or ignore God's promptings?

As you continue your faith walk with God, ask Him to reveal areas in your life where you need a reevaluation, change in direction, or new path, one that will lead you to the best possible destination.

Lord, help me to stay on Your straight and narrow path.
Please fully examine my heart and mind. If there is anything
within me that is not moving toward You, give me Your strength
to reconsider my route, hit the brakes, and drive down a new road.

When the Lord Speaks

"You and your brother Aaron are to speak to the rock while they watch, and it will yield its water. You will bring out water for them from the rock and provide drink for the community and their livestock."

Numbers 20:8 HCSB

The Israelites were giving Moses and Aaron a hard time for there was no water for the people to drink. Humbled by the situation, Moses and Aaron went to God. The Lord told Moses to take the staff and assemble His people. Then, he and Aaron were to speak to the rock, telling it to yield its water. But instead, Moses struck the rock twice. Water still gushed out, but not by the process God had commanded.

Afterward, the Lord told Moses and Aaron that because they didn't trust God to show His holiness in the sight of the Israelites, the brothers wouldn't be the leaders bringing Israel into the Promised Land.

When the Lord speaks, He wants you to totally trust Him in every detail, no matter how strange His request. So, if and when you find yourself doubting, humble yourself and ask for forgiveness. Then walk forward, trusting your Creator, taking Him at His word.

Lord, please forgive me for not trusting You at times. Keep my ears open to what You have spoken to me through Your Word, through the prompting of Your Holy Spirit, and through the testimonies of others. Keep my ears open, Lord, to what You're saying.

Great Lengths

And God said to Balaam, You shall not go with them;
you shall not curse the people, for they are blessed.

NUMBERS 22:12 AMPC

B alak wanted Balaam to curse Israel, but God wouldn't allow it for He loved His chosen people. So, God went to great lengths to ensure the thoughts and planned attempts of Balak and Balaam wouldn't succeed.

Precious daughter of the Most High, the same holds true for you. God loves you with an everlasting love. Although, at times, you might wonder or question Him, He loves you unconditionally. He watches over you, never sleeping nor slumbering. His ways are perfect and true.

If the same God who went to great lengths for the Israelites is the same God you follow today, to what great lengths are you willing to go to express your love and devotion to Him?

Today take some time to inventory your relationship with God. How have you seen Him come through for you? What miracles has He performed? What prayers has He answered? How can you praise Him for all that He has done and will yet do? Thank Him for being available right now, in this moment, to hear you, love you, and lavish you.

Father God, You are worthy of my praise and admiration.
Thank You for continuing to pursue me even when I forget to
look up and pursue You! Reveal to me the areas in my life
where I can worship You with praise and thanksgiving.

Commissioned Leader

*Moses spake unto the LORD, saying, Let the LORD,
the God of the spirits of all flesh, set a man over the
congregation, which may go out before them, and which
may go in before them, and which may lead them out,
and which may bring them in; that the congregation of
the LORD be not as sheep which have no shepherd.*
NUMBERS 27:15–17 KJV

M oses had been a faithful, obedient, servant to God and a leader to an at times quite challenging community of people. Now it was time for someone to succeed him.

Moses was humble in his prayers for a new leader. Interesting how he prayed that the people would not be like sheep without a shepherd, a similar description of what Jesus—the long-awaited Messiah—would one day be for all of His people (Matthew 9:36). In answer to his prayer, the Lord told Moses to lay hands on Joshua and commission him before the assembly.

Like Moses, you may be in a position of leadership or someday will be. At some point you may have to mentor and pray in a new leader. Or, conversely, perhaps you aren't a leader now, but a time may come when someone in leadership will ask *you* to step up and be obedient to the call. Either way, be faithful in praying about unique opportunities in which you may serve God and others for His glory.

*Lord, show me the ways You would
have me serve and lead others well.*

Yeast-Free?

*"On the fourteenth day of the first month the LORD's Passover
is to be held. On the fifteenth day of this month there is to be
a festival; for seven days eat bread made without yeast."*

NUMBERS 28:16–17 NIV

P assover was a sacred time for God's people, one during which they
would eat bread made without yeast—the agent that causes the
bread to rise—resulting in flat, cracker-like bread. Removing the yeast
exemplified what life needed to be like in order to let God rule and rein
in His people.

According to CompellingTruth.org's article, "How Is Unleavened
Bread Significant in the Bible?" Passover "was symbolic of the haste
with which the Israelites fled Egypt during the Exodus—they left so
quickly that the bread did not have time to rise." The article goes on to
say, "Leaven is also a symbol of sin, and the way sin spreads through
its host, affecting the entire organism. Even a small amount of leaven
is sufficient to affect an entire lump of dough, and likewise, a little sin
will affect an entire church, nation, or the whole of a person's life."

Are there ingredients in your own life that resemble yeast? You need
God's help to aid in overcoming obstacles, doing impossible things, and
turning away from sin.

Today consider areas in your life where you can eliminate the
figurative yeast. Turn to God for answers. He will honor you for doing so.

*Father, show me areas in my life that I need to
change to be a better witness for You. Give me Your
supernatural strength and ability to obey You alone.*

Faithful to the End

Then the LORD said to Moses, "On behalf of the people of Israel, take revenge on the Midianites for leading them into idolatry. After that, you will die and join your ancestors."

NUMBERS 31:1–2 NLT

Moses had been a faithful leader and example of what it meant to listen wholeheartedly to God. Yes, he had his imperfections. At times, Moses felt inadequate. Many times, he was humbled by the people he was leading. Yet he was a servant to the end. A faithful ambassador for the assembly, praying in and commissioning Joshua, the Israelites' new leader.

Here, Moses is faced with another task: to enter into war with the Midianites. Afterward, he'd be able to rest.

Has God ever brought you through a challenging season? Chances are He has. As you went through it, it most likely felt hard and overwhelming. You might have questioned God or even thrown your hands up and railed at Him, asking, "How long, Lord? When will my situation *finally* change?"

Dear sister in Christ, stay faithful until the end. Your time of rest is coming, both now here on earth and later, when you get to spend eternity with God in heaven.

Lord, help me remain faithful. When I'm in seasons of blessing and harvest, help me remember it was You who provided abundantly. When I'm in seasons that are humbling, help me remember that life is fragile and shaky, but You are stable and solid!

A Godly Inheritance

"Command the People of Israel. Tell them, When you
enter Canaan, these are the borders of the land you
are getting as an inheritance."

NUMBERS 34:1–2 MSG

God gave Moses specific instructions on how to divide the Promised Land. God loved His people and considered this land their inheritance from Him.

Yesterday's devotion asked you to think back on a season in your life that presented numerous challenges, times during which you might have nagged, railed at, or grumbled to God, perhaps the way the Israelites did. Maybe you spent hours wondering when your wanderings or wantings would end. You might have even asked God, "What are You trying to teach me in all of this? What are You doing, God? Where are You in all of this calamity and chaos?"

Yet then, as soon as the dust settled around your challenges, did you start to see blessings emerge? Did you witness a godly inheritance unfolding? Perhaps things you had been praying about for years were finally taken care of. Blessings started to blossom right before your eyes. What God promised for you in the Bible became real and apparent to you. God kept His word! In return, it's time for you to consider your words of praise to Him!

Lord, You're awesome! Thank You for the many ways You choose
to refine me for Your glory and my good. Then, when times get tough,
help me keep my eyes and mind fixed and focused on You!

Caring for Future Generations

"None of the territorial land may pass from tribe to tribe,
for all the land given to each tribe must remain within
the tribe to which it was first allotted."

NUMBERS 36:7 NLT

If you've ever read any of Jane Austen's masterpieces, you probably picked up on the fact that inheritance of land and estate was always one of the primary issues facing each family, particularly single daughters, who had no right to inherit. Keeping the land in the family was key, for the stability of the family depended on the ownership of land and home.

The same was true in ancient times, dating back to the Israelites. When God gave instructions for the allotment of territory in the Promised Land, He added a very interesting note: all of the territory given to a particular tribe must remain within that tribe. To that end, God also made a special provision for men who had only daughters. For those daughters, God commanded, "Let them marry anyone they like, as long as it is within their own ancestral tribe" (Numbers 36:6). The Lord wanted to ensure the people had stability, not just for a moment but for generations.

God cares about your future generations too. In fact, He's already made spiritual provision for them through the blood of His Son, Jesus.

Father, thank You for caring about Your children
enough to ensure our stability for this generation
and many more to come. Amen.

It's Time to Move On

*"When we were at Mount Sinai, the LORD our God said to us,
'You have stayed at this mountain long enough.'"*

DEUTERONOMY 1:6 NLT

~~~~

Traveling in a large group is never easy. If you've ever tried to take your extended family on a vacation, you understand the old expression "It's like herding cats."

Surely Moses felt this same way at times. Even under his leadership, the Israelites seemed to get confused or lost. In a sense, they froze in place. Because they were unable to move forward, they often stayed much longer than expected in any given place. The trip from Egypt to the Promised Land could have been made in weeks. Instead it took forty years. (And you think some of the people in your world are slowpokes! Can you imagine taking the Israelites to an amusement park for the day?)

What about you? Have you ever gotten stuck? Maybe grief kept you locked in place. Perhaps fear played a role in keeping you immovable. It's time to move on. You've circled that mountain long enough. Speak to it, tell it to go in Jesus' name, and then take deliberate steps forward.

*I've stayed too long at this mountain, Lord.
I need Your help to move forward. Please give
me the courage to do so now. Amen.*

There Is No Other

*"He showed you these things so you would know
that the Lord is God and there is no other."*

Deuteronomy 4:35 nlt

B efore the Israelites could possess the Promised Land, Moses decided a little chat was in order. He wanted to remind them that the point of their journey, the reason they were moving forward to a new location, was their dedication to the Lord. What would be the point of coming all that way to abandon the most important relationship of all?

Perhaps you're in the same position even now. You've got opportunities. You want to cross over into your Promised Land. Be reminded, even now, that following hard after God is far more important than following after your hopes, wishes, and dreams. They have their rightful place, of course, but what if you gained all of that only to wane in your relationship with Him?

Go. . .but go with God.

*I'm ready to cross over into my Promised Land, Lord,
but I want You to know that I'm following hard after You,
the dream-giver. For You alone are God. There is no other
I wish to follow, obey, and fashion my life after. Amen.*

Learn, Obey, and Live

Moses called all the people of Israel together and said,
"Listen carefully, Israel. Hear the decrees and regulations
I am giving you today, so you may learn them and obey them!"
DEUTERONOMY 5:1 NLT

When Moses called the people together to share the commandments God had given Him, he had one motivation—to pass on a message that would bring life and hope to the Israelites.

Some people might look at the commandments (put God first, don't commit adultery, don't steal, don't bear false witness, etc.) and think, *Whoa, God is really making things tough on me*. Yet nothing could be further from the truth. God gives His commands so that you can experience freedom and life in Him.

When you tell your children to stay away from the upstairs railing, it's to keep them from falling. Your great love propels you to give that step-away-from-the-risk rule. God's motivation is the same as yours. It is rooted in the deepest love you will ever know.

Father, I get it! Your commands protect me. They bring life.
Today I choose to obey not out of fear but out of my love for You.
Daddy God, thank You for allowing me to experience not only
freedom because of Your commands but a sense of Your great
protection of and deep love for me. Amen.

It's Not Your Goodness

*"Do not say in your heart, after the LORD your God
has thrust them out before you, 'It is because of my
righteousness that the LORD has brought me in to possess
this land,' whereas it is because of the wickedness of these
nations that the LORD is driving them out before you."*

DEUTERONOMY 9:4 ESV

It might have been easy for the Israelites to look at the Promised Land as a gift from God, given because of their goodness. (Why wouldn't they? He'd already made it clear they were His chosen people.) But Moses made sure they understood God's gift had nothing to do with their good deeds. He didn't want it to go to their heads, perhaps. Or maybe he knew their penchant for trouble. After all, they were obedient for some seasons and disobedient for others.

It's easy to let pride get in the way. Have you ever struggled with that? Perhaps you go through a season of favor and think it's a result of something you've done.

Your goodness can only take you so far, for just about the time you think you've got your act together, you're sure to stumble and fall. So, don't put that nose too high up in the air. You still have a lot of living (and learning) to do.

*Father, I want to please You with my actions,
but thank You for the reminder that I don't win
any brownie points with my good deeds. Amen.*

A Total Purge

*"When you drive out the nations that live there, you must
destroy all the places where they worship their gods—high on
the mountains, up on the hills, and under every green tree."*
DEUTERONOMY 12:2 NLT

When the Israelites took possession of the Promised Land, they were instructed to thoroughly purge the area: to drive out the people who currently lived there and to destroy all of the places where idol worship had taken place. Any semblance of wickedness had to go.

This story might not make much sense to you (or even seem fair). Maybe you're thinking, *Wow, that's not very nice to the people who already lived there.*

God knew what He was doing when He asked His children to purge their lives of any idols—and their land of any idol worshipers. And nothing has changed since that time. All around, the temptation of modern-day idols remains—money, materialistic gain, jobs, relationships, social media, Hollywood movies, and so on. These things can get in the way of your relationship with God.

Has the time come to purge the idols from your own life? Are you spending too much time playing games on your cell phone? Do you spend hours watching TV or streaming movies on your laptop? Has money become too important? If so, it might be time for an idol purge.

*Help me, Lord. I need to do inventory of the areas of
my life that are pulling me away from You. Amen.*

True Justice

"You must never twist justice or show partiality. Never accept a bribe, for bribes blind the eyes of the wise and corrupt the decisions of the godly. Let true justice prevail, so you may live and occupy the land that the LORD your God is giving you."
DEUTERONOMY 16:19–20 NLT

Why do you suppose God has always been so interested in justice—not just for His people but for the downtrodden?

From the time the Israelites entered the Promised Land until now, God's thoughts on this subject haven't changed. He doesn't abide partiality. He's not keen on seeing the down-and-out hurt by those who have ulterior motives.

Take a look at your own life. Do you show favoritism to any one person or any one thing? Are you equally just to all of the people you work with, even the people in your family or inner circle? Allow God to show you areas where you might be treating others unjustly.

And while you're at it, this would be a good time to forgive those who've treated you unfairly. Release them. Set them free. God will, in His own time, bring proper justice to all people and all situations.

Father, I want to reflect Your goodness in how I treat others—justly, fairly, and with great love. Amen.

Holy Living

*"When you enter the land the LORD your God
is giving you, be very careful not to imitate the
detestable customs of the nations living there."*

DEUTERONOMY 18:9 NLT

Monkey see, monkey do. Perhaps you remember that expression from childhood. When you hang out with the wrong people, it's easy to take on their customs, their ways. And even when you don't mean to copycat the wicked, it's far too easy to give yourself over to their ways, inch by inch, compromise by compromise.

This was true of the Israelites. They tended to settle in with other nations and absorb the culture to the detriment of their own faith. They just couldn't seem to stay on the straight and narrow, no matter how hard they tried.

God cared a great deal about this. He insisted His people set themselves apart and not imitate the current inhabitants of the Promised Land. He feels just as strong about this now as He did then.

What about you? Have you noticed that you're becoming less and less like Jesus and more and more like your coworkers, your neighbors, or your worldly friends? Take a hint from the Israelites. Acclimating to others will only compromise your faith and pull you away from the One who desires you most.

*Lord, I don't want to be an imitator of those around me.
May I shine as a light for You. Amen.*

Caring for Your Neighbors

"If you see your neighbor's ox or sheep or
goat wandering away, don't ignore your
responsibility. Take it back to its owner."
DEUTERONOMY 22:1 NLT

It's fascinating to see how God has always cared about our relationships with our neighbors. Even the "little things," like caring for our neighbor's animals, is important to the Lord. Doesn't it touch your heart to know that He cares about all of His creation?

If you're part of a neighborhood group, no doubt you've spent time helping with the search when a dog has gone missing or a stray turns up on someone's doorstep. Everyone gets involved to bring the runaways back to their owners. And it doesn't stop at finding and returning lost animals. God even wants you to return "your neighbor's. . .clothing, or anything else your neighbor loses. Don't ignore your responsibility" (Deuteronomy 22:3).

Caring about the things that concern your neighbors is easy when you love them. And isn't that at the heart of what God is saying here? Love others as you love yourself, and you'll care about the things that matter to them most.

I'm so glad You've placed people in my life who care about
me, Father. Give me the same heart toward others, I pray.

A Spirit of Generosity

"When you reap your harvest in your field and forget a sheaf in the field, you shall not go back to get it. It shall be for the sojourner, the fatherless, and the widow, that the LORD your God may bless you in all the work of your hands."

DEUTERONOMY 24:19 ESV

We see the beautiful heart of God at work in these instructions regarding the leftovers at harvest. He knew there'd be those less fortunate, so leaving the fallen bits would serve two purposes—it would feed those who needed food and would clear the fields as well.

If God cared about the foreigners, orphans, and widows in Old Testament times, it's certain He cares about them now. That's why He expects us to treat others with an extended hand, palm open, always ready to give, to meet needs.

There are so many practical ways you can help. You can donate to your local food bank, start a food pantry at your church, or help storm victims replenish their kitchens when they return home. You can make sure the homeless man on the corner has a to-go meal from a local restaurant. You can hand out donuts to your coworkers. . .just for fun. You can surprise a friend with a fruit basket.

Choose to spread your generosity with God's love leading the way.

What fun ideas, Lord! I want to be known as a woman who is generous to the core. Amen.

Faithful Obedience

"If you fully obey the LORD your God and carefully keep all his commands that I am giving you today, the LORD your God will set you high above all the nations of the world."

DEUTERONOMY 28:1 NLT

We often ask God to elevate us. We look for higher positions at work, greater favor with our bosses, even higher status with our friends. We take on positions of leadership with the Parent Teacher Organization, the garden club, the women's Bible study group. . .all sorts of things.

Oh, how we love to rise to the top. It's interesting though to think that God's elevation plan begins with our submission. Ouch. In fact, His plan hinges on one simple word: *obedience*. If you obey Him, then you free His hands to bless you.

What have you set your sights on? What area of your life are you hoping to elevate? Ask God to show you if there are any areas where you need to buckle down and obey Him. Perhaps that simple act of obedience will open the door to that next big thing.

I set my heart to obey You, Lord, not that I might be elevated, but that I might please Your heart. Show me, Lord, any areas where I need to buckle down and obey You. Amen.

He Delights in You

"The LORD your God will delight in you if you obey his
voice and keep the commands and decrees written in this
Book of Instruction, and if you turn to the LORD your
God with all your heart and soul."

DEUTERONOMY 30:10 NLT

~~~

N o doubt the Israelites were intrigued to hear that God actually took
delight in them, especially after all of their mess-ups. Like any
good father, His heart warmed at the sight of His children, no matter
how naughty they'd been. They gave Him that wonderful fuzzy feeling
that all parents get when they watch their little ones do the simplest
things. (Remember how you felt when your child took her first steps
or learned to drink from a straw?)

Did you know that God delights in You too? It's true! You bring
such joy to your Daddy-God's heart.

For some women, that might be hard to hear. . .or believe. Many
are convinced that they are a disappointment to the Lord, that their
mistakes have somehow separated them from Him. Nothing could
be further from the truth. Today and every day, turn to God and see that
He has a sparkle in His eye and hands extended. You're His daughter,
and you bring Him such joy!

I'm so glad my presence brings You joy, Daddy-God!

His Special Possession

"For the people of Israel belong to the LORD; Jacob is his special possession. He found them in a desert land, in an empty, howling wasteland. He surrounded them and watched over them; he guarded them as he would guard his own eyes."

DEUTERONOMY 32:9–10 NLT

Imagine a family heirloom—a crystal bowl that's been handed down for multiple generations. It's priceless to you. You keep it in a special place on display for all to see. When people stop by, you point it out and tell the story behind it. If you lost this special treasure, you would be devastated. If broken, you would never forgive yourself.

The Israelites were priceless to God, and so are you. He took great care, moving them from place to place. Just as you wrapped that fragile crystal bowl, He took the time to make special provision for His people. As we learn in today's verses, God surrounded His children and watched over them. He guarded them at every turn (crossing the Red Sea, fleeing from the Egyptians, and so on).

God cares just as much about you and is watching over you even now. How priceless you are to your heavenly Father!

Lord, I'm so grateful for the reminder that You see me as priceless. I am Your treasure and You are mine.

Spring Forward

Joshua then commanded the officers of Israel, "Go through the camp and tell the people to get their provisions ready. In three days you will cross the Jordan River and take possession of the land the Lord your God is giving you."

JOSHUA 1:10–11 NLT

Have you ever experienced a sense of expectation? Maybe you've waited on the arrival of a baby or anticipated an upcoming trip or cruise. Perhaps you're excited about the return of a child who's been away at college or a visit from a best friend you haven't seen for years. Regardless, you surely know what it feels like to have that sense of anticipation.

The Israelites knew this feeling well. After years of wandering in the desert, they now stood at the edge of the Promised Land. Their hearts must've been beating out of their chests as they glanced across the river at the place they'd only dreamed of.

Surely they could hardly sleep the night before their crossing. All they had dreamed of was about to come true.

God places that sense of expectation inside each of us when He's about to do something magnificent. As you "spring forward," see yourself springing into new seasons with Him.

You're up to something, Lord. I can sense it. I can't wait to see what You have on the horizon. Amen.

A Memorial

When all the people had crossed the Jordan, the LORD said to Joshua, "Now choose twelve men, one from each tribe. Tell them, 'Take twelve stones from the very place where the priests are standing in the middle of the Jordan. Carry them out and pile them up at the place where you will camp tonight.'"

JOSHUA 4:1–3 NLT

Why do you suppose God instructed the Israelites to take twelve stones from the river and place them at their campsite? Was it possible He wanted to give them a visual reminder of what He had just done?

When God has moved mightily on your part, it's easy to celebrate and then walk away and forget it. That time He healed you? How thrilled you were, and yet how quickly you moved on with life. That time He healed the marriage of your good friends? Time has passed, and few people talk about it anymore. That time He brought you through a heartbreaking loss or illness? God's help and comfort were amazing, something you told others about, yet then it became something you took for granted.

God doesn't want us to forget the miracles He's performed in our lives. The next time you witness one, picture yourself taking twelve stones and placing them at the edge of your proverbial river. That way you'll never forget.

Thank You, God, for the reminders of how You have moved in my life.

And the Walls Came Tumbling Down

*When the people heard the sound of the rams' horns,
they shouted as loud as they could. Suddenly,
the walls of Jericho collapsed, and the Israelites
charged straight into the town and captured it.*

JOSHUA 6:20 NLT

The Israelites witnessed miracle after miracle as they crossed the desert. But when they arrived at the edge of Jericho, there was still one more obstacle, and it was a doozie. The walls around the city were massive and strong. And God's plan for bringing them down was a little, well, unusual.

Joshua and the Israelites marched around the city for seven days, just as the Lord instructed. Then, when the moment was right, the ram's horn was blown, and the walls collapsed right in front of them. Amazing!

Maybe you've faced some walls in your own life. There are areas you feel are impenetrable. That job you'll never get. That marriage you'll never have. That home you'll never own. Those children you'll never raise. Perhaps it's time to march around those "nevers" a few times and blow the ram's horn. If you have faith as the Israelites did, those walls might just come tumbling down!

*Thank You for knocking down the walls in my life,
Father! Please increase my faith as, with Your help,
I march around the "nevers" in my life. Amen.*

Faith for Victory

*So Joshua went up from Gilgal, he and all the people of war
with him, and all the mighty men of valor. And the LORD
said to Joshua, "Do not fear them, for I have given them into
your hands. Not a man of them shall stand before you."*

JOSHUA 10:7–8 ESV

H appy Saint Patrick's Day! Patrick, much like Moses, entered his Promised Land (Ireland) after years away. He came to bring the Gospel message and to do away with paganism. This brave man ministered for nearly thirty years, baptizing more than 120,000 Irishmen and planting 300 churches. Wow!

Do you suppose Patrick knew he would be victorious? The Israelites often knew in advance. Whenever they were headed into a battle that God had ordained, He let them know before they ever lifted a sword that they would have the victory. That way, when things got scary, they would have the reminder of His promise, and their courage would be boosted. In today's scripture, God went so far as to say that not one of their opponents would be able to stand up to His people. Wow!

Maybe you're facing some battles. Maybe you've been given a poor diagnosis or perhaps your marriage is on the rocks. You're not as confident as Moses or St. Patrick. Can you hear God's still small voice? He's gone ahead of you and is battling on your behalf.

*I'm so glad You've given me confidence
for the battles ahead, Lord. Amen.*

There's Still Work to Be Done

When Joshua was an old man, the LORD said to him,
"You are growing old, and much land remains to be conquered."

JOSHUA 13:1 NLT

P icture Joshua. After a lifetime of living for God, after serving Moses and the Israelites and leading them across the Jordan to the land of milk and honey, Joshua was finally facing old age. Likely weary and in pain, he felt the work was behind him. But God had other ideas. He reminded Joshua about the lands yet to be conquered.

Maybe you are reaching the point in your journey where you feel your best days are behind you. You don't know what—if anything—is next. Your "glory days" were wonderful, but you're just tired. Depleted.

God still has plenty of adventure ahead for you. The work isn't done yet and neither is His plan for your goodness. Get the rest you need, but don't give up. Rise up from that bed and face new adventures, new joys.

Lord, I confess I've often felt my expiration date
has passed. Thank You for the reminder that
there are still adventures ahead. Amen.

Dwelling Together

But the tribe of Judah could not drive out the Jebusites,
who lived in the city of Jerusalem, so the Jebusites live
there among the people of Judah to this day.
Joshua 15:63 nlt

U nlike the Israelites, God hasn't called us to avoid people of different cultures and beliefs. In fact, New Testament teachings urge us to love and care for all people, regardless of their beliefs or differences.

Perhaps you're having a hard time fitting in your community because you're in the minority where your faith is concerned. Don't give up. God can surely use you to shine as a light before those who need to know Him.

Who do you need to minister to today? Do the neighborly thing. Bake some cookies and take them over. Offer to pick up groceries for someone who's homebound. Shovel a driveway of snow, rake a yard, or give someone a ride to the doctor.

Love people unconditionally and then watch as God uses you to open doors to share about your faith. It can happen if love leads the way.

You can use me to reach others with Your love, Lord,
even those who don't put their trust in You. Thank You
for the reminder that I am a light meant to reflect You.
Show me where and how to shine. Amen.

While You're Waiting

*But the descendants of Manasseh were unable
to occupy these towns because the Canaanites
were determined to stay in that region.*

JOSHUA 17:12 NLT

I t's officially the first day of spring. Maybe you live in a region where the snow hasn't started to melt yet. Or perhaps you're in a warmer climate where the leaves on the trees are already beginning to green up. Maybe flowers are peeking through in colorful array.

If you're like many, you're so excited about the change of seasons that you're already making arrangements for spring break or for the upcoming summer. You can hardly wait to set your plans in action.

Maybe you're not in a position to take that big trip like the one your neighbors are taking. And maybe you're not able to cruise the Caribbean. But while you're waiting, God can still do amazing things.

The Israelites knew what it was like to wait. Even after they entered the Promised Land, the descendants of Manasseh ran into a hitch. Surely it dashed their hopes to realize they would have to wait to occupy their portion of land. Still, they didn't give up in the waiting, and God doesn't want you to give up either. . .no matter how long it takes.

*I won't give up while I'm waiting, Lord. I'll keep the
faith no matter how things look in the natural. Amen.*

Cities of Refuge

*The following cities were designated as cities of refuge:
Kedesh of Galilee, in the hill country of Naphtali; Shechem,
in the hill country of Ephraim; and Kiriath-arba (that is,
Hebron), in the hill country of Judah.*

JOSHUA 20:7 NLT

No doubt everything felt foreign to the Israelites when they crossed over into the Promised Land. At any point, something could go wrong. (They must have been frightened at and hesitant because of all the unknown variables.) So, God designated refuge (sanctuary) cities, places of safety, healing, and recuperation. The Israelites could always run to these safe places to rest and catch their breath.

God is still in the "cities of refuge" business. When things happen that are out of your control, He provides a safety net, a place you can run to. Jesus is your safe place. He's your city of refuge, your shelter from the storm. When you're in trouble, run to Him. When you're feeling lost, race to His arms for guidance. When you're broken, confused, and unsteady on your feet, let Him be that city of refuge to undergird you.

And while you're at it, keep proclaiming the message that God is a sanctuary for all. Let love lead the way as you guide others to Him so that they too can find rest.

*Thank You for being my city of refuge, Lord.
I'm so grateful to have a place to run. Amen.*

Your Family Can Change

Joshua said to the people, "This is what the LORD, the God of Israel, says: Long ago your ancestors, including Terah, the father of Abraham and Nahor, lived beyond the Euphrates River, and they worshiped other gods. But I took your ancestor Abraham from the land beyond the Euphrates and led him into the land of Canaan. I gave him many descendants through his son Isaac."

JOSHUA 24:2–3 NLT

Maybe you've heard it said "Her grandpa was a drunk, her daddy was a drunk, she'll probably turn out to be a drunk too." Or maybe you've heard "His brothers all failed out of school. He's probably a flunky too."

People can be so cruel and judgmental, especially when looking at one's whole family. They often judge individuals based on the mistakes of others, and that's not fair.

Consider the words of Joshua to the Israelites in today's passage. He tells them where they came from (beyond the Euphrates River) and where they are now (the land of Canaan).

Perhaps it's time to remind yourself (and others) that you're not where your family once was. Those things your parents, grandparents, and siblings did? They're not yours to contend with. You're in the Promised Land now, and God is only concerned about right here, right now.

Welcome to Canaan, woman of God!

Thank You for the reminder that the sins of my family have no bearing on me, Lord! I'm free in You! Amen.

A Rescuer

*But when the people of Israel cried out to the LORD for help,
the LORD raised up a rescuer to save them. His name was
Othniel, the son of Caleb's younger brother, Kenaz. The Spirit
of the LORD came upon him, and he became Israel's judge.
He went to war against King Cushan-rishathaim of Aram,
and the LORD gave Othniel victory over him.*

JUDGES 3:9–10 NLT

God has always been in the business of rescuing people—from calamities, from each other, from illness, from breakdowns in relationships, from unforeseen weather events, from starvation, and sometimes even from themselves.

Take a look at the motivational statement at the beginning of this verse: "when the people of Israel cried out to the LORD for help." That's where it starts. God hears the cries, the prayers, the pleas of His people and raises up a rescuer.

Over two thousand years ago, God heard the cries of His people and sent His Son, Jesus, as the ultimate rescuer. He did what none of the former "gods" could do—He offered eternal rescue to all who would place their trust in Him.

Today, when you cry out to God, trust that He will hear your prayer. Know that Jesus will rescue you from whatever's coming against you. For that's His business today, tomorrow, and forever.

*Thank You for hearing the words of my prayer, Lord.
Jesus, how can I ever thank You for coming to save me? Amen.*

A Woman of Honor

Deborah, the wife of Lappidoth, was a prophet who was judging
Israel at that time. She would sit under the Palm of Deborah,
between Ramah and Bethel in the hill country of Ephraim,
and the Israelites would go to her for judgment.

JUDGES 4:4–5 NLT

Deborah wasn't just in the business of prophesying; she was well respected among the leaders of the day. The Israelites (presumably men) would go to her for judgment. They listened to her advice and acted accordingly.

Think about that for a moment. Long before the days of women's lib, long before women had the right to vote, God was already in the business of using women to speak into the lives of others.

God hasn't changed. He still uses women today. They speak into the lives of their children, friends, loved ones, and the church body. They write and teach Bible studies, direct plays, lead ministries. They manage companies, travel the globe, and impact people world-round.

What a blessing to know that God values the giftings inside of His women. What gift is He stirring in you right now?

Thank You for using women, Lord. I'm so grateful for
the gifts You've placed inside of all of us. Amen.

The "Why?" Question

*"Sir," Gideon replied, "if the LORD is with us, why has
all this happened to us? And where are all the miracles
our ancestors told us about? Didn't they say, 'The LORD
brought us up out of Egypt'? But now the LORD has
abandoned us and handed us over to the Midianites."*

JUDGES 6:13 NLT

You've heard it hundreds of times: "If God really cared, then why did this happen?" "If He really loved me, why did that happen?"

The "why" question has plagued humankind all along. We've somehow convinced ourselves that God is cruel for not rescuing us from our hard times.

Yet life is hard. That's a fact. An indisputable one. Parents lose children. Loved ones pass away unexpectedly. Injustices occur. We can cry out to the heavens, "Why, Lord?" or we can continue to trust God even during the hardest seasons.

The truth is we won't have all the answers in this life. But there's a day coming when we will, and He can heal our broken hearts in the interim.

God, the only "why" question I feel compelled to ask today is "Why did You love me so much that You sent Your only Son to die for me?" I'm humbled and grateful for You and all You've done for me, Lord. Amen.

Put Your Money Where Your Mouth Is

Then Zebul turned on him and asked, "Now where is that big mouth of yours? Wasn't it you that said, 'Who is Abimelech, and why should we be his servants?' The men you mocked are right outside the city! Go out and fight them!"

JUDGES 9:38 NLT

You hear them all the time. . .the braggers. They talk a big game—shoulders squared, jaws set, smirks on their faces. Then, when the rubber meets the road, they're nowhere to be found. Where is their courage now? They've run, with their tails tucked between their legs.

God is looking for people who will put their money where their mouths are. People of faith talk a big game too because they trust in a big God. And they don't turn and run when things get scary. Instead, they turn to Him and trust that He's got things under control.

Today, why not rehearse with a few statements of faith: "the Spirit who lives in you is greater than the spirit who lives in the world" (1 John 4:4). "I can do everything through Christ, who gives me strength" (Philippians 4:13).

When the going gets tough, believers stick around for the fight.

I'm not running, Lord! You're fighting my battles for me, and I want to stick around to see the victory!

He's Done It Before

*The LORD replied, "Did I not rescue you from the
Egyptians, the Amorites, the Ammonites, the Philistines,
the Sidonians, the Amalekites, and the Maonites? When they
oppressed you, you cried out to me for help, and I rescued you."*

JUDGES 10:11–12 NLT

How sad God must be when we walk away from the many miracles He's performed in our lives and forget them. . .and Him! That time He delivered your friend from alcohol. That time He healed your broken friendship. That time you felt sure you wouldn't get the job and yet you did.

The Israelites were in the same boat. They just couldn't seem to remember the work He had already done.

God started their journey with the ultimate miracle—Passover (which we commemorate beginning at sundown tonight). He fed them manna and quail, split the Red Sea so that they could walk through on dry land, and gave Moses a mountaintop experience unlike any other. But at the end of it all, the Israelites suffered from memory loss, responding time after time as if He'd never done anything for them at all.

Whatever you're facing in your life today, instead of giving in to defeat, make a list of the many, many times God has come through for you in the past. He did it before. . .and He'll do it again.

*May I never forget the many times You've come through
for me, God. I'm so grateful. I know You'll do it again. Amen.*

A Celebration with Friends

His father went down to the woman, and Samson prepared a feast there, for so the young men used to do. As soon as the people saw him, they brought thirty companions to be with him.

JUDGES 14:10–11 ESV

On Palm Sunday, Jesus was ushered into Jerusalem with His disciples at His side, singing and shouting His praises in front of the residents of the city. Did Jesus' followers have any idea He would give His life less than a week later? If so, would they have clung to Him a little tighter? Worshipped Him a little deeper?

Like Jesus, Samson was surrounded by his peers. Unlike the disciples, these men were strangers to him. They were "assigned" companions. They didn't know each other.

But isn't that how all relationships begin, with total strangers? Didn't the disciples come to Jesus as unknowns? Didn't your friendships start the same way?

Think of one or two of your favorite friends. Aren't you glad God brought them along when He did, how He did? Today, let those friends know how grateful you are to have them in your life.

Lord, thank You for turning strangers into friends. I love my companions! Amen.

Right in Their Eyes

In those days Israel had no king; all the people
did whatever seemed right in their own eyes.
JUDGES 17:6 NLT

During the "kingless" years, Israel decided to have a free-for-all. Because there was no one to hold them accountable, they operated under an "anything goes" mentality. (Sounds a bit like kids leaving the routine of home to go away to college, doesn't it?)

The problem is, when left to our own devices, we rarely stick with obedience or sacrifice. Instead, we seek to please ourselves. Those things we promised our parents we'd never do? We try many of them. And, after they become pleasurable to us, we do anything we can to justify them.

Take a close look at your life. Are there any areas that are out of alignment? Perhaps it's time to take those issues to the Lord, to make yourself accountable to Him once more. Admit that you've been doing what felt right in your own eyes, then submit yourself to God's will, His plan.

Father, I want to do what is right in Your eyes, not my own.
When I look to myself as the plumb line, I lose my way every time.
But You will lead and guide me in Your truth, Lord. Amen.

United as One

*Then all the Israelites were united as one man, from Dan in
the north to Beersheba in the south, including those from
across the Jordan in the land of Gilead. The entire community
assembled in the presence of the LORD at Mizpah.*

JUDGES 20:1 NLT

To walk united with your brothers and sisters in Christ is a lovely thing. Perhaps you've experienced the opposite. You've been through a church split. You've had a falling out with a good friend. Those you thought you could count on have abandoned you, and you're not sure you'll ever get back to where you were.

Today, God wants you to work on being united with those you do life with. It's not always possible (and there are relationships you should steer clear of), but as much as you are able, live at peace with those around you.

Think about Jesus during that final week of His life, leading up to the cross. He needed His disciples more than ever. And though they didn't realize how short the time was, they needed Him too.

You need your tribe. They need you. Stick with it, and trust God to mend any broken places.

*God, show me how to walk with my brothers and sisters
in a way that brings glory and honor to You. Amen.*

Where You Go, I'll Go

But Ruth replied, "Don't ask me to leave you and turn back.
Wherever you go, I will go; wherever you live, I will live.
Your people will be my people, and your God will be my
God. Wherever you die, I will die, and there I will be
buried. May the LORD punish me severely if I allow
anything but death to separate us!"
RUTH 1:16–18 NLT

Naomi and her daughters-in-law were facing a terrible dilemma. After losing her husband and two sons in Moab, she felt led to go back to Bethlehem to her people. She encouraged Ruth and Orpah to go back to their homes as well.

Orpah said she'd remain with her family, but Ruth had a different answer, likely one that surprised Naomi: "Where you go, I'll go. Where you stay, I'll stay. Your people will be my people; your God my God."

Wow. Naomi must've been shocked. Ruth was so bonded with her mother-in-law that Ruth couldn't bear the idea of separating from her.

God wants us to be as bonded to Him as Ruth was to Naomi. When He moves to the right, He wants us to move to the right. When He moves to the left. . .well, you get the point. Where He goes, we go. Where He stays, we stay.

Wherever You go, Lord, I'm going too. You might
lead me to places I've never been, but I know I
can trust You to take me there. Amen.

Provoking or Peace?

*This went on year after year. Whenever Hannah
went up to the house of the LORD, her rival provoked
her till she wept and would not eat.*

1 SAMUEL 1:7 NIV

L et's face it. Girls can be catty and cruel to one another. We've been pitted against each other for so long that if we were honest, we'd admit we often see other women as competition. This mind-set has caused us to be jealous. And in the end, we are busy rooting against others because it's just too painful to watch them win.

It's a sad reality, really.

Hannah experienced this bully-mentality herself. She wasn't able to get pregnant after years and years of trying, and her husband's other wife exploited Hannah's barrenness. While we don't know exactly how Peninnah did it, we can assume she made fun of Hannah, muttered rude comments, and pointed out her failures. And because Hannah had such favor with their husband, we can also assume Peninnah was flat-out jealous.

What might have happened had she comforted Hannah instead? What if Peninnah had affirmed Hannah's womanhood instead of degrading it?

Let's choose to be women who stand in support of one another and encourage each other through hard times. Let's not be intimidated by the successes of others, because that's usually what ignites competition to begin with. Instead, let's band together so we can live in peace.

*Lord, rather than provoke other women so I can
feel better about myself, help me promote peace.*

No Other Gods

But when they arose early the next morning, behold, Dagon had
again fallen on his face on the ground before the ark of the Lord,
and [his] head and both the palms of his hands were lying cut off
on the threshold; only the trunk of Dagon was left him.

1 SAMUEL 5:4 AMPC

Dagon was the Philistines' god. And when the stolen ark of the Lord was placed in the same room with it, the statue itself bowed to God. Not once but twice. The Philistines' god couldn't even *stand* in the presence of ours. And it scared the Philistines enough to come up with plans to return the ark to the Israelites.

The truth is there's no other god worthy of our praise and worship. Yes, there are lots of religions with their own deities, but none of them can stand up to *the* God. He requires faith in Jesus while every other god requires excessive works.

Yet let's look closer to home. We create our own gods often without even realizing it. Our calendars would reveal the things we worship— coffee dates, club sports, vacations, workouts—because they get the majority of our time. We prioritize them above our relationship with God.

Ask the Lord to help rearrange your priorities to reflect your faith. Show Him there's no other god but Him in your life.

Lord, I'm sorry I've put other things ahead of my
time with You. Help me make You my priority!

The Am I Not Kind of Insecurity

Saul said, Am I not a Benjamite, of the smallest of the tribes of Israel? And is not my family the least of all the families of the clans of Benjamin? Why then do you speak this way to me?

1 SAMUEL 9:21 AMPC

When we feel insecure, we tend to see ourselves *less than* in every way possible. Saul plays this out perfectly. In confusion, he's wondering why the prophet Samuel is treating him the way he is. Saul wants to make sure Samuel understands who he's talking to. Saul is sure the prophet has the wrong person.

Notice how Saul points out that other tribes are more important than his, how other families within the Benjamite tribe are more noble than his own. Saul's insecurity has him underestimating his worth in spades. And it triggers his "am I not?" insecurity.

When we allow ourselves to entertain it, this kind of self-doubt will keep us sidelined in life. It will stop us from trying new things. And it will make us close the door of opportunity because we don't think we're good enough. Unless we activate our faith.

God used Samuel to help Saul overcome his fears so he could step into his kingship. And God will give you the confidence you need to take your next right step, if you ask Him.

Lord, I don't want to live insecurely. Please fill me with the truth of who I am—in You!

Consider All the Things

"But be sure to fear the LORD and serve him faithfully with all your heart; consider what great things he has done for you."

1 SAMUEL 12:24 NIV

God has been your constant companion. Not only did He create you and plan your exact entrance onto the kingdom calendar, He gave you hope and a future. His love has always been there, although sometimes hard to see. But through the ups and downs of life, He's been right next to you, going before you, or carrying you.

Think about the great things God's done in your life. Can you remember the doors He opened for you, as well as all the doors He closed? What about the times money showed up unexpectedly or a bill was paid anonymously? Maybe your health battle was miraculously healed or a prodigal child came home. Have you been able to look back on a tough season of life and see why God allowed the things He did? Was a marriage restored? Did an unexpected friendship develop?

Spend some time this week considering all the wonderful ways God has impacted your life, then thank Him. Let Him know you see His fingerprints on your life. Tell God all the ways He's been an amazing Father to you!

Lord, looking back at all the things You've done for me is humbling. Forgive me for not recognizing and acknowledging Your hand in my life more. I'm going to change that.

Our Unstoppable God

And Jonathan said to his young armor-bearer, Come,
and let us go over to the garrison of these uncircumcised;
it may be that the Lord will work for us. For there is nothing
to prevent the Lord from saving by many or by few.

1 SAMUEL 14:6 AMPC

We serve a mighty God who always wins. He has been, He is, and He will always be victorious because He is above all. God's plans are perfect, and His will is wonderful. There is nothing to prevent the Lord from doing what He sees fit to do.

Nothing.

Please let that truth comfort you. The Word clearly states over and over again that God is for you, that He loves you, and that His plans for you are good! That means that if you take a wrong turn in life or have a bad season of sinning, God's plans still win. If it's His will, *it will happen*.

Talk about taking away the pressure to perform or be perfect! Friend, your job is to keep taking the next right step, developing a relationship with Him, confessing and repenting your struggles, and trusting God's power over your circumstances. He's inviting you to live in a place of rest in Him.

Let God do the heavy lifting. Activate your faith in His abilities, because, unlike you, He is unstoppable.

Lord, what a relief to know that Your will. . .will be done.
Thankfully, You're God and I am not.

Whose Opinion Matters Most?

Saul gave in and confessed, "I've sinned. I've trampled roughshod over GOD's Word and your instructions. I cared more about pleasing the people. I let them tell me what to do."
1 SAMUEL 15:24 MSG

We often fall into the same pit of pleasing others as Saul did. It's something we, as womankind, all struggle with. Rather than focus on God's hope and desire for us, we decide to follow the ideas and recommendations of others. And it gets us into trouble.

It's hard to not worry about what friends think. Your husband, who wants to see you thrive, is a great influencer on you as well. And chances are you still want to please your parents, no matter how old you get. So following God's plan often puts you in a hard place, especially when it goes against the advice of those you care about.

Ask God for courage to stand up for yourself and the decision you're committed to make, even if it goes against the well-intended guidance of others. Don't ignore Him to avoid an argument with someone else. And don't turn your back on God's will because you want someone's approval or acceptance. In the end, it's just not worth it.

God is good all the time. That means His *plans* for you are good all the time. Trust that when you're faced with a choice between Him and them.

Lord, help me live concerned only with what You want for my life. Your opinion matters most.

Declare It Out Loud

*David answered, "You come at me with sword and spear
and battle-ax. I come at you in the name of GOD-of-the-
Angel-Armies, the God of Israel's troops, whom you curse
and mock. This very day GOD is handing you over to me."*

1 SAMUEL 17:45 MSG

Goliath was a champion. He had the very best tactical training and the most advanced weaponry available. And he was huge, standing taller than anyone else on that battlefield. His protective gear was revolutionary—gear made specifically for this beast of a man. To look at him, one would've thought he had the clear advantage, which is why no Israelite had the guts to face him.

But the one thing Goliath didn't have was God.

While the entire Israeli army was losing their ever-lovin' mind over this behemoth and his daily jeers, David didn't blink an eye. He wasn't intimidated. He wasn't worried in the least. Not for one second did he consider himself the underdog. Instead, David had complete faith in the Lord. He knew the victory was his, and he was confident in that truth enough to declare it out loud for all to hear.

It's one thing to believe God will give you victory over the giants you face. It's another thing altogether to speak it.

Trust God enough to voice your faith in Him. Tell others you believe in Him. It's encouraging when you're bold enough to declare your faith in God.

Lord, I believe You. I trust You. My faith will always be in You.

Have Their Back

But Jonathan, Saul's son, delighted much in David,
and he told David, Saul my father is seeking to kill you.
Now therefore, take heed to yourself in the morning,
and stay in a secret place and hide yourself.

1 SAMUEL 19:2 AMPC

Jonathan was an amazing young man who loved his friend well. The prince, willing to risk his life to save David from harm, was fiercely protective of him. And because Jonathan's father—King Saul—didn't care for David, Jonathan had to walk the tension between being a good friend and being a good son. Not an easy task.

Yet David trusted him. He knew that no matter what, Jonathan had his back. He believed in their friendship, and that helped build confidence in it.

The relationship between these two men offers a beautiful example of what we should strive for in ours. What kind of a friend are you? Are you trustworthy? Reliable? Do your friends have to worry if their secrets are safe with you? Have you betrayed their confidence? Are you quick to ask for forgiveness as well as give it? Do they know you have their back?

One of the kindest things we can do for others is be a safe place. God built us for community, but finding a good one can be challenging. Choose to be the kind of friend you'd want for yourself.

Lord, help me be the kind of friend others can trust.
And help me find friends like that too.

Back to Prayer

So David went back to GOD in prayer. GOD said, "Get going.
Head for Keilah. I'm placing the Philistines in your hands."

1 SAMUEL 23:4 MSG

Prayer is a direct communication with God. It's how we nurture and build a relationship with our heavenly Father. No matter what situation you find yourself in, no matter whose fault it is, no matter how embarrassing it may be, no matter how many times you've already talked to Him about it, regardless of what got you to this place, God is always ready to listen. You can always go back to prayer.

Others may grow tired of hearing you unpack your feelings again, but not God. He made you to be in a relationship with Him. And while He already knows your heart and the ins and outs of the circumstances you're facing, nothing delights Him more than hearing you share your troubles with him.

God puts no limits on your sharing. He doesn't roll His eyes when "that topic" comes up again and again. He never grows weary of your requests. God wants to hear all, all the time.

What are the lies you've been believing about prayer? What are the misconceptions you've been entertaining? Do you believe God is "all ears" for you?

Woman of the Way, you are God's daughter. Because you're the daughter of the King, you can always come back to prayer.

Lord, thank You for the open invitation
to pray to You anytime, anywhere.

A Woman of Wise Advice

*And blessed be your discretion and advice, and blessed
be you who have kept me today from bloodguiltiness
and from avenging myself with my own hand.*
1 SAMUEL 25:33 AMPC

D avid had the wherewithal to see that Abigail was a wise woman married to a foolish man. Rather than seek the Lord, Nabal spoke out of turn to David's men, which almost brought certain death to his household. But Abigail knew just what to do to turn things around.

As women, we are very influential in the world around us. We're often the glue that holds families together and the ones who help point our husbands and children toward the right path. Many of us have lived enough life to speak from a place of hard-won wisdom. Even more, God has given us the Holy Spirit, who guides us to make good decisions and choices. And when we spend time with the Lord in prayer and reading His Word, we're given divine wisdom that is unmatched.

You don't have to figure everything out on your own. And you don't have to have all the answers. Wisdom comes from God, and your pressing into Him for it will help you speak with confidence.

Who are the wise ones in your life? Make sure your counsel comes from faith-filled women. Then be ready to offer the equivalent divine direction to them.

*Lord, please fill me with wisdom that comes from You.
I want to offer truth and hope with You as the source for it.*

Don't Dabble

*So Saul ordered his officials, "Find me someone who can call
up spirits so I may go and seek counsel from those spirits."
His servants said, "There's a witch at Endor."*

1 SAMUEL 28:7 MSG

Saul was playing with fire. The prophet Samuel—a trusted friend—had died. Saul had been asking God for guidance but had no response yet to his prayers. And he was wracked with fear as the Philistine army was approaching. These three factors were the perfect storm to drive him to seek guidance from the occult.

There is no good reason to look for anything from witchcraft or other pagan religions. The Word tells us there is a real enemy who wants to seek us and destroy our life. His plans for us are not good, and we are to rebuke him in the name of Jesus. God is clear in His command for us to never dabble in anything that defiles His name.

Friend, God is Lord over everything. There is none above Him and none beside Him. God alone rules the heavens and the earth, and He determines your next steps. Don't allow anything to pull you away from Him. Have faith that He loves you fully and completely. And decide today to trust God even when you don't understand His ways and will.

*Lord, I believe You're 100 percent for me and will never
leave nor forsake me. Forgive me for the times I've
doubted You. You alone I'll seek and trust.*

Strengthening Yourself in Him

*David was greatly distressed, for the men spoke of stoning
him because the souls of them all were bitterly grieved,
each man for his sons and daughters. But David encouraged
and strengthened himself in the Lord his God.*

1 SAMUEL 30:6 AMPC

Upon their return from battle, not only had David's family been kidnapped, but also the families of his men. In their grief, they blamed David and plotted his death. He had no one to help him process his own sorrow. Except God.

Have you ever navigated a tough situation alone? There are times we have to walk through the valley without anyone by our side. No one there to encourage us or share hard-won wisdom. No one available to hold our hand through the hard parts. No one around to give us a hug or sit and listen as we talk it out. Sometimes it's just us. Going solo.

Like David, it's vital we know how to strengthen ourselves in the Lord. It might consist of desperate conversations with Him. It might entail reading His Word or speaking out scriptures that remind us who He is. It might be listening to worship music or figuratively crawling into our Daddy's lap and crying those big crocodile tears.

Remember, you have everything you need to encourage and strengthen yourself in God as you walk out this hard season.

*Lord, help me learn to strengthen myself when no one is around.
I'm so thankful that You always make a way.*

It's Okay to Be Sad

They mourned and wept and fasted till evening for Saul and his son Jonathan, and for the army of the LORD and for the nation of Israel, because they had fallen by the sword.

2 SAMUEL 1:12 NIV

Sometimes we think we must be brave when the storms of life hit. We put a smile on our face as if nothing is wrong. We see sadness as weakness, and we don't want that adjective to define us.

Yet life is rough, friend. We face heartache on a regular basis. Maybe it's working through divorce, death, or disease. It could be an unexpected betrayal or a child having to suffer the natural consequences of his or her bad decisions. There are addictions, lawsuits, cross-country moves, and the loss of a job.

Life isn't fair or easy for anyone. Sorrow is something we all face. And it's okay to be sad. It's healthy to mourn. God gave you that powerful emotion to help you process upsetting situations. It's in those sad times He will help heal your heart.

But you can't live there. Life moves forward and so must you.

Embrace the sadness. Invite God into it. Ask for Him to heal your heart. And know that in time you will smile again.

Lord, it's hard for me to be honest about my sadness. I don't want to be a burden or seen as overly dramatic. Will You give me courage to feel those emotions and trust You for healing?

Living in Peace with Others

*There was a long war between the house of Saul and the
house of David. But David grew stronger and stronger,
and the house of Saul grew weaker and weaker.*

2 SAMUEL 3:1 AMPC

Have you ever been in a long war with someone? Maybe you are right now. Maybe your sister is manipulating the family and you've ended up as the black sheep. Maybe your stepson won't accept you into the family and it's affecting your marriage. Maybe in-laws are bickering and you're forced to take sides. Yep, it can get ugly.

Being at odds is a painful reality that can often have far-reaching effects that are hard to manage. The tension becomes an issue at get-togethers, making them something to avoid. And it can trickle down to other people, causing even more stress and strain.

But God wants you to be an agent for peace. It's a fruit of the Spirit you can pluck any time you need it. And while you cannot control how others respond, you can most certainly choose your response. You can speak kindly. You can be quick to extend grace. And you can refuse to hold on to offense.

When you choose to live this way, it will show others peace is possible.

*Lord, I don't want to get stuck in feuds with those I love. Life is hard
enough without adding to it. Would You help me be an agent for
peace? With Your help, let me model kindness and forgiveness.*

Worship with Abandon

When David returned home to bless his household,
Michal daughter of Saul came out to meet him and said,
"How the king of Israel has distinguished himself today,
going around half-naked in full view of the slave girls
of his servants as any vulgar fellow would!"

2 SAMUEL 6:20 NIV

Don't let anyone put a damper on your worship. However you feel led to show your love and reverence to the Lord is between you and Him, and it just doesn't matter if others don't like it. They have a right to their opinion just like you have a right to yours.

Worship with abandon. Like David, you may dance before God. You may sing with arms raised and tears streaming down your face. You might use an instrument or turn the volume up on your praise music to an epic level. Maybe you make up your own words to the song or you pray right through it. You may even sing your own song a cappella while down on your knees.

Regardless of how you do it, you have the ability and right to worship with freedom like David. You can make a joyful noise however you see fit.

Don't worry about the judgers. It's okay if they don't understand. Don't concern yourself with nay-sayers. God is worthy of your praise, and He delights to receive it from you in authentic and intentional ways.

Lord, give me the confidence to worship You my way—our way.

The Gift of Kindness

"Don't be afraid," David said to him, "for I will surely
show you kindness for the sake of your father Jonathan.
I will restore to you all the land that belonged to your
grandfather Saul, and you will always eat at my table."
2 SAMUEL 9:7 NIV

David was a fearless warrior. He was also a radical worshipper, known for dancing with abandonment in the streets. As a kid, he defeated Goliath with nothing but a slingshot, and he fought off lions and bears as he shepherded the family's flock. And this multifaceted man was also the king of Israel.

Yet it's important we see that even with all this testosterone-fueled strength and bold confidence, David was kind. And kindness is a powerful weapon.

Think of people who have been kind to you. Maybe it was a teacher or coach. It could have been a grandparent or family friend. Maybe your youth leader, neighbor, or doctor. Maybe it was a random act of kindness from a stranger that left an imprint on your heart.

In this often-harsh world, kindness means so much. Find opportunities to be generous with your words and actions. Be someone's blessing. Help put a smile on their face with a genuine compliment. Make them feel special and seen and loved. And ask God for these kinds of opportunities every day.

Lord, help me see people who need a dose of kindness.
Give me the chance to impact their day with Your goodness.

The Temptation of Lovely

One evening David arose from his couch and was walking
on the roof of the king's house, when from there he saw a
woman bathing; and she was very lovely to behold.

2 SAMUEL 11:2 AMPC

David didn't go looking to be tempted by something lovely, but it presented itself nonetheless. And when he saw the object of his desire, everything changed. He went against his morals, sinned against God, ruined a marriage, plotted a death, and found himself in a pickle.

What are the lovely things that tempt you? What do you find so irresistible that you compromise what you know is good and right? Do you struggle to stay on a healthy eating plan when the holidays hit? Do you overspend way past your budget for the sake of a "good deal"? Do you justify drinking too much because it's a celebration for a job well done? What lovely things tempt you?

The truth is that we won't escape this life without being enticed by something or someone. It's common to every one of us. Let's just settle that right now. But, sister, when the pressure to compromise feels too much, God will help you hold steady and not give in.

Remember that you're not alone. And you don't have to rely on your own strength to stay strong.

Lord, there are lovely things that weaken my resolve.
On my own, I can't always withstand their pull,
so thank You for Your promise to help me.

Your Voice Matters

Her brother Absalom said to her, "Has your brother
Amnon had his way with you? Now, my dear sister,
let's keep it quiet—a family matter. He is, after all, your
brother. Don't take this so hard." Tamar lived in her
brother Absalom's home, bitter and desolate.
2 SAMUEL 13:20 MSG

Tamar's story is hard to read. Sexual assault and rape are heinous crimes that often go without punishment. But just as horrible is her brother's command to keep quiet.

Sweet one, your voice matters. You have the right to stand up for yourself. God would never ask you to stay silent so others feel more comfortable. He wants you to advocate for yourself because you have immeasurable worth. But God doesn't want you to sin when you do. Be wise with your words, and choose when to use them and what to say when you do.

Sometimes we think that to be a good Christian girl, we must always turn the other cheek. And while that's biblical to a point, God didn't create you to be a doormat for others to walk all over. His desire isn't for you to be used or abused. You're His child, and His plans for you are good. And while that doesn't mean evil won't come your way, it does mean He's given you a voice to stand up for what's right.

Lord, thank You for my voice. Help me use it
at the right time and in the right way.

Cleansing Tears

And David went up over the Mount of Olives and wept as he
went, barefoot and his head covered. And all the people who
were with him covered their heads, weeping as they went.

2 SAMUEL 15:30 AMPC

Tears are such a gift. They help release our emotions and cleanse us of heartache. It's been said that every tear we cry is one less hour of therapy we'll need. Yes, they are that powerful. Even Jesus wept.

Yet sometimes tears are seen as a sign of weakness. Many of us weren't allowed to cry growing up, so we learned to stuff our emotions deep down inside. We learned to be stoic and unmoved by the sorrow we felt. And rather than processing our feelings in healthy ways, we buried them. We put on a brave (and fake) smile. Do you still live this way?

David was never one to shy away from his emotions, and maybe God included him in the Bible in part because of it. Maybe He wanted to show us the value of cleansing tears. Maybe He wanted us to understand the healing it would bring.

Don't be afraid to let your feelings spill out of your eyes. Everyone needs a good cry from time to time. Tears are God's gift, and they serve a beautiful purpose when you're walking through grief.

Lord, sometimes I'm overwhelmed by situations
I'm walking through. Thank You for the reminder
I can be real with my emotions through tears.

Love for Your Enemies

The king was shaken. He went up to the room over the
gateway and wept. As he went, he said: "O my son Absalom!
My son, my son Absalom! If only I had died instead of
you—O Absalom, my son, my son!"
2 SAMUEL 18:33 NIV

A bsalom had schemed to overthrow King David—his father—and was on a mission to have him killed. Full of rage and anger, Absalom directed his animosity toward his dad. Nevertheless, David's heart was full of unwavering love for his son.

It's hard to understand how people can be tender toward their enemies. It seems impossible to care about those trying to take you down, doesn't it? Just how do you love someone attempting to steal your job, wreck your marriage, entice your child, sue your business, or ruin your reputation? The reality is that in your own strength, you can't.

David was able to love his wayward son because the Lord moved in his heart. God is what made it possible for him to overlook evil and find compassion for Absalom. And it's God who will make it possible for you to do the same.

There may be healthy boundaries in place to protect you, but God will open your heart to love those who come against you. And that love will keep your heart full of compassion so you can be a powerful testimony of God's love.

Lord, show me the way to love my enemies.

Be the Voice of Reason

And when he came near her, the woman said, Are you Joab?
He answered, I am. Then she said to him, Hear the words
of your handmaid. He answered, I am listening.

2 SAMUEL 20:17 AMPC

At David's command, Joab was tracking down Sheba, a troublemaker who'd rebelled against the king. They tracked him to the town of Abel of Beth-maacah, where he was hiding. As the Israeli forces began tearing down the city wall, a wise woman spoke up as a voice of reason. She reminded Joab the city was peaceful, and she offered to deliver the fugitive in a different way. Later that day, Sheba's head was thrown over the wall.

Had the wise woman of Abel not spoken up, chances are the historic city would have been left in shambles. It was her courage to come forward and the perspective she shared that preserved the wall from further damage. This lone woman had the wherewithal to set emotions aside and speak with wisdom.

It's not always easy to take a step back from a situation to get a thirty-thousand-foot view. But when we do, it allows us to see the big picture. We're removed from the chaos of high emotions and able to see things more clearly. And it's in that clarity we can bring logic and truth to the discussion.

Lord, I want to be the voice of reason within my circle of influence.
Help me take a breath so I can offer sound advice and good sense.

Let Him Be Your Everything

My God, my Rock, in Him will I take refuge; my Shield and
the Horn of my salvation; my Stronghold and my Refuge,
my Savior—You save me from violence.

2 SAMUEL 22:3 AMPC

What is God's role in your life? Take a moment and think of all the things He is to you. Say them out loud. Maybe jot them down on this page as a reminder when you need it. Because you will.

There is power in the spoken word. Many of us are audible learners, and so hearing the different ways God has blessed us is powerful. David knew that. As a matter of fact, he spoke today's verse (and full chapter) to the Lord. It was a form of worship, an acknowledgment, and a reminder.

So, friend, who is God to you? Like David, would you say He's your Refuge and Rock? Is He your Stronghold, Shield, and Savior? Maybe He's been your Provider and Physician, or Friend and Fortress? Is God your Healer and Hope? Is He your Deliverer and Delight?

Tell God your list, and thank Him for all the ways He's shown up for you and how He's impacted your life. Share with God your needs, and ask for His help. Let Him be your everything.

Lord, thank You for being involved in my life. I'm so grateful
for who You are to me. I see it now. My heart is so full!

Is It Guilt or Shame?

*But when it was all done, David was overwhelmed
with guilt because he had counted the people, replacing
trust with statistics. And David prayed to GOD, "I have
sinned badly in what I have just done. But now GOD
forgive my guilt—I've been really stupid."*

2 SAMUEL 24:10 MSG

D o you know the difference between guilt and shame? Guilt is feeling bad about something you've done (like David in today's verse). But shame is a whole other beast. It's when you feel bad about who you are.

Guilt says you've *done* something bad. Shame says you *are* bad.

It's important to know the difference because shame is often a hidden belief that operates within without you even knowing it. Unless it's uncovered, it will be the lens you look at life through. It will decide what you think about yourself. And it will beat you down until you feel unlovable, unwanted, and insignificant.

Just as David took his guilt to God, you can too. Even more importantly, you can take the shame you're feeling to Him as well. Confess them both, and then ask for the Lord to remove them and remind you of your value. Neither guilt nor shame are beneficial to living your one and only life well.

*Lord, I realize I'm living with both of these joy-draining
feelings. Please either remove them or break their hold over me.
Then, Lord, restore my value as I live and breathe in You.*

How to Be Wise and Prosper

Keep the charge of the Lord your God, walk in His
ways, keep His statutes, His commandments,
His precepts, and His testimonies, as it is written
in the Law of Moses, that you may do wisely and
prosper in all that you do and wherever you turn.
1 KINGS 2:3 AMPC

O n his deathbed, David was passing along some valuable, hard-won wisdom to his son, Solomon, who was about to be crowned king. From a shepherd boy to the ruler of Israel, David had lived such a rich life, full of ups and downs. Yet he never once doubted God through it. And because of David's radical faith, God considered David a man after His own heart (Acts 13:22).

In today's verse, we're given the secret to living a life marked by wisdom and blessed by prosperity. David doesn't mince words. He bottom-lines it. And his hope is to take the guesswork out of living right with God. David simply reminds his son (and us, thousands of years later) of the value of obeying the Lord.

It's a daily choice that brings about His blessing. It's deciding to do the right thing, which is also usually the hard thing. It's following God's commands over your selfish desires. Woman, it doesn't mean life will be perfect. But it will be full of purpose.

Lord, I want to be obedient to Your will and ways.
Give me courage to focus on the right things so
my choices will bless You, me, and others.

What Do You Want the Most?

"Here's what I want: Give me a God-listening heart so I can lead your people well, discerning the difference between good and evil. For who on their own is capable of leading your glorious people?"

1 KINGS 3:9 MSG

Solomon had a big decision. God was pleased with his kingship, and because of that, He asked, "What can I give you?" He was a proud Father who wanted to bless Solomon for his choices.

Think about it. Given the opportunity, many would have used the occasion to ask for riches or popularity. They may have requested more territory or servants. Maybe more power or good health for a long life. What might you have asked for?

But Solomon's request deeply delighted the Lord. Rather than a shallow response, this new king asked for wisdom to lead God's children well. He wanted discernment to know good from evil. And he then asked a profoundly accurate question: "Who on their own is capable?"

The truth is that we all need God's direction to live and love well. Sure, we can manage on our own for a while, but the Lord created us to need Him. We were made to be in a relationship. And when we decide we have life all figured out on our own, we'll eventually end up a hot mess.

Where do you need God's direction? Why not ask Him for help right now?

Lord, I need Your wisdom today and every day.

The Proof Is in the Pudding

*When Hiram heard the words of Solomon, he rejoiced
greatly and said, Blessed be the Lord this day, Who has
given David a wise son to be over this great people.*

1 KINGS 5:7 AMPC

You may say you're a Jesus-girl. You may spend time with God on a regular basis, cultivating a strong relationship with Him. There might be praise music blaring through your speakers—music that often reduces you to tears because you feel so close to Him. You may be involved in Bible studies or small groups weekly where you dig deep into the Word of God. And you may even be in the pews every Sunday, ready for a fresh word from the pastor.

But if no one can see the fruit of your time with Jesus, if those around you have no idea you love the Lord, if your life doesn't look any different than the rest of the world's, you may need to take another look at how you're living.

People should notice something distinctive about the way you live and love. They should see your care for others. There should be a beautiful grace about you, and they should see how you stay tucked in peace no matter what. Your life should reflect your faith.

Oh yes, the proof is always in the pudding. Would others know you love the Lord by how you live?

Lord, help my life reflect my relationship with You in all I do!

What Has God Promised?

"The LORD has kept the promise he made: I have succeeded David my father and now I sit on the throne of Israel, just as the LORD promised, and I have built the temple for the Name of the LORD, the God of Israel."

1 KINGS 8:20 NIV

I f God makes a promise, He'll keep it. He's incapable of breaking a vow. So even though it seems He's moved on or forgotten you, keep believing Him for it. Flex that faith muscle and hold on to the promise.

Write down things God shares with you, dating them. Journal every time you see another step toward Him fulfilling those promises. Whether it be something He pledged to you specifically or an assurance you've read in His Word, trust God will come through for you.

What's He been whispering into your heart lately? What doors has God been opening or closing? What new excitement for your career has been stirring? Has God put a dream or a hope into your spirit, something you're equally excited for and scared to death of? Do you have new flashes of creativity? Are you wanting to step out and try a new thing?

Sister in Christ, ask God if He is making a new promise. Ask Him to show you the next right step to take. Tell God you are ready and excited. And then bathe it in prayer!

Lord, I know You will keep Your promises.
Thank You for being faithful and trustworthy!

A Need to Be Noticed

Jeroboam stood out during the construction as
strong and able. When Solomon observed what a
good worker he was, he put the young man in charge
of the entire workforce of the tribe of Joseph.

1 KINGS 11:28 MSG

We all want to be noticed. Deep down, we women have a strong desire to be seen by others. While sometimes it's for selfish reasons, it isn't always so. Often, it's born from a desire to know that others see our heart for them and feel blessed by us.

We want our family to see the selfless sacrifices we make for them every day. We want friends to recognize our loyalty and reward it with a stronger friendship. We want our employer to see the extra hours we put in to meet the deadline. And sometimes, we just want someone to recognize our efforts and applaud a job well done.

It may not be the only reason we do what we do, but it encourages us to know we're contributing to the world and it's noticed.

In what role do you long to be seen and recognized? As an attentive wife or a fun-loving mom? A dependable daughter or a dedicated employee? Maybe a trustworthy friend or steadfast sister? Know that even if no one else notices, God does. And He is pleased with the ways you purpose to bless those around you!

Lord, when no one else does,
thank You for noticing me and my efforts.

Praying for Others

Then the king said to the man of God, "Intercede with the LORD your God and pray for me that my hand may be restored." So the man of God interceded with the LORD, and the king's hand was restored and became as it was before.

1 KINGS 13:6 NIV

Praying for others is a privilege. It's an opportunity to take someone to the Lord's throne room and plead on her behalf. We get to join in prayer with other loyal friends and family. And it helps those asking for prayer because we're agreeing to help carry the torch of hope with them. But sometimes we consider it a burden.

Have you been asked to pray for someone and it frustrated you? Or have you thought you were too busy and already praying for enough people? Maybe you had every good intention when you agreed to be a prayer partner, but it slipped your mind altogether.

Ask God to help you embrace the opportunity, because the Bible tells us prayer matters. The Lord hears every word, every request, every plea. Not only does He listen, we're told in the pages of His Word that we will be answered. Sometimes He says, "Yes," other times He says, "No," or "Wait for it," but God will answer.

Lord, prayer is tricky for me at times. I want to be open to praying for others when they need it, without their request feeling too heavy. Change my heart when needed.

Generational Curses and Blessings

He walked in all the sins of his father [Rehoboam]
before him; and his heart was not blameless with the
Lord his God, as the heart of David his father [forefather].

1 Kings 15:3 ampc

Did you realize that your actions today will affect generations to come? What truths and lies you lay down here and now will continue with your children and grandchildren. Let this be a great encouragement to you!

That means you can change the course of generational curses that have been passed down for years in your family. It might be alcoholism or pornography. It could be godlessness or pagan religions. Or it could be some other addiction or sin. But, friend, you can break that curse today. Through tactical prayer, professional help, or sheer willpower, you can stop those curses from affecting those who come next.

In the same vein, you can also continue to nurture the blessings. Is your family known for its faith-filled women? Have you all been recognized throughout the years as prayer warriors? Maybe there are generations of missionaries in your history. These are amazing blessings you can continue to cultivate and pass along.

You have the ability to make changes for generations to come. And with Jesus, all things are possible.

Lord, I want to leave a legacy of faith for my family. Help me be the right kind of witness so my family line will be full of Jesus-followers.

True to His Word

The jar of meal was not spent nor did the bottle of oil fail,
according to the word which the Lord spoke through Elijah.
1 KINGS 17:16 AMPC

God rewards you when you have faith in Him and His Word, no matter how far-fetched His commands seem. Case in point: Elijah and the widow.

God told Elijah to go to Zarephath because He'd commanded a widow there to provide for him (1 Kings 17:9). So, the ever-obedient Elijah goes to Zarephath. There he sees a widow gathering sticks. He asks her to bring him some water and bread. Imagine Elijah's surprise when she tells him she has nothing but a "handful of meal in the jar and a little oil in the bottle" (1 Kings 17:12) and was now gathering sticks to make herself and her son a last meal.

Yet Elijah knows his God is a god of His word, a doer of the seemingly impossible. He tells the widow not to fear but to make him a cake and *then* prepare some for her and her son. Because God has said that during the famine, the widow's jar of meal and her bottle of oil would not run out! So, the widow followed Elijah's advice and found God was true to His word.

Just as God came through for the widow of Zarephath, God will come through for you. *Simply believe!*

Thank You, God, for being true to Your word! Help me believe!

In the Silence and Stillness

The Lord was not in the fire; and after the fire
[a sound of gentle stillness and] a still, small voice.
When Elijah heard the voice, he. . .went out.
1 KINGS 19:12–13 AMPC

Right after an amazing demonstration of God's power, during which several of Queen Jezebel's pagan priests were killed, Elijah's life was threatened by the queen herself. Panicked, the prophet ran for his life, traveling "to Beersheba. . .[over eighty miles, and out of Jezebel's realm]" (1 Kings 19:3). Then Elijah traveled even farther, going into the wilderness, where he sat under a tree and asked God to take his life! Instead of killing His prophet, God sent him an angel with food and water. And it was in the strength of that food that Elijah made the forty-day journey to Horeb. There, God passed by him and a huge wind tore apart the mountains. But God wasn't in the wind. Then came an earthquake and a fire, but God wasn't in those either.

Elijah finally found God after the fire. For it was then that he heard "[a sound of gentle stillness and] a still, small voice." Hearing that voice, Elijah went out to meet and converse with his Lord.

Need to hear a word from God? Find a place that's quiet. There, in the silence and stillness, you will not only find God but hear His voice.

I come to You, Lord, in the quiet of this moment. Speak, Lord. Speak.

The Limitless God

"Thus says the LORD, 'Because the Syrians have said,
"The LORD is a god of the hills but he is not a god of the
valleys," therefore I will give all this great multitude into
your hand, and you shall know that I am the LORD.' "

1 KINGS 20:28 ESV

God doesn't like it when His creatures try to put Him in a box or imply that He's limited in some way. Yet that's just what the Syrians did. They claimed that the Israelites' God was a god of the mountains but not the valleys. Irked, God decided to prove just how wrong the Syrians were. So, even though Ahab, the current king of Israel, was evil, God gave him the victory anyway. In that battle, God's army killed 100,000 Syrian foot soldiers—in one day!!!

God wants you to know that He can do anything, be anywhere, and reigns over all things, creatures, and places—in heaven and on earth. Your God is bigger, greater, mightier, and more wonderful than anything or anyone you could ever meet or imagine.

If you have a problem, don't fear. Just look to God. Know that He's bigger than any obstacle that stands before You. And He will give you the victory, the ways, the means to overcome it.

Lord, I rejoice that You are so mighty, so much bigger than any
obstacle looming before me! Because of You, I fear nothing and no one!

Before You Do Anything. . .

He turned to Jehoshaphat and said, "Will you join me
in fighting for Ramoth Gilead?" Jehoshaphat said,
"You bet. I'm with you all the way—my troops are your
troops, my horses are your horses. . . . But before you
do anything, ask GOD for guidance."

1 KINGS 22:4–5 MSG

So, you have a decision to make. You've done some research, thought long and hard about the situation, and now think you're ready to act. But first you run it by a few people. Perhaps your parent, sibling, husband, friend, pastor, fellow churchgoer, peer, or coworker might have some good advice, give you some direction.

It's all well and good that you're not rushing the decision and have sought counsel from your fellow humans. The Word says that although plans without advice may fail, with many advisers, they'll succeed (Proverbs 15:22). That whoever listens to the counsel of others is wise (Proverbs 12:15). But there's a major source of wisdom you've yet to consider: God.

James 1:5–6 says, "If you don't know what you're doing, pray to the Father. He loves to help. You'll get his help, and won't be condescended to when you ask for it. Ask boldly, believingly, without a second thought."

Today, before you do anything, ask God for guidance. He'll be sure to head you in the right direction, from here to eternity.

Lord, I'm in need of Your guidance.
What would You have me do?

God the Miracle Worker

*Then Elisha went to the spring of the waters and cast
the salt in it and said, Thus says the Lord: I [not the salt]
have healed these waters; there shall not be any more
death, miscarriage or barrenness [and bereavement]
because of it. So the waters were healed to this day.*
2 KINGS 2:21–22 AMPC

When a miracle occurs in your life, to whom do you give the credit?
The miracle worker or God?

In today's reading, the men of Jericho said to the prophet Elisha,
"You can see for yourself, master, how well our city is located. But the
water is polluted and nothing grows" (2 Kings 2:19 MSG). Even animals
were miscarrying and becoming barren. So, Elisha told the men of the
city to bring him a bowl with some salt in it. He then cast some of the
salt into the spring and proclaimed God's Word, telling them it was not
the salt or Elisha that had healed the water but God Himself!

Today, as you look at the miracles in your life and beyond, seek to
understand that it is God who is behind all the great works. He is the
source of all creation, healing, and wonders on heaven and earth.

*As I look around me, Lord, I see Your hand, Your love,
Your healing in it all. Thank You, Lord of wonder,
for all things. In Jesus' name I pray, amen.*

The Source of Success

When Elisha arrived in the house, the child was dead
and laid upon his bed. So he went in, shut the door
on the two of them, and prayed to the Lord.
2 KINGS 4:32–33 AMPC

A wealthy woman in Shunem often invited Elisha into her home for food whenever he passed her way. Later, after discussing the idea with her husband, she had a room built for the prophet so that he would have a place to rest.

To repay the Shunammite woman's kindness, Elisha told her she'd have a son next year. And she did! But one day, while out in the field with his father, the boy became ill. Later, he died in his mother's arms.

Telling others everything would be all right (2 Kings 3:23, 26), the woman sought out Elisha, who returned to her house. After entering his room and shutting the door, the very next thing Elisha did was pray to God and become the channel through which a miracle was wrought.

You and other humans are the creatures God works through to bring His blessings down to earth. Today, on this National Day of Prayer, open yourself up to God, the source of your success.

Lord, the source of all success, on this day and
every day, work Your will and way through me.
Make me a channel of Your blessings.

Opened Eyes

"Do not be afraid, for those who are with us are more than
those who are with them." Then Elisha prayed and said,
"O LORD, please open his eyes that he may see." So the
LORD opened the eyes of the young man, and he saw.
2 KINGS 6:16–17 ESV

The prophet Elisha's servant had gotten up early one morning. He headed outside, when he was stunned by the sight of the Syrian army with its horses and chariots surrounding the city! Panicked, he yelled to Elisha, "Alas, my master! What shall we do?" (2 Kings 6:15).

Elisha told his servant not to fear because the heavenly agents with them were way more numerous than the earthly army beyond their door. Elisha then prayed and asked God to open his servant's eyes so he could see God's army surrounding them!

As the Syrians approached, Elisha prayed for God to blind the soldiers. "So He struck them with blindness, according to Elisha's word" (2 Kings 6:18 HCSB). And Elisha led the temporarily God-blind army back to Samaria.

As a servant of God, you need never fear for God is with you. All. The. Time. No matter what you do or where you go, God is there. And so is His army, His angels, His heavenly host—whether you see them or not.

It feels so good, Lord, to know You are always surrounding
me with Your presence and power. In You, I can rest easy.

Promises Kept

"Know, then, that not a word the LORD spoke against
the house of Ahab will fail, for the LORD has done
what He promised through His servant Elijah."

2 KINGS 10:10 HCSB

K ing Ahab of Israel had devoted himself "to do what is evil in the LORD's sight" (1 Kings 21:20). And because of Ahab's extreme wickedness, because he had provoked God's anger and led Israel to sin, the Lord, speaking through Elijah, told the king, "I am about to bring disaster on you and will sweep away your descendants" (1 Kings 21:21). But God didn't stop there. He included Ahab's wife, Jezebel, in His retribution, saying she would be eaten by dogs. All because God had determined that she, Jezebel, had prompted Ahab to do wicked things.

And, in the end, all that God said would happen to Ahab and his family happened. They were wiped out, and Jezebel went to the dogs.

This story is a reminder that you can take God at His word. Because God means what He says, the promises He makes He keeps. Today, consider a promise that God has made, one that's recorded in His Word (consider Jeremiah 29:11; Matthew 11:29; Isaiah 40:29–31; Philippians 4:19, to name a few). And pray that promise back to God, fully assured that He will make good on His vows to you.

Thank You, Lord, for making good on Your
promises to me, for You are as good as Your Word.

God as a Mother

But the Lord was gracious to them and had compassion
on them and turned toward them because of His covenant
with Abraham, Isaac, and Jacob, and would not destroy
them or cast them from His presence yet.

2 KINGS 13:23 AMPC

E very human goes through stages. Born helpless, a babe's unable to feed itself, walk, or talk. Months later, she may begin to crawl, then walk, talk, and run. Soon the child is in school, learning to read, write, and do arithmetic. Eventually she goes through puberty, becomes an adult, and starts a family, strikes out on a career path, or both. Decades later, she goes through menopause and finds herself plucking out gray hairs. In a blink, she's a senior citizen, running the final lap of life. Yes, humans go through an amazing amount of change. But God never does: "Because I, Yahweh, have not changed, you descendants of Jacob have not been destroyed" (Malachi 3:6 HCSB).

Just as God was gracious to His people and had compassion on them thousands of years ago, your God-who-never-changes has grace and compassion for you today. As a Christ-follower, rest assured your God is waiting to hold you in His arms, to love and comfort you just as "a mother comforts her child" (Isaiah 66:13 NIV).

Today, on this Mother's Day, seek out your God. When you do, He'll turn to you, arms and heart open wide.

Lord, hold me. Love me. Be to me as a mother. Amen.

Help on the Way

GOD was fully aware of the trouble in Israel, its bitterly hard times. No one was exempt, whether slave or citizen, and no hope of help anywhere was in sight. But GOD wasn't yet ready to blot out the name of Israel from history, so he used Jeroboam son of Jehoash to save them.

2 KINGS 14:26–27 MSG

Going through a difficult time? If so, are you wondering where God is? No matter what you're going through or when, God sees. He is fully aware of the troubles that have come into your life. He knows the hard times you—and others around you—may be facing. And because God sees what's happening, He's sending help. It may come from an unexpected place, from someone who isn't a believer in Christ, someone who doesn't follow God, someone who is downright evil.

That's what happened thousands of years ago. God saw the trouble His people were in. He realized there was no one else around to help them. So, God used the evil King Jeroboam to save His people.

God isn't choosey when He sends you help, so keep your eyes, ears, and heart open. God works in mysterious ways. Expect that help from your Lord is on the way.

I know, Lord, that You see what's happening in my life. Please send help. And please open my eyes, ears, and heart to that help.

Personal Deliverer

*"Worship GOD, the God who delivered you from Egypt in great
and personal power. Reverence and fear him. Worship him.
Sacrifice to him. . . . Worship GOD, and GOD only—he's the
one who will save you from enemy oppression."*

2 KINGS 17:36, 39 MSG

There was a time in Israel when God's people would not count on Him alone. Instead, they looked to other gods for help. Even after God warned them not to, the Israelites turned away from Him, His commandments, and His promises. Their disbelief that God could do anything and everything resulted in their disobeying the one true God, the one with all the power to deliver them from all their enemies.

Perhaps you too have found yourself trusting in, worshipping, or following other gods. Maybe you are trusting that next new job to solve all your problems. Or perhaps you're dabbling in the occult, checking your horoscope, or using tarot cards to glean advice and wisdom. Or maybe you're trusting in a fellow human—a parent, partner, friend, pastor, spouse, or schoolmate—to get you out of a fix.

Woman, God is making clear who you are to turn to and trust in time of trouble: Him—the all great and powerful God. He alone can save you from every enemy and all oppression. In Jesus' name.

*I come to worship You alone, Lord. For it is You alone
who can save me. For You are my personal Deliverer.*

Presence and Prosperity

Hezekiah trusted in, leaned on, and was confident in
the Lord. . . . For he clung and held fast to the Lord and
ceased not to follow Him, but kept His commandments,
as the Lord commanded Moses. And the Lord was with
Hezekiah; he prospered wherever he went.

2 KINGS 18:5–7 AMPC

Only six out of twenty kings of Judah did right in God's eyes, and Hezekiah was one of those six. Hezekiah was a good king because he trusted totally in God, clinging to Him, keeping His commandments. His relationship with God is what shielded this king from trouble and evil. And because Hezekiah was close to God, God was close to him, walking with him every step of the way and prospering him wherever he went.

What's your relationship with God like? What do you trust Him with? How close do you cling to Him—in good times and bad? How well do you keep His Son's commandments?

Woman, there is a connection between God's presence in your life and your prosperity. Today contemplate your answers to the forgoing questions. Then pray for God to increase your faith, trust, and confidence in Him.

Lord, I want to grow my trust and faith in You alone. Please help me
follow You no matter what, for I desire Your presence in my life here
and beyond! So please be with me, Lord, prospering me wherever I go.

The Power of Heartfelt Prayer

*Hezekiah turned his face to the wall and prayed to the
Lord, "Please LORD, remember how I have walked before
You faithfully and wholeheartedly and have done what
pleases You. . . ." " 'The Lord God. . .says: I have heard your
prayer; I have seen your tears. Look, I will heal you.' "*

2 KINGS 20:2–3, 5 HCSB

When Hezekiah became ill, the prophet Isaiah told him to put his affairs in order, because from this illness, the king would die. That news prompted Hezekiah to pray to God, putting his case before the Lord of his life. The king reminded God of how faithful he'd been, how he'd followed God with all his heart, doing what pleases Him. Then he had himself a good cry.

God, meanwhile, hearing that heartfelt prayer, sent Isaiah back to tell Hezekiah that He had heard his prayer, seen his tears, and would heal him. To prove it, Hezekiah asked God to reverse the course of a shadow, making it go back ten steps. And He did!

When you find yourself in dire straits, follow the wisdom of good King Hezekiah. Go directly to God. Put your case before Him. Allow the tears to flow and the heart to speak. Then know that God has heard you. He has seen your tears. And He will heal you—if not in this life, then the next.

Lord, You have my heart. Now hear my prayer.

Read and Pray

"Go and pray to GOD for me and for this people—for all Judah! Find out what we must do in response to what is written in this book that has just been found! GOD's anger must be burning furiously against us—our ancestors haven't obeyed a thing written in this book."

2 KINGS 22:13 MSG

Ten years into good King Josiah's reign, the temple of the Lord was being repaired under his orders. That's when the high priest Hilkiah found the "Book of the Law in the house of the Lord!" (2 Kings 22:8 AMPC). Hilkiah handed the book over to the scribe Shaphan, who then read it before the king. Hearing God's Word, Josiah realized how far his people, the people of God, had wandered away from their Lord!

Can you imagine trying to live life without the Bible, God's voice, His words to train you, inform you, advise you, and call you ever closer to Him? Can you imagine losing His precious Word? Yet having a Bible but not even opening it is even worse.

Today, grab your Bible. Pray that God will open your eyes, ears, mind, and heart to the message meant for you today. Then read God's words. Allow His direction and wisdom to flow into you. Then pray once more, seeking what God would have you do with this new knowledge.

Open Your Word to me, Lord. Show me what You would have me know, see, hear, and do.

No Comparison

There was no king to compare with Josiah—neither before
nor after—a king who turned in total and repentant
obedience to GOD, heart and mind and strength, following
the instructions revealed to and written by Moses.
The world would never again see a king like Josiah.

2 KINGS 23:25 MSG

King Josiah was a rare king for he put all of himself—his mind, his heart, and his strength—into following the Lord and His law as penned by Moses. But he didn't stop there. He read the book to his people so they would know what it contained and how far they'd fallen. Then King Josiah renewed the deal, the covenant the people had with God, telling them to "follow GOD believingly and obediently; to follow his instructions, heart and soul, on what to believe and do; to put into practice the entire covenant, all that was written in the book" (2 Kings 23:3). Then he "swept the country clean of the polluting stench" (2 Kings 23:5) of foreign gods, idols, and high places.

Jesus said the greatest commandment is to love God with all your heart, soul, mind, and strength (Mark 12:30; Matthew 22:37; Luke 10:27), and God Himself stated this in Deuteronomy 6:5–7. When you do, you, like Josiah, will stand apart from the rest. In God's eyes, no one else will compare with you.

Help me, Lord, to truly follow You with all
my heart, soul, mind, and strength.

From Pain to Provision

Jabez was a better man than his brothers, a man of honor.
His mother had named him Jabez (Oh, the pain!), saying,
"A painful birth! I bore him in great pain!" Jabez prayed to
the God of Israel: "Bless me, O bless me! Give me land, large
tracts of land. And provide your personal protection—
don't let evil hurt me." God gave him what he asked.
1 Chronicles 4:9–10 MSG

The first book of Chronicles lists the genealogy of the people of Israel, beginning with Adam (1 Chronicles 1:1)! And every once in a while, amid the names of fathers, brothers, and sons, and the occasional mention of mothers, sisters, and daughters, comes an insight into the people who traveled this road long before your feet touched the ground. And one of those people was Jabez.

Jabez means "pain." That's what his mother suffered during his delivery. Yet even with this misnomer attached to him, Jabez turned out to be an honorable man, a better man than his brothers. So, he prayed to God, asking God to bless him with land and His personal protection. And God gave Jabez what he'd asked for.

No matter what burdens you carry, you have an amazing tool at your fingertips. It's called prayer. Today, be like Jabez. Consider what you need. Then go to God with your specific requests, allowing Him to remove your pain and supply you with provisions.

Lord, thanks for hearing my prayer. Please bless me with. . .

Courage and Conviction

Zelophehad had daughters [only].
1 CHRONICLES 7:15 AMPC

A mid the wealth of genealogical data in 1 Chronicles, we find this little, seemingly innocuous bit of information about a man named Zelophehad from the clan of Manasseh. He had no sons, only daughters named Mahlah, Noah, Hoglah, Milcah, and Tirzah (Numbers 27:1). Yet these same five daughters had the courage to take a stand for their family's rights and, in the process, changed the laws and the Jewish culture.

It began when the Lord told Moses to take a census of the Israelites after their wilderness venture. Soon afterward, these five courageous women, brimming with conviction, stated their case before Moses, the priest, the leaders, and the entire community. Their father, Zelophehad, had died in the wilderness. Yet now, because he had no sons, his ancestral name would be forgotten and his legacy divided among other clan members, as women couldn't inherit. They then said, "Since he had no son, give us property among our father's brothers" (Numbers 27:4 HCSB).

Moses took the issue to God, and God agreed with the sisters. From that day on, under Jewish law, if a man was blessed with daughters only, those daughters could inherit.

Sister, if you see an injustice, take a shot of courage and discuss the issue with your spiritual leader and the Lord. If God agrees with your position, He'll help you find a way to make things right.

Lord, help me become a woman of courage and conviction.

Raise a Praise

And then there were the musicians, all heads of Levite families. They had permanent living quarters in The Temple; because they were on twenty-four-hour duty, they were exempt from all other duties.

1 Chronicles 9:33 MSG

God loves to be praised! And music is a big part of that process. That's why all the Levite musicians lived permanently in The Temple. For twenty-four hours a day, they were to write, sing, and play songs and teach others to do the same so there would be constant praise music before the Lord their God.

The Bible explicitly tells us to praise God for His glory and strength (1 Chronicles 16:28), for His wisdom and power (Daniel 2:20), for His rescuing the downtrodden from evil (Jeremiah 20:13), and for His gift of grace to those who believe in Jesus (Ephesians 1:6), to name just a few.

When was the last time you praised God, making a joyful noise to Him with songs of praise (Psalm 95:1–11)? James tells you to pray if you're suffering and sing praise if you're cheerful (James 5:13). Yet can you imagine how wonderful it would be if you'd praise God even on your down days? If you do, if you burst into song when you're unhappy, your sorrow will soon fade away because you'll be focusing on the Lord instead of yourself or your troubles.

Lord, I lift my voice in praise to You each day and, in so doing, lift myself in You!

Prayer Precedes Breakthroughs

*So [Israel] came up to Baal-perazim, and David smote [the Philistines]
there. Then David said, God has broken my enemies by my hand,
like the bursting forth of waters. Therefore they called the name
of that place Baal-perazim [Lord of breaking through].*

1 CHRONICLES 14:11 AMPC

King Saul and his son, Jonathan, had been killed and buried. David was finally king of Judah and Israel. Hearing about his promotion, the Philistines searched him out. And when David heard they were on their way, he went out to face them. But before he did anything more, David went to God in prayer, asking, "Shall I go up against the Philistines? And will You deliver them into my hand? And the Lord said, Go up, and I will deliver them into your hand" (1 Chronicles 14:10).

So, in the confidence that God was with Him and would be true to His word, David stepped out and went after the Philistines. And God broke through His enemies by David's hand.

Perhaps you need God to give you the go-ahead for a certain battle or endeavor. Perhaps you're looking for a breakthrough only God can accomplish. Whatever the case, before stepping out, lift your hands in prayer and praise to God. Ask Him what you should do. Then allow Him to help you win the day!

*I need a breakthrough, Lord.
Please, tell me, what should I do?*

Thursday of Thanksgiving

Thank GOD! Call out his Name! Tell the whole world who he is and what he's done! . . . Study GOD and his strength, seek his presence day and night; remember all the wonders he performed.

1 CHRONICLES 16:8, 11–12 MSG

On the day he brought the ark of God to Jerusalem, David, the shepherd-boy-who-became-king, "first appointed Asaph and his associates to give praise to the LORD" (1 Chronicles 16:7 NIV). In honor of that august occasion, David introduced a psalm of praise to God. Yet this same song/psalm, written over three thousand years ago, can be easily sung by you today. For just like God, David's song is timeless.

David begins his psalm by suggesting you thank God for all He's done, which brings up an interesting question: When was the last time you really sat still and gave some thought as to what God has done for you, *is* doing for you, or *will* do for you in the future? Or when was the last time you made a list of all the ways He's helped you by working miracles for you or others?

Why not make today—and every Thursday—your day for expressing thanksgiving to God? Begin by making a list of at least five things God has done for you personally. Soon you'll find yourself overflowing with praise!

I praise You, Lord, for all You've done for me. Thank You for. . .

Courage

*"If the Arameans are too much for me, you help me; and if
the Ammonites prove too much for you, I'll come and help you.
Courage! We'll fight might and main for our people and for the
cities of our God. And GOD will do whatever he sees needs doing!"*

1 CHRONICLES 19:12–13 MSG

❦

Joab, David's general, was trapped between two enemy armies—the
Arameans and the Ammonites. So, he split up his army. His group
would fight the Arameans, and his brother Abishai would command a
group to fight the Ammonites. If either got into trouble, the other would
help. After Joab relayed this game plan to his brother, he followed it
with a giant word: *Courage!* This was backed up with the knowledge that
no matter what happened, "GOD will do whatever he sees needs doing!"
In the end, both enemy armies were defeated.

When you find yourself between a rock and a hard place, don't allow
yourself to feel defeated. Instead, look for or give help where needed.
Then remind yourself that you can find all the courage you need in the
God you trust. At the same time, be sure to acknowledge that your victory
lies in knowing God Himself will do whatever else He sees needs doing.

*I'm stuck in a tough situation, Lord. Yet in You I find the courage
I need and the knowledge that You'll do whatever I cannot.*

Success

"You will succeed if you carefully follow the statutes and ordinances the LORD commanded Moses for Israel. Be strong and courageous. Don't be afraid or discouraged. . . . Now determine in your mind and heart to seek the LORD your God."

1 CHRONICLES 22:13, 19 HCSB

King David had made lots of preparations for building a temple for God. Yet God had made it clear that David's son, Solomon, would build the Lord's house. Why? Because David had too much blood on his hands (1 Chronicles 22:8).

So, David, knowing his days were numbered, gave Solomon the best advice any father, king or no king, could give his son. He told him that if he followed God's statutes and ordinances, he would be a successful king. Then he urged Solomon to be strong and courageous. Later David spoke to the leaders of Israel, telling them to not only help his son in his kingship but to set their own minds and hearts to seek the Lord.

People define *success* with a certain income, job, or social status. But God and His people describe it as a dying David did to Solomon: "Do what GOD tells you. Walk in the paths he shows you: Follow the life-map absolutely, keep an eye out for the signposts, his course for life. . .then you'll get on well in whatever you do and wherever you go" (1 Kings 2:3 MSG). How do *you* define *success*?

Lord, help me be a success in Your eyes.

Equal Roles

These divisions of the gatekeepers, under their leading men, had duties for ministering in the LORD's temple, just as their brothers did. They cast lots for each gate according to their ancestral houses, young and old alike.

1 CHRONICLES 26:12–13 HCSB

Before he departed from the earth, King David made sure that all those who were to serve in the Temple of the Lord—Levites, priests, musicians, gatekeepers, and treasurers—knew their roles. So he began to divide 38,000 Levites over the age of 30, saying "24,000 are to be in charge of the work on the LORD's temple, 6,000 are to be officers and judges, 4,000 are to be gatekeepers, and 4,000 are to praise the LORD with the instruments that I have made for worship" (1 Chronicles 23:4–5).

Yet the author of Chronicles makes it clear that each ministry role and each person who filled that role was not greater or lesser than any other. The gatekeeper's job was just as important as the musician's.

You too have a ministry role to fill at your place of worship. If you want to build God's Church, you must offer yourself and do the best you can. What role do or might you fill for God?

I do some things at church, Lord, but I'm not sure if I'm fulfilling the role You would have me fill. Speak to me, Lord. Tell me what You would have me do, no matter how little or great.

Enough Time

Be strong and courageous, and do it. Fear not, be not
dismayed, for the Lord God, my God, is with you. He will
not fail or forsake you until you have finished all the
work for the service of the house of the Lord.

1 CHRONICLES 28:20 AMPC

I n his waning days of life, David once more addressed the leaders, commanders, officials, and warriors of his kingdom. After encouraging them to continue to follow God, David then addressed his son, Solomon, telling him once more to be strong and courageous and to do what needed to be done, remembering that God would continue to be with him until he'd finished his work.

Have you ever considered you would never have enough time to do all you wanted to do in your day or lifetime? If so, take heart. God has a certain purpose for you, a role He would have only you fill, work that you alone can accomplish. And He will not leave or fail you until you've done what He created you to do. So, woman, let go of that "I'll never have enough time to do what needs to be done" feeling. Stop rushing to accomplish what God has put in your hands. Instead, be calm, quiet, and confident that your Lord is with you, helping you, and allowing you all the time you need.

Lord, help me to slow down, to seek to live for and
serve You, knowing You'll stick with me till the end.

The Heart of the Matter

"This is what has come out of your heart: You didn't grasp for money, wealth, fame, and the doom of your enemies; you didn't even ask for a long life. You asked for wisdom and knowledge so you could govern well my people over whom I've made you king. Because of this, you get what you asked for—wisdom and knowledge. And I'm presenting you the rest as a bonus."

2 CHRONICLES 1:11–12 MSG

What you ask God for tells Him quite a bit about you.

The night after Solomon had offered sacrifices in God's temple, God came to him and said, "What do you want from me? Ask" (2 Chronicles 1:7). In response, the young king asked God for wisdom and knowledge so that he could rule God's people well. Hearing this, God realized who Solomon was: a man who spoke from his heart. And because this new king didn't ask for money, wealth, fame, and honor, God gave him those things on top of the wisdom and knowledge he'd requested.

Today, consider making a wish list of all the things your heart desires. Then look deeply into your soul. Is your wish list one that reflects the true you? If so, "may He grant you according to your heart's desire and fulfill all your plans" (Psalm 20:4 AMPC).

Lord, let's get down to the heart of the matter as I share with You my desires.

Your Heart and God's Hand

*Blessed be the Lord, the God of Israel, Who has fulfilled
with His hands what He promised with His mouth to
David my father. . . . You Who have kept Your promises to
my father David and fulfilled with Your hand what You
spoke with Your mouth, as it is today.*

2 CHRONICLES 6:4, 15 AMPC

I n his song "Life Changes," country music star Thomas Rhett sings, "You never know what's gonna happen. You make your plans and you hear God laughing." King David may have shared that sentiment when God told him, "Since it was in your heart to build a house for My Name and renown, you did well that it was in your heart. Yet you shall not build the house, but your son, who shall be born to you—he shall build the house for My Name" (2 Chronicles 6:8–9). And that son was Solomon.

You too may have certain plans in your head and heart, goals you want to reach, plans you want to succeed. But God may have other ideas for you. So be patient, knowing you are working, living, and serving on God's timeline, not your own. And trust the Lord your God, because you, like David, will see God's hand fulfill every promise He has shared with you.

*Help me, Lord, to be patient and trust You, Your promises,
Your timing, and Your plans for me, today and every day. Amen.*

All That You Are

King Solomon surpassed all the kings of the earth in riches and wisdom. And all the kings of the earth sought the presence of Solomon to hear his wisdom which God had put into his mind.

2 CHRONICLES 9:22–23 AMPC

King Solomon's wisdom and wealth were lauded by many other kings and queens alike. They sought him out to hear what he had to say time and time again. Perhaps the praise and reverence he received from others led to Solomon's trusting in his God-given gifts more than God Himself.

All that you have, all that you are, all that you do, in fact, your very life itself are gifts from God. He is the one who created you, then breathed life into you. He is the one who sustains, protects, and provides for you. And He is the one who will, at some point, bring you back to Himself. So, when others laud you for your talents, possessions, insights, knowledge, etc., remind yourself (and perhaps them) that what others admire about you is from God, giving credit where credit is due. Doing so will not only help you keep things in perspective but will keep you modest as well.

You are the One who has made me what I am, Lord. So, when others praise me, remind me to give all of the credit to You alone!

Prevailing with God

But as for us, the Lord is our God, and we have not forsaken Him. . . . Behold, God Himself is with us at our head. . . . Thus. . .the people of Judah prevailed because they relied upon the Lord.
2 Chronicles 13:10, 12, 18 AMPC

Under the reign of Solomon's son, Rehoboam, the kingdom was torn into two nations—Judah and Israel. At Rehoboam's death, his son, Abijah, became king of Judah and soon found himself warring against King Jeroboam of Israel.

When the two nations faced each other, Abijah stood on Mount Zemaraim and addressed Jeroboam and the warriors of Israel. Abijah told them that Judah still worships the Lord, unlike the people of Israel, who worship "the golden calves which Jeroboam made for you for gods" (2 Chronicles 13:8). Abijah explained that God was with Judah, leading them, then said, "O Israelites, fight not against the Lord, the God of your fathers, for you cannot prosper" (2 Chronicles 13:12).

Afterward, Judah found themselves trapped before and behind Israel's army. Yet when the men of Judah cried out to God, He routed the army of Israel and handed it over to those loyal to Him.

When you find yourself either in or out of the thick of battle, don't panic. God has you covered. He'll route your enemies before and behind and lead you to victory.

On You alone do I rely, Lord. With You, I know I'll prevail.

Take Courage

*"Take courage! Do not let your hands be weak, for your work
shall be rewarded." As soon as Asa heard these words,
the prophecy of Azariah the son of Oded, he took courage.*

2 CHRONICLES 15:7–8 ESV

W hen the spirit of God came upon the prophet Azariah, he relayed His message to King Asa of Judah. Azariah told him: "The LORD is with you while you are with him. If you seek him, he will be found by you, but if you forsake him, he will forsake you" (2 Chronicles 15:2 ESV). Then he told Asa that, in the past, when the disobedient people of Israel had turned to God in their distress, they'd found Him. So, King Asa should take courage and be strong. God would reward him.

When Asa heard these encouraging words, he "rolled up his sleeves, and went to work" (2 Chronicles 15:8 MSG) removing idols and renovating altars. As a result of his endeavors, the Judeans sought God with all their hearts and minds and found Him. And "the LORD gave them rest all around" (2 Chronicles 15:15 ESV).

You have the truth and wisdom of God at your fingertips, so when you need some extra courage, seek out His good Word. Look for Him with all your heart and mind. And you too will find God, as well as His strength, courage, peace, and rest.

*Lord, as I seek You, please give me the courage and
strength to do what You've called me to do.*

Eyes on God

*For we have no might to stand against this great
company that is coming against us. We do not know what
to do, but our eyes are upon You. . . . The Lord says this to
you: Be not afraid or dismayed at this great multitude;
for the battle is not yours, but God's.*
2 Chronicles 20:12, 15 ampc

One of the best and most inspirational stories in the Bible is found in 2 Chronicles 20. There we find Judah's King Jehoshaphat being told that a huge army is coming to attack him and his people. Immediately after hearing this news, Jehoshaphat sets himself to seek God. He tells Him what's happening, then lets God know that although Judah doesn't have the strength to stand against these enemy armies, and although he and his people don't know what to do, their eyes are on God.

Hearing these words from Jehoshaphat, God tells him not to be worried or afraid of this great mass of warriors at Judah's gate for this battle is His. All His people need to do is "take your positions, stand still, and see the deliverance of the Lord [Who is] with you" (2 Chronicles 20:17).

When you find yourself about to panic, stop. Let God know your situation. Then, with your eyes on Him and your faith in Him, stand still and witness the victory.

*I don't know what to do, Lord. But my eyes
are on You, and my faith is in You.*

Courage Waiting in the Wings

*So Jehosheba daughter of King Jehoram, sister of Ahaziah, and wife
of Jehoiada the priest, hid [Joash] from [his grandmother] Athaliah,
so that she did not slay him. And Joash was with them hidden in
the house of God six years, and Athaliah reigned over the land.*

2 CHRONICLES 22:11–12 AMPC

I magine your power-hungry, murderous, evil grandma was out to get you. Yikes! Yet that's just what was happening in Joash's house.

Joash's grandfather, Jehoram, had died "to no one's regret" (2 Chronicles 21:20 HCSB). After him had come King Ahaziah, who only reigned for one year. "He walked in the ways of the house of Ahab, for his mother gave him evil advice" (2 Chronicles 22:3 HCSB). When Ahaziah was killed, his mother, Athaliah (daughter of Ahab and Jezebel), started murdering all the heirs to the throne. But she missed murdering Joash because his aunt Jehosheba (his dad Ahaziah's half-sister) hid him.

For six years Joash remained hidden. Then his uncle and priest Jehoiada called up his own courage and began working to put Joash on the throne. Once Athaliah was dead, Joash did indeed take the throne and began repairing God's temple.

Yes, evil may be running rampant in the world. But for every evil Athaliah who comes into the picture, God makes sure there's a courageous Jehosheba on the scene.

*I thank You, Lord, that amid this world's evil, You
have courageous people waiting in the wings, ready
to usurp ne'er-do-wells when needed.*

Notorious

He did what was right in the eyes of the LORD, just as
his father Amaziah had done. He sought God during the
days of Zechariah, who instructed him in the fear of God.
As long as he sought the LORD, God gave him success.
2 Chronicles 26:4–5 niv

In Old Testament times, the kings of Israel became notorious for disobeying God. The occasions when we do read of their humility and conformity to the Lord's will are unfortunately as scarce as water in a parched desert.

Humankind has changed little over the centuries. We too have become notorious when it comes to surrendering to God and His perfect will. We neglect Him, dishonor Him, and act as if on many occasions we do not even need Him!

Pride seems to be the most monstrous spiritual culprit, for it has the capacity to bring down kings as well as every person ever born on this fallen earth.

Amazingly, we expect all good and lovely things to come to us, even when we brazenly follow our own desires without considering the precepts of God. May we always seek to please God in all we do that we might know His favor.

Mighty God, Maker of all, please show me how to stay
humble and not succumb to the temptation of pride for I
aim to please You in all I do. In Jesus' name I pray. Amen.

A Holy Hallelujah

There was great joy in Jerusalem, for since the days of Solomon son of David king of Israel there had been nothing like this in Jerusalem. The priests and the Levites stood to bless the people, and God heard them, for their prayer reached heaven, his holy dwelling place.

2 CHRONICLES 30:26–27 NIV

When Hezekiah became king, there was a glorious time of repentance, consecration, worship, sacrifices, praises, healing, and jubilation. This young king was determined to make things right with God. And you could say that there was indeed a real hallelujah time that flowed through the land and the hearts of the Israelites!

Yes, for a time, all was made right. The people's prayers reached heaven. Healing and restoration came down from God's holy dwelling place. The music of cymbals, harps, lyres, trumpets, and singing filled the temple. Rejoicing and happiness reigned.

Today, with Christ's help, may we take a prayerful and heartfelt assessment of our transgressions. May we respond to that divine nudge toward repentance and experience the fresh freedom of forgiveness. May our land be healed and our souls transformed into the likeness of Christ. This dark and hurting world is in great need of a holy hallelujah!

Oh Lord, my Redeemer and Friend, together may we transform this day into a holy hallelujah. Amen.

Choose God

*He sacrificed his children in the fire in the Valley of Ben
Hinnom, practiced divination and witchcraft, sought omens,
and consulted mediums and spiritists. He did much evil in the
eyes of the LORD, arousing his anger.*

2 Chronicles 33:6 niv

H ezekiah's son, Manasseh, brazenly embraced all kinds of practices
that God considered to be an abomination. Today, we might tilt our
chins with a bit of smugness, knowing we could not possibly be guilty
of such barbaric behaviors or detestable practices. And yet.

Year by year, we have gotten worn down to the pressures and lures
of New Age practices, infanticide, horoscopes, amulets, witchcraft, and
the seeking out of fortune tellers to name a few. We tend to trail after
whatever is put in front of us. We are a fickle and stiff-necked people,
no different really than the ancient folk of the Bible. But God will not
be mocked. He will humble us as a nation as He did King Manasseh.

However, whatever the Lord does in disciplining us, He does out of
great love for us. Why do we flee from love so pure and luminous and
passionate? Why creep around in the darkness, playing with the toys
of destruction and death, when we can step into the light of life—into
all things beautiful, all things good and lovely?

May we choose light, choose love—choose God.

Lord, give me wisdom and help me to always follow You! Amen.

The Best Life There Is

*While they were bringing out the money that had been taken
into the temple of the LORD, Hilkiah the priest found the Book
of the Law of the LORD that had been given through Moses.
Hilkiah said to Shaphan the secretary, "I have found the Book
of the Law in the temple of the LORD." He gave it to Shaphan.*

2 CHRONICLES 34:14–15 NIV

What would happen if the most vital book in the world had gotten lost or forgotten or ignored? Second Chronicles proves that the Word of God can indeed be forgotten. And when the Israelites forgot about God and the Book of the Law, well, life didn't go well. The people found themselves in spiritual peril.

Running from the truth hasn't changed. Today, we have done a great job of snubbing the Word of God and even removing parts of the Bible that make us squirm. We've extracted the Good Book from our schools, businesses, and even our hotel rooms. And now, the Word of God is fading from the hearts of people, leaving each of them in spiritual peril.

The great news is that what was lost can be found. Look for that family Bible or buy a new one. Open its pages and discover real life in Christ—the best life there is—both now and forevermore.

*Lord, at times we're guilty of ignoring You and the Bible.
Please awaken us to the truth of Your Word. Amen.*

A Coming Home of the Soul

But many of the older priests and Levites and family heads,
who had seen the former temple, wept aloud when they saw the
foundation of this temple being laid, while many others shouted
for joy. No one could distinguish the sound of the shouts of joy
from the sound of weeping, because the people made so much
noise. And the sound was heard far away.

EZRA 3:12–13 NIV

When the Jews did what was right before God—that is, began the rebuilding of the temple by laying its foundation—some wept and others shouted for joy. The mingling of the sounds made so much noise that it could be heard from far away.

Making things right with God, well, there's nothing else like that divine reconnection. One might come to think of remorseful or joyous weeping or jubilant shouts before God as a sacred song or a "coming home of the soul."

Have you connected to God lately? Have you confessed your sins? Have you come to know that "coming home of the soul"? It is only a prayer away.

God, please forgive me for all that I've done to harm
our relationship. I want to be close to You both now
and forevermore. In Jesus' holy name I pray. Amen.

From Discouragement to Joy

Then the peoples around them set out to discourage the
people of Judah and make them afraid to go on building.
They bribed officials to work against them and frustrate their
plans during the entire reign of Cyrus king of Persia and
down to the reign of Darius king of Persia.
EZRA 4:4–5 NIV

When the Jewish exiles began to rebuild the temple, the people of the land—who were Samaritans as well as their enemies—asked to help them. But the Jews were wise and declined their aid. Then the true motivation of the Samaritans came to be known as they tried to obstruct the rebuilding of the temple. But even then, with all the opposition, eventually the temple was indeed completed and dedicated.

In our modern world, there will be people who will pretend to help us in our endeavors, but in the end, we may discover their hidden motives might not be so pure or helpful. Yet just as God allowed the Jewish exiles to succeed in the end, may we always pray for His will to be done in our lives no matter the worldly hostilities and the ploys of the enemy. May God give us wisdom and perseverance as we follow His lead in helping to build His kingdom!

Lord, please allow me to know Your will and follow through with it no matter the oppositions. Please turn my discouragements into joy!

Choosing to Honor God

Praise be to the LORD, the God of our ancestors, who has put it into the king's heart to bring honor to the house of the LORD in Jerusalem in this way and who has extended his good favor to me before the king and his advisers and all the king's powerful officials. Because the hand of the LORD my God was on me, I took courage and gathered leaders from Israel to go up with me.

EZRA 7:27–28 NIV

The Old Testament is riddled with accounts of bad kings who made the people groan in misery. But there are also instances of kings who followed God and who made life better for the Jews.

Today, we do not have a king ruling over us. We can choose who will be our lawmakers from the voting booth. Are we prayerfully considering who we select to lead us? Does the person running for office love the Lord? Does he or she follow scripture, including honoring the biblical view of marriage, the sanctity of life, and watching out for the needy and elderly? Or do the people running for office call good evil and evil good?

God wants wonderful and lovely things for us. With His help, may we be diligent in finding godly leaders.

Lord, I want to honor You in all that I do, including choosing the right people to lead our nation. Please give me wisdom and discernment to do just that. Amen.

Appalled!

After these things had been done, the leaders came to me and said, "The people of Israel, including the priests and the Levites, have not kept themselves separate from the neighboring peoples with their detestable practices, like those of the Canaanites, Hittites, Perizzites, Jebusites, Ammonites, Moabites, Egyptians and Amorites. They have taken some of their daughters as wives for themselves and their sons, and have mingled the holy race with the peoples around them. And the leaders and officials have led the way in this unfaithfulness." When I heard this, I tore my tunic and cloak, pulled hair from my head and beard and sat down appalled.

EZRA 9:1–3 NIV

As we read in Ezra, it appears there's a time to be appalled with one's behavior! Today, we should be equally distraught over our many offenses against God. So many nations have allowed themselves to be influenced by the peoples and cultures around them, and some of the practices embraced are far from biblical. Like the frog that finds itself cooked to death because the heat has been turned up so gradually that it doesn't notice, too many of us have unwittingly crept closer and closer to destruction.

Sister, let's remember the Bible isn't a rule book meant to spoil our fun—it's God's way for us to live truly free, abundant lives!

*Lord, show me all the ways I have strayed from Your precepts.
Help me love and honor You alone as the One true living God. Amen.*

The Sweetness of Tears

When I heard these things, I sat down and wept. For some days I
mourned and fasted and prayed before the God of heaven. Then I said:
"LORD, the God of heaven, the great and awesome God, who keeps his
covenant of love with those who love him and keep his commandments,
let your ear be attentive and your eyes open to hear the prayer your
servant is praying before you day and night for your servants,
the people of Israel. I confess the sins we Israelites, including myself
and my father's family, have committed against you."

NEHEMIAH 1:4–6 NIV

Humans tend to quickly swipe away tears of any kind. And yet there
can be a cleansing effect to tears and a benefit to some kinds of
sorrow. That is, if our hearts are trying to get right with God, then those
tears are sweet, and that kind of remorsefulness is beautiful.

Nehemiah wept over the sins committed by the Israelites. He
mourned and fasted and prayed. And when he prayed, he added himself to the confessions, which was right and good.

Yes, tears and repentance and heartfelt prayers can be good and
lovely things because they can bring you closer to God—which will
ultimately bring you joy!

Lord God, I'm sorry for the wrongs I've done and how they have
grieved Your Holy Spirit. But I also know that because of Your
divine mercy, You will forgive me! In Jesus' name I pray. Amen.

God Will Fight for Us

When all our enemies heard about this, all the surrounding nations were afraid and lost their self-confidence, because they realized that this work had been done with the help of our God.

NEHEMIAH 6:16 NIV

The Israelites faced much opposition when rebuilding the wall of Jerusalem—insults, threats, weariness, and hardships. But they knew that their God would fight for them. And He was indeed faithful.

We may not be building a city wall, but we will face any number of hardships in our lives. Perhaps a wayward teenaged daughter will come home pregnant. Or you will face the sudden disloyalty within a lifelong friendship. Maybe you will suffer the bullying of a boss or the tremendous challenges and disappointments in a career you thought was tailormade by God. Perhaps the painful issues will be health or marriage related, or you may have bouts of poverty or depression or experience ridicule because of your faith in Christ. Life can be brutal at times, but God *will* fight for us, for you.

Stay close to God and ask Him to come alongside you. The Lord is willing and waiting, and He is full of love and mercy.

Dearest Lord, in this troubled world, please be my stronghold and my courage. In Jesus' powerful and holy name I pray. Amen.

Our Bumbling Ways

They refused to listen and failed to remember the miracles you performed among them. They became stiff-necked and in their rebellion appointed a leader in order to return to their slavery. But you are a forgiving God, gracious and compassionate, slow to anger and abounding in love. Therefore you did not desert them.
NEHEMIAH 9:17 NIV

At times, this life is much like a mountain climb. Some of the trails might be pleasant, while others are rough, foggy, and downright treacherous. Unfortunately, we humans sometimes make the way harder than it is with our rebellion. We might choose a route that we know is deadly, just because it appears enticing. And then that's it—we traipse off on our own without ropes or a compass or our Guide. Like sheep gone astray, we find ourselves stumbling into an abyss or a patch of razor-sharp brambles. And then later, bloodied and bone weary, we wonder bitterly what went wrong. We rail at the world, at everyone around us, and even at God.

Throughout history, we've been those bumbling sheep. Thank the Lord—truly—that He is forgiving, gracious, and compassionate, slow to anger and abounding in love. Even in our sheeplike ways, we can rest in those good and lovely truths.

Dearest Lord Jesus, I admit that at times I am one of those bumbling sheep stuck in the brambles. Please keep me on Your path—the one that leads to eternal life. Amen.

The Light of Life

*"We assume the responsibility for carrying out the commands to
give a third of a shekel each year for the service of the house of
our God: for the bread set out on the table; for the regular grain
offerings and burnt offerings; for the offerings on the Sabbaths,
at the New Moon feasts and at the appointed festivals; for the
holy offerings; for sin offerings to make atonement for Israel;
and for all the duties of the house of our God."*

NEHEMIAH 10:32–33 NIV

The more we read the Old Testament, the more we see how very
difficult it must have been for the Jews to fulfill the law in its
entirety. It was so extensive and precise in its commands, it seemed
humanly impossible to carry them all out fully. But perhaps that is the
point. Only God can accomplish the impossible task of redemption.
He offered us a flawless sacrifice in His Son, Jesus Christ, and in that
offering we can know forgiveness and reconciliation. We can know—Him.

It's as if we were living in a dank, dark prison, and Christ alone
lovingly showed us the way out. Out into the bright light of life and
love and eternity!

*Lord of life, thank You for setting the captives free,
including me. I love You more than words can say. Amen.*

Soul Celebrations

*And on that day they offered great sacrifices, rejoicing
because God had given them great joy. The women
and children also rejoiced. The sound of rejoicing in
Jerusalem could be heard far away.*

NEHEMIAH 12:43 NIV

Oh, when we get it right with God, ahh yes, our souls can't help but
rejoice—just as they did in the days of old. What have your unique
times of "soul celebrations" looked like? Did they come as a praise, a
shout, or a song? And how did you come by that joy? Was it the day you
walked away from a temptation that had previously tangled you in its
web? Or was it in the moment when you genuinely cheered for a friend's
engagement even though that dream of marriage has always eluded you?
Perhaps it was when you went back to the store to pay for an item that
had accidentally gotten left off your bill. Or could it be the deliberate
pause amid a harried life to take in the wonder of God's creation?

The world may not delight in these kinds of life happenings, but
the Lord does. May we ever rejoice in what is good and right and lovely
in the sight of God. May we all fall into step with the Lord, bring Him
delight, and know joy everlasting.

*Lord, may my life delight You and my soul
celebrations bring attention to Your majesty
and mercy. In Jesus' name I pray. Amen.*

The Gift

Then Haman said to King Xerxes, "There is a certain people dispersed among the peoples in all the provinces of your kingdom who keep themselves separate. Their customs are different from those of all other people, and they do not obey the king's laws; it is not in the king's best interest to tolerate them. If it pleases the king, let a decree be issued to destroy them, and I will give ten thousand talents of silver to the king's administrators for the royal treasury." So the king took his signet ring from his finger and gave it to Haman son of Hammedatha, the Agagite, the enemy of the Jews. "Keep the money," the king said to Haman, "and do with the people as you please."

ESTHER 3:8–11 NIV

Through history, the Jews have known great tribulations. But during all these many hardships and rebellions, the Jews have continued to be a people set apart by God.

As Christ followers, we too are set apart but in a different way. There is no faith on earth like ours, for Christianity is not so much a religion as it is reconciliation with the one true God. Through Christ, God has offered us the gift of redemption, which leads to eternal life, and He desires that all people embrace this gift. Shall we then partake of this divine present of the soul?

Jesus, thank You for the gift of salvation. I love You! Amen.

Divine Courage

"For if you remain silent at this time, relief and deliverance for the Jews will arise from another place, but you and your father's family will perish. And who knows but that you have come to your royal position for such a time as this?" Then Esther sent this reply to Mordecai: "Go, gather together all the Jews who are in Susa, and fast for me. Do not eat or drink for three days, night or day. I and my attendants will fast as you do. When this is done, I will go to the king, even though it is against the law. And if I perish, I perish."

ESTHER 4:14–16 NIV

It took great courage for Esther to go before the king with her request to save the Jewish people from annihilation. She chose to step out in faith even though her actions could have resulted in her death. Esther's bravery was rewarded with a mighty miracle, and now her heroic story is repeated throughout time.

What does God ask of you that requires courage? Is it to stand up for the sanctity of life? Is it to watch out for the needy? Is it to walk away from vengeful gossip? Or maybe it's a little-big thing, such as not hollering at your kids when they're forcing you to peddle on the last fumes of your patience! Whatever God asks of you, He will provide you with the strength and courage to fulfill it.

Lord, give me divine courage! Amen.

Choices

King Xerxes imposed tribute throughout the empire, to its distant shores. And all his acts of power and might, together with a full account of the greatness of Mordecai, whom the king had promoted, are they not written in the book of the annals of the kings of Media and Persia? Mordecai the Jew was second in rank to King Xerxes, preeminent among the Jews, and held in high esteem by his many fellow Jews, because he worked for the good of his people and spoke up for the welfare of all the Jews.

ESTHER 10:1–3 NIV

When the heroic story of Queen Esther concludes in the Bible, Mordecai is also held in high esteem by not only the king but by Mordecai's fellow Jews. If you have never read the whole book of Esther, allow yourself to be taken up into its fullness, to be awed by its drama—to be inspired and challenged by the way God uses humanity to alter the flow of history.

Today, every choice you make is not only remembered by God but has the potential to change the flow of history—for good or for evil.

What will your choices be today?

Dearest Lord Jesus, please help my choices to be good and lovely ones. Help them to shine Your light in a world that is in great need of Your radiant presence. Amen.

Trials

*Then the LORD said to Satan, "Have you considered my servant
Job? There is no one on earth like him; he is blameless and
upright, a man who fears God and shuns evil." "Does Job fear God
for nothing?" Satan replied. "Have you not put a hedge around
him and his household and everything he has? You have blessed
the work of his hands, so that his flocks and herds are spread
throughout the land. But now stretch out your hand and strike
everything he has, and he will surely curse you to your face."*

JOB 1:8–11 NIV

S ome might say that Job is one of the most uncomfortable books in
the Bible. A book no one really wants to think about. Not because
it's hard to understand but because the message might appear too
fearsomely clear. God and Satan have a conversation, which brings about
a wager of sorts, and a man named Job will have to prove himself as
a true lover of God amid tremendous suffering. As we know from the
story, Job passes the test fairly well.

If we endured a few Job-like catastrophes, how would we fare?
Would we curse God? Would we doubt His power, sovereignty, or love
for us? Or in the end would we, like Job, still find ourselves in love with
God, no matter our circumstances?

*Lord, help me to stay true to You even
during the rough patches. Amen.*

A Promise of Great Things

*"Why then did you bring me out of the womb? I wish I
had died before any eye saw me. If only I had never come
into being or had been carried straight from the womb
to the grave! Are not my few days almost over? Turn
away from me so I can have a moment's joy before I go
to the place of no return, to the land of gloom and utter
darkness, to the land of deepest night, of utter darkness
and disorder, where even the light is like darkness."*

JOB 10:18–22 NIV

When we walk through the darkest valley, God is there. And even if we don't receive the help, the healing, the complete victory on this side of eternity, we will on the other side. As followers of Christ, we have promises of much more to come, promises that no mere man or woman on earth can make. Only Jesus says, "And if I go and prepare a place for you, I will come back and take you to be with me that you also may be where I am" (John 14:3).

When all is lost, and even when the light here has become like darkness, Christ comes with truth, assurances, and hope.

Know. Cling. Celebrate!

Lord, thank You for the beautiful promise of heaven. Amen.

Good and Lovely Friends

*Then Job replied: "Doubtless you are the only people who
matter, and wisdom will die with you! But I have a mind
as well as you; I am not inferior to you. Who does not
know all these things? I have become a laughingstock to
my friends, though I called on God and he answered—
a mere laughingstock, though righteous and blameless!"*

JOB 12:1–4 NIV

The human heart-cry in the book of Job is deeply painful to read.
Job wishes he had never been born so that he could have escaped
his many hardships.

How many times in your own life have you known various losses
and sorrows? This broken life can act like a bludgeoning hammer on
the body, mind, and soul. Job had been hit so hard, he could barely
function. Amazingly though, he could still state his case with clarity,
passion, and maybe even a bit of wit!

The back-and-forth arguments between Job and his friends are also
heartbreaking to read. His friends clearly didn't provide the healing
words that Job needed. They failed so much so that God reprimanded
Job's friends.

So, what kind of friendship do you provide when someone is stricken
with sorrows? Do you arrive with judgment or with a lovely spirit of
compassion?

*Lord, please help me be a real and true friend,
one who can be a help and not a hindrance. Amen.*

To Speak Life

*Then Job replied: "How long will you torment me
and crush me with words? Ten times now you have
reproached me; shamelessly you attack me. If it is true
that I have gone astray, my error remains my concern
alone. If indeed you would exalt yourselves above me and
use my humiliation against me, then know that God has
wronged me and drawn his net around me."*

JOB 19:1–6 NIV

As we live out our days on this earth, whether we're at home, work, church, traveling, or wherever, do we ever step back to study the way we react to various people and happenings in our lives? It's easy to be Miss Sweety Pie—and speak words of life—when we are loved, understood, and handed good things. But throw some inconvenience our way or toss some crabby individuals in our path, or perhaps even people who are broken or needy, well, our words of life might morph into something else—something that isn't so good and lovely.

Job's visitors spoke words that judged, discouraged, and tore him down even though he was already as low as any human could be. The people around him could have chosen to speak truth with compassionate doses of life and love, but they did not.

Today, consider how you choose to speak as you go about, to and fro.

*Holy Spirit, show me how to offer people the truth as well
as words of life, encouragement, and great hope. Amen.*

Wily Ways of Pride

*"Listen carefully to my words; let this be the
consolation you give me. Bear with me while I speak,
and after I have spoken, mock on."*

JOB 21:2–3 NIV

Reading the book of Job is quite a fascinating, challenging, and inspiring ride. In the verses above—showing Job's curt reply—we can see that the dialogue between Job and his friends is still quite heated.

One of the problems with Job's false comforters is that they were puffed up with self-righteousness. In fact, one could say they were blinded by it. Proverbs 16:18 reminds us, "Pride goes before destruction, a haughty spirit before a fall."

From reading all the various passages in the Bible that denounce pride, it is obvious that God does not like a haughty heart. He instead loves humility. And Job's friends were sorely lacking in the latter.

One of the many pieces of wisdom that can be gleaned from Job is to be watchful for the wily ways of pride. The strange paradox is that people can be haughty even about their humility! That would be amusing if it weren't so true.

*Lord, give me a humble heart—the real thing—
so that I might bring glory to Your name
and be usable in Your kingdom. Amen.*

Some Is Left to Mystery

"Oh, that I had someone to hear me! I sign now
my defense—let the Almighty answer me; let my
accuser put his indictment in writing. Surely I would
wear it on my shoulder, I would put it on like a
crown. I would give him an account of my every step;
I would present it to him as to a ruler."

JOB 31:35–37 NIV

Job said his piece before God and man and then left his plight in the hands of the Almighty. Job was forced to make a decision about suffering. A choice we all must face. That is, in times of trouble and travail, whom do we turn to in faith? Job chose God. No matter what.

Later, we find great mystery in God's response since He didn't really explain the "whys" of Job's suffering. As frustrating as that might seem, if all the majesty and supernatural power and creative wonder and holiness of God could be unpuzzled by humans, then He would no longer be God. Yet in the midst of mystery, we can know that our God is good and He is love. That is what we can hold on to. That is what can and will bring us peace in times of peril.

Dear Lord, may I always choose You even
when I don't understand Your will. Amen.

Good News

So these three men stopped answering Job, because he was righteous in his own eyes. But Elihu son of Barakel the Buzite, of the family of Ram, became very angry with Job for justifying himself rather than God. He was also angry with the three friends, because they had found no way to refute Job, and yet had condemned him. Now Elihu had waited before speaking to Job because they were older than he. But when he saw that the three men had nothing more to say, his anger was aroused.

JOB 32:1–5 NIV

If you read the whole book of Job, you may eventually wonder, "I thought Job's friends were finally finished with their onslaught of accusations, but it seems to never end. Do these men have more words than sense? They never stop spewing against poor old Job." And yet, the visitors do have some fascinating points to make. From the outside, they could be seen as wise. But God sees man's heart and his deepest yearnings and secrets, and He knows what is happening in the unseen world. Even though we may not understand the ways of the Almighty, we can be thankful that we are judged by God and not by man.

Yes, God is the final judge, not your neighbor, not your boss, not even your friends. That is our good news!

I trust in Your judgments, Lord, for You are a God of mercy. Amen.

Love

The LORD blessed the latter part of Job's life more than the former part. He had fourteen thousand sheep, six thousand camels, a thousand yoke of oxen and a thousand donkeys. And he also had seven sons and three daughters. The first daughter he named Jemimah, the second Keziah and the third Keren-Happuch. Nowhere in all the land were there found women as beautiful as Job's daughters, and their father granted them an inheritance along with their brothers. After this, Job lived a hundred and forty years; he saw his children and their children to the fourth generation. And so Job died, an old man and full of years.

JOB 42:12–17 NIV

O ur Creator has always wanted a relationship with us—a complete circle of love. The real thing.

God poses the question, "Do you love Me only because I bless you with many good things?" If we're honest, this may be a similar thought we have about our children. That is, if we stopped showering them with toys, fun times, and treats, would they still care for us? As parents, we hope that as our children mature, they'll come to want a relationship with us that goes far beyond what we can give them.

After Job's time of testing—when the blessings were removed—his love was proven to be real, and God rewarded him mightily again. It makes us wonder, "Why do *we* love God?"

Lord, show me how to love You with all my heart! Amen.

What Is Excellent!

LORD, our Lord, how majestic is your name in all the earth!
You have set your glory in the heavens. Through the praise of
children and infants you have established a stronghold against
your enemies, to silence the foe and the avenger. When I
consider your heavens, the work of your fingers, the moon and
the stars, which you have set in place, what is mankind that you
are mindful of them, human beings that you care for them?

PSALM 8:1–4 NIV

It is easy to get bogged down in the mire of daily living, isn't it? Sometimes this world makes us so negative, harried, and downtrodden, we even forget about God and how deeply we are cherished by Him.

Yet Philippians 4:8 tells us, "Finally, brothers and sisters, whatever is true, whatever is noble, whatever is right, whatever is pure, whatever is lovely, whatever is admirable—if anything is excellent or praiseworthy— think about such things."

God has provided us with many things to think about that are true, noble, right, pure, lovely, admirable, excellent, and praiseworthy. We have the blessing of family and friends, good work with divine purpose, as well as the vast wonderment of His creation. And, of course, most excellent of all—we have Christ's mercy and grace!

Lord, thank You for providing so many
excellent things to think on. Amen.

Flinging Flattery

*Help, LORD, for no one is faithful anymore; those
who are loyal have vanished from the human race.
Everyone lies to their neighbor; they flatter with their
lips but harbor deception in their hearts.*

PSALM 12:1–2 NIV

H ave you ever met a gusher? You can't miss them. You might meet one at a party, or church, or at work. They stand out because they are usually a bit on the showy side, and they fling flattery around like verbal confetti. Face it, the same women who tell you they adore you and they will move heaven and earth for you may turn out to be the same women who refuse to even acknowledge you the very next day. Yikes!

As you can see in Psalms, God is not amused with flattery. He knows what lies behind such talk. God knows that flattery is worse than useless. It is deceptive and damaging because it's simply not the truth. Flattery comes with sly motivations, which turn out to be self-serving and manipulative. Oh, may our words be loving and real, pure and noble.

*Father God, in all my conversations, please help me not to
give into the temptation of flattery, but may I instead reflect
You in all I say and do. In Jesus' name I pray. Amen.*

Divine Timing

Wait for the LORD; be strong and take
heart and wait for the LORD.

PSALM 27:14 NIV

Our society has become more and more high-speed. We want instant everything—from food to news to cars to technology. We are taught life is short, time is money, and if people slow us down or cause us to lose our focus, well, maybe they should just get out of our way!

Amid the world's fast pace though, sometimes the Lord asks us to wait. And our spirits cry out, "No, not that word—*wait*—anything but that." And yet, sometimes God desires that we should wait on Him. Not because the Almighty is fickle or enjoys watching us squirm in frustration but because God is the One who made time. He is the Creator and Master of all of eternity. Only He knows the exact time when something should happen so that it can truly work for our good.

Take a moment to look back on your life at all the times God came to your rescue, gifted you with amazing blessings, and was your comfort and strength. What loveliness there is in the divine timing of God!

Jesus, please give me the patience to wait on You.
I love You and I trust You with all my tomorrows! Amen.

Rejoicing in the Morning

Sing the praises of the LORD, you his faithful people;
praise his holy name. For his anger lasts only a moment,
but his favor lasts a lifetime; weeping may stay for the
night, but rejoicing comes in the morning.

PSALM 30:4–5 NIV

There is a soul-sting that comes from being disciplined. Nobody likes it. Being told that we did something bad or didn't do something we should have, well, how many people respond to that reprimand with "I am so very happy you came to me with your rebukes. You are so right. I am a fortunate woman indeed. Thank you!" Hmmm. Bit of a stretch for most folks.

Yet when God is speaking to us in love, telling us how we can improve in our walk with Him on this earth, we should listen. We should make the necessary changes. And we should even be grateful, yes, thankful that the Lord cares for us like the doting parent who loves us deeply enough to correct us. We may be sad for a time, but His favor lasts for a lifetime, and there will be rejoicing in the morning!

Holy Spirit, in all honesty, I don't always relish Your divine
discipline, but help me to be grateful for it and to learn and grow
from these lessons. Thank You for being a good parent. Amen.

River of Delights

*Your love, LORD, reaches to the heavens, your faithfulness to
the skies. Your righteousness is like the highest mountains, your
justice like the great deep. You, LORD, preserve both people and
animals. How priceless is your unfailing love, O God! People take
refuge in the shadow of your wings. They feast on the abundance
of your house; you give them drink from your river of delights.
For with you is the fountain of life; in your light we see light.*

PSALM 36:5–9 NIV

Since humankind chose to rebel and fall from grace in the Garden
of Eden, we have known great sin, destruction, and death. Life
has not gone well, and yet in the midst of all that travail and misery,
there is light still—God's holy light. In fact, when we follow the Lord,
we can drink from a river of delights. What can that be? How can that
be possible, and what does it mean?

Read and reread this passage in Psalms, and embrace the delights
of God Almighty.

Remember, of course, that the greatest delight comes from Jesus
Christ Himself, whose sacrifice and redemption make for the most
radiant light and most irresistible goodness and most powerful love
this world will ever know.

*Father God, be ever near me. Walk with me. Talk with me.
I want to know You. I want to drink from Your river
of delights. I love You! In Jesus' name I pray. Amen.*

My Soul Thirsts for You!

As the deer pants for streams of water, so my soul pants
for you, my God. My soul thirsts for God, for the
living God. When can I go and meet with God?
PSALM 42:1–2 NIV

What a lovely image in Psalms, comparing a deer that pants for streams of water with the way one's soul thirsts for the Lord. For humans, we might experience a smoldering and sweaty day of yardwork, which ends in a terrible thirst. We can't wait to drink down that tall glass of lemonade or iced tea and be fully satisfied. How much more should we thirst for the company of our Lord? May it become our focus, our drive, and even our passion.

How do we love our God? Do we long to meet with Him? Do we look forward to those moments and call them precious? Do we savor them, learn from them, come away challenged, inspired, and refreshed by them? Then, do we long to tell others about our living God?

Dearest heavenly Father, I long for Your beautiful and pure and
glorious presence, and I acknowledge that there is nothing
on earth that will satisfy like You. My soul thirsts for You!
Please be ever near me. In Jesus' name I pray. Amen.

This Is God

Walk about Zion, go around her, number her towers,
consider well her ramparts, go through her citadels, that
you may tell the next generation that this is God, our God
forever and ever. He will guide us forever.

PSALM 48:12–14 ESV

In Psalm 48, we see two very different responses to Zion. Those who were against God panicked; they trembled and fled. But the people of God praised Him. In God's great city, His people saw God's greatness. In Zion's citadels and temple, they saw proof of His protection and love. They were to look at Zion and think of their God.

As we walk this earth, our responses to life could run the gamut—from wonder and joy to apathy, gloom, fear, and so on. Regardless of what we face, positivity and praise are possible if we keep our thoughts fixed on God.

What "landmarks" can you recall—times when God has shown who He is or come through for you or others in little or big ways? Where have you seen God's hand in the past—His generosity, compassion, and power? Think on those times in your mind every day. And when you have a burden to bear, don't dwell on the burden. Give it to God! Be assured that He will take care of you—as He has always done (Psalm 55:22).

Lord, help me focus on the many evidences of You.
You are God, and I praise You. Amen.

For Us

You keep track of all my sorrows. You have collected all
my tears in your bottle. You have recorded each one in
your book. . . . This I know: God is on my side! I praise
God for what he has promised; yes, I praise the LORD
for what he has promised. I trust in God, so why should
I be afraid? What can mere mortals do to me?

PSALM 56:8–11 NLT

When you're in the middle of a rough season, does it ever feel as if no one else, including God, notices what you're going through?

In Psalm 56, David recounted when he was in a tough spot. From morning till night, the Philistines lurked and threatened and trampled him. Yes, David was greatly troubled, *but* he knew one thing: God was for him. God had not overlooked what was happening; in fact, He was keeping track of *every* sorrow and collecting *every* tear. In his trouble, David trusted God all the more, because only that trust—only God Himself—could rescue him from despair. No wonder the shepherd-boy-turned-king advised, "O my people, trust in him at all times. Pour out your heart to him, for God is our refuge" (Psalm 62:8).

God is on your side! Turn to Him when rough times pull you down. He'll pull you back up.

God, You see everything that's going on, and You care.
I can put my trust in You always. Amen.

Old and Gray

For you have been my hope, Sovereign LORD, my confidence
since my youth. From birth I have relied on you; you brought
me forth from my mother's womb. I will ever praise you.

PSALM 71:5–6 NIV

A*ging*. That word doesn't always bring positive thoughts to mind. After all, each year adds wrinkles and aches. Each year makes the list of trials we've lived through get longer. Yet growing older is a blessing also.

The writer of Psalm 71 had experienced hardship, and it wasn't letting up in his old age. Yet God was still faithful. It was God whom he depended on the day he was born, and it would be God whom he depended on to revive him every day of his life. He wrote of God: "Though you have made me see troubles, many and bitter, you will restore my life *again*; from the depths of the earth you will *again* bring me up" (v. 20 NIV, emphasis added). With each passing year, the psalmist witnessed God's faithfulness firsthand, over and over, and that boosted his faith. In fact, the good things God had done were so far beyond number and knowledge that the psalmist could "hope continually" and praise God "more and more" despite any trouble (vv. 14–15 ESV).

If you allow it, growing older can increase your faith too.

God, help me grow closer to You as I grow older.
You are faithful, and I will ever praise You! Amen.

Our Everything

My flesh and my heart faileth: but God is the
strength of my heart, and my portion for ever.
PSALM 73:26 KJV

᠁

The psalmist tried to do his best, but what he got back was trouble. Then he started looking around, and wouldn't you know it, the people who weren't trying to be good at all weren't troubled by anything. How did he handle the situation? With grace and maturity? Nope. A whole lot of ugliness surfaced. But when he was at his worst, he learned something about himself and God:

> *I realized that my heart was bitter, and I was all torn up inside.*
> *I was so foolish and ignorant—I must have seemed like a*
> *senseless animal to you. Yet I still belong to you; you hold my*
> *right hand. . . . Whom have I in heaven but you? I desire you*
> *more than anything on earth. . . . My spirit may grow weak,*
> *but God remains the strength of my heart; he is mine forever*
> *(Psalm 73:21–23, 25–26 NLT).*

Maybe you've seen things in this life that don't make sense and don't seem fair. Maybe you've questioned and struggled, and a whole lot of ugliness surfaced. But through it all, God remains. You are still His. He is still yours. And, oh, "how good it is to be near God" (v. 28 NLT)!

God, when I'm torn up inside, may I turn to You. Amen.

Remember When

So each generation should set its hope anew on God, not forgetting his glorious miracles and obeying his commands. Then they will not be like their ancestors—stubborn, rebellious, and unfaithful, refusing to give their hearts to God.

PSALM 78:7–8 NLT

The psalmist began Psalm 78 with a plea: "O my people, listen to my instructions. Open your ears to what I am saying, for I will speak to you in a parable. I will teach you hidden lessons from our past—stories we have heard and known, stories our ancestors handed down to us" (vv. 1–3). What follows is a brief retelling of God's mighty deeds and Israel's misdeeds, of how God took care of His people and how His people turned their backs on Him. It's a true-life cautionary tale. "Listen up!" the psalmist could have said. "Take these things to heart!"

That's good advice for us too. We have those stories and more that are handed down to us, all neatly printed and bound in the cover of a Bible (or digitally displayed on a device). Chunks of the Bible may be tedious to read, it's true; but let's not forget God's Word is a gift. It's an ages-long record of what God has done—and what people have done in response, both good and bad.

Your mission? Pattern your life on the good.

Lord, help me listen and learn as I read the Bible. Amen.

Rocky Road, Steady Faith

Blessed be the LORD forever! Amen and Amen.
PSALM 89:52 ESV

The psalms cover a lot of ground—from laments to worship. They show the human side of faith as God's people try to live out their beliefs each day, even when they wonder about what's happening. Psalms 88 and 89 are examples of this tension.

The writer of Psalm 88 didn't know why he had been plagued by an illness. "O LORD, why do you reject me?" he wrote. "Why do you turn your face from me?" (Psalm 88:14 NLT). The writer of Psalm 89 had a question too. He knew God's promises about Israel, but he didn't see God's promises being fulfilled, and asked, "Lord, where is your unfailing love? You promised it to David with a faithful pledge" (Psalm 89:49 NLT).

Yet despite uncertainty, both psalmists chose to trust God to work *everything* out. His sickness may not be explained, but he would continue to turn to God: "O LORD, I cry out to you. I will keep on pleading day by day" (Psalm 88:13 NLT). What God promised may seem unlikely, but he would still believe: "I will sing of the LORD's unfailing love forever! . . . Your faithfulness is as enduring as the heavens" (Psalm 89:1–2 NLT). Both psalmists chose faith. What do you choose?

My world might be stretched by questions, but I choose to put my faith in You, blessed Lord. Amen and amen!

Unforsaken

But the LORD is my fortress; my God is
the mighty rock where I hide. God will
turn the sins of evil people back on them.

PSALM 94:22–23 NLT

A lot has changed since the psalms were written. But while modern society is different from the ancient world, a lot remains the same. Reading through the psalms, we see that the people of biblical times were no strangers to just how wicked humankind could be. Evil people were doing evil things way back then too, and God's people called out to Him to make things right.

Yet even before God righted the wrongs, His people observed how He was still active in positive ways in their individual lives: "Joyful are those you discipline, LORD, those you teach with your instructions. You give them relief from troubled times until a pit is dug to capture the wicked" (Psalm 94:12–13). And again, "Unless the LORD had helped me, I would soon have settled in the silence of the grave. I cried out, 'I am slipping!' but your unfailing love, O LORD, supported me. When doubts filled my mind, your comfort gave me renewed hope and cheer" (vv. 17–19). God *always* brings His goodness into the bad. Until that day when He abolishes all evil, we can look to Him, our fortress and rock of refuge.

God, sometimes it seems like wickedness is everywhere.
Help me find good things in You. Amen.

Take a Look

Bless the LORD, O my soul! O LORD my God, you are
very great! You are clothed with splendor and majesty,
covering yourself with light as with a garment,
stretching out the heavens like a tent.
PSALM 104:1–2 ESV

When the psalmists felt overwhelmed and needed to be reminded of God's greatness, they looked around them—past the busyness of life, past the day-to-day toils and troubles, past the evil that abounded . . .past all of that to the ways God was revealed in His creation.

Psalm 104 gives a panoramic view of how God created and cares for the earth and everything on it. His many acts include forming the solid ground, shaping the mountains and valleys and seas with a command, making gushing springs and plentiful vegetation, and ordering the days and seasons. Yes, God's fingerprints are everywhere! So much so that the psalmist declared, "O LORD, how manifold are your works!"; "O LORD my God, you are very great!" (v. 24; v. 1).

What do you do when you're overwhelmed? Do you head to the spa? Do you hunker down with a good book or a gooey brownie? Do you hit the gym or maybe some high notes while singing in the shower? For a change, do what the psalmists did. Step outside. Look around at God's creation. And let your heart praise Him.

God, I see Your greatness in the sky, in the ocean. . .
in this whole world. How awesome You are! Amen.

He Saves!

Has the LORD redeemed you? Then speak out! Tell others he has redeemed you from your enemies. For he has gathered the exiles from many lands, from east and west, from north and south.

PSALM 107:2–3 NLT

Our Lord is a redeemer. He is *the* Redeemer, the One who saves us from spending eternity in hell. Yet He also rescues us from hairy situations throughout our lives.

Psalm 107 says to tell those life-saving stories and it gets the ball rolling. The psalmist used four examples of how God redeemed His people. Some wandered in the desert. Some were imprisoned. Some suffered from sickness. Some battled a storm at sea. In each situation though, the people sought God for deliverance. Four times we see the request—"Then they cried to the LORD in their trouble." And four times we see God's response—"and he delivered them from their distress" (vv. 6, 13, 19, 28 ESV). He led the wanderers to a city. He broke the chains that held the prisoners. He healed the sick. He calmed the storm.

Yet the stories don't end there. Four times we see the reaction—"Let them give thanks to the LORD for his unfailing love and his wonderful deeds for mankind" (vv. 8, 15, 21, 31 NIV). Our Lord is a redeemer. And that's worth praising about!

Lord, You reach out to save us in so many ways.
Thank You! I can't wait to share the stories. Amen.

No Fear

*Surely the righteous will never be shaken; they will
be remembered forever. They will have no fear of bad
news; their hearts are steadfast, trusting in the LORD.
Their hearts are secure, they will have no fear; in the
end they will look in triumph on their foes.*

PSALM 112:6–8 NIV

We dread the phone call. We wait anxiously for the test results. We have nightmares about the stories we see on the internet. We fret over what tomorrow will bring, because there never seems to be a shortage of bad news, right? But here's the good news! The Bible says that the righteous—people who revere God and want to obey Him (Psalm 112:1)—can be fearless in the face of bad news. Their hearts stay steadfast and secure by trusting in God, who watches over them and is sovereign over all. God is so very great that our biggest fears vanish in His shadow.

Each time you feel your heart tugged toward fear, tug it back toward God with these words: "The LORD is high above all nations, and his glory above the heavens! Who is like the LORD our God, who is seated on high, who looks far down on the heavens and the earth? He raises the poor from the dust and lifts the needy from the ash heap, to make them sit with princes" (Psalm 113:4–8 ESV).

Lord God, in Your presence every fear fades! Amen.

Good for Us

*I used to wander off until you disciplined me; but now
I closely follow your word. . . . My suffering was good for
me, for it taught me to pay attention to your decrees.*

PSALM 119:67, 71 NLT

You're not alone if you don't think of "discipline" and "suffering" as good. Maybe it's because of time-outs when we were kids or being grounded as teenagers. Maybe it's because suffering is just plain unpleasant. But for the psalmist, pain led to a positive outcome. All the unpleasantness led to pleasure because there's nothing sweeter than living a life in line with God (Psalm 119:103)!

So, how did the psalmist go about living a pure life? "By guarding it according to your word" (v. 9 ESV). To God, he writes, "I have stored up your word in my heart, that I might not sin against you. . . . I will meditate on your precepts and fix my eyes on your ways" (vv. 11, 15 ESV). We need God's words to shield us from the inside, and they do that when we soak our minds in them. We need something else too. Multiple times the psalmist asked for God to teach him, to lead him, to uphold him, et cetera. We *can't* live this life on our own. Isn't it good that our Helper is ready, willing, and able to help us live?

God, use all things to show me how to live by Your Word. Amen.

Be Glad!

The Lord has done great things for us! We are glad!
PSALM 126:3 AMPC

Years of captivity, years of being unwilling residents in a foreign land, were suddenly over. The writer of Psalm 126 described the incredible event like this: "When the LORD brought back his exiles to Jerusalem, it was like a dream! We were filled with laughter, and we sang for joy. And the other nations said, 'What amazing things the LORD has done for them.' Yes, the LORD has done amazing things for us! What joy!" (vv. 1–3 NLT). But years of captivity meant everything wasn't perfection in Jerusalem. So the psalmist prayed for God to bring prosperity back just as He had brought the people back home, while anticipating the good times that spring out of the bad: "Restore our fortunes, LORD, as streams renew the desert. Those who plant in tears will harvest with shouts of joy. They weep as they go to plant their seed, but they sing as they return with the harvest" (vv. 4–6 NLT).

Are you running low on this kind of hope? By focusing on all God has done, you can learn to praise Him beforehand for things He is yet to do. Because the Lord *does* amazing things for you still today. What a reason to be glad!

Bring back good times, Lord. And until then, I am and will be glad because of the amazing things You do. Amen.

In the Midst of Trouble

*Though I am surrounded by troubles, you will protect
me. . . . The LORD will work out his plans for my life—
for your faithful love, O LORD, endures forever.*
PSALM 138:7–8 NLT

Sometimes when we feel the walls of a tough situation closing
in on us, we lose sight of God. We fail to see that He is with us
absolutely everywhere—no matter what situation we find ourselves
in or put ourselves in—and He never stops intervening in our lives.
David expressed wonder at the thought, saying, "You know everything I
do. . . . You go before me and follow me. You place your hand of blessing on my head. Such knowledge is too wonderful for me, too great for
me to understand!" (Psalm 139:3, 5–6 NLT).

David could go no place where God wasn't already present, waiting
to shepherd him. "Where can I go from your Spirit? Where can I flee
from your presence?" David asked. "If I rise on the wings of the dawn,
if I settle on the far side of the sea, even there your hand will guide me,
your right hand will hold me fast" (vv. 7, 9–10 NIV).

Are troubles making you claustrophobic? Shift your focus to
the One who is ever present, ever faithful, and ever working out His
plans for you.

*Lord, You've not abandoned me in
my troubles. Help me see You. Amen.*

Praise Him!

Praise the LORD!
PSALM 150:6 ESV

You see them throughout Psalms, and they are the book's final words: *Praise the Lord.* This last psalm is a call to praise almighty God with music and dance and voices. Every verse is like a shout: "Praise the LORD! Praise God in his sanctuary; praise him in his mighty heavens! Praise him for his mighty deeds; praise him according to his excellent greatness! Praise him with trumpet sound; praise him with lute and harp! Praise him with tambourine and dance; praise him with strings and pipe! Praise him with sounding cymbals; praise him with loud clashing cymbals! Let everything that has breath praise the LORD!" (Psalm 150:1–6 ESV).

"Let everything that has breath. . ." Praise can be our refrain too. When we're feeling up or down—praise the Lord! In good times and bad—praise the Lord! At the beginning of each new morning, at the end of our longest days—praise the Lord! Maybe praising God doesn't come naturally to you, or maybe your praise muscles are a little out of shape—praise the Lord anyway! It's amazing what praise can do. And God deserves nothing less. As the psalmist declared, "Hallelujah! It's a good thing to sing praise to our God; praise is beautiful, praise is fitting" (Psalm 147:1 MSG).

Lord, there's so much to praise You for. Oh, that praise would fill my life and rise straight to You! Amen.

Straight Paths

Trust in the LORD with all your heart, and do not lean on your own understanding. In all your ways acknowledge him, and he will make straight your paths.

PROVERBS 3:5–6 ESV

*I*t doesn't make sense! . . . Why is this happening? Have thoughts like that ever gone through your mind during difficult times? Or maybe you've been trying to figure out a particular situation, and no matter how much you ruminate, you just *cannot* make sense of it. In fact, the more you think on something, the more unclear that something becomes! You're left frustrated and discouraged, which starts your mind going all over again.

Ready for the solution? You won't find it in yourself—in what you can think up—but in God Himself. Proverbs 3 reminds us to trust in God with all that we have, to acknowledge Him in everything we do—yes, even when we can't make heads or tails of things. While our thinking may lead us astray, God's way always leads to blessedness.

Following godly teaching results in a full and fulfilling life (vv. 1–2), so we'd do well to listen to Solomon's words: "Don't be impressed with your own wisdom. Instead, fear the LORD and turn away from evil" (v. 7 NLT). And as you trust and acknowledge Him, God will make those paths straight!

Lord, my mind's a muddle! I choose to lean on You and not my understanding. Amen.

Oh Wisdom!

Instruct the wise and they will be wiser still.
PROVERBS 9:9 NIV

T he book of Proverbs has a lot to say about wisdom. It's filled with practical insights and spiritual truths. In its beginning chapters, the book also explores wisdom in general, often comparing it with its antithesis, folly. Both call out for devotees. But while Folly's call comes with warnings, Wisdom's call is an invitation to blessing. If Folly is the wicked stepmother, Wisdom is the fairy godmother! "With me are riches and honor, enduring wealth and prosperity," says Wisdom. "My fruit is better than fine gold; what I yield surpasses choice silver. I walk in the way of righteousness, along the paths of justice, bestowing a rich inheritance on those who love me and making their treasuries full" (Proverbs 8:18–21 NIV).

Terrific! But just *how* do we choose wisdom over folly—especially when this world of ours practically clanks and clatters with so many voices? Step one is to fear God: "Skilled living gets its start in the Fear-of-GOD, insight into life from knowing a Holy God" (Proverbs 9:10 MSG). And step two is to actually seek wisdom. Keep reading God's Word! The Bible promises that the ones who search for wisdom will find it (Proverbs 8:17). What's more, when we let God's words train us, we will become even wiser.

*God, teach me how to filter out foolishness
so I can live with wisdom. Amen.*

In the End

When the tempest passes, the wicked is no more,
but the righteous is established forever.

Proverbs 10:25 esv

❦

As you read through Solomon's proverbs, you might notice a pattern. On the one hand, you have the righteous. On the other hand, you have the wicked. In each of these righteous-versus-wicked proverbs, the righteous person's behavior produces something positive; the wicked person's behavior, something negative. The righteous win out, and the wicked give out! Yet, looking around, that's not always what we see. Negative things befall good people. And, yes, positive things seem to come to the bad. But what we see happening now doesn't have to spoil our optimism about what is going to happen. When all the storms of this life pass, the righteous will end in good, and the wicked will end period. It's a promise:

Count on this: The wicked won't get off scot-free, and God's loyal people will triumph (Proverbs 11:21 msg).

The godly can look forward to a reward, while the wicked can expect only judgment (Proverbs 11:23 nlt).

The light of the righteous rejoices, but the lamp of the wicked will be put out (Proverbs 13:9 esv).

All that goes on—well, it makes me mad, and it makes me sad. But I trust You for the future, God of justice. Amen.

"Take My Advice!"

Get all the advice and instruction you can,
so you will be wise the rest of your life.
PROVERBS 19:20 NLT

A dvice and criticism—things we're probably better at dishing out than taking in. Who likes to admit that they don't have all the answers? Who likes to hear that they're wrong? But in the Bible's book of wisdom, we're told to welcome instruction—to get all that we can, in fact—and that includes correction. The advice that initially tears us down can ultimately build us up.

God can also use others to guide us into the best life: "If you listen to constructive criticism, you will be at home among the wise. If you reject discipline, you only harm yourself; but if you listen to correction, you grow in understanding" (Proverbs 15:31–32). Or, as The Message translates the verses: "Listen to good advice if you want to live well. . . . An undisciplined, self-willed life is puny; an obedient, God-willed life is spacious."

Just one word of caution concerning words of advice: be sure to weigh any advice against God's Word. We are to heed constructive, godly counsel, not personal opinions or nitpicking. Wisdom from above gives *life*—rich, vital, beautiful life. And who doesn't want more of that, even if the advice is hard to swallow?

God, I'm not very good at taking advice.
Open my ears to hear what comes from You. Amen.

Holy Controller

A person's steps are directed by the LORD.
How then can anyone understand their own way?
PROVERBS 20:24 NIV

Lots of successful people pride themselves on knowing where they're headed. Just going where the wind blows? No way! They've set the trajectory, and that's where they'll land. But sometimes even best-laid plans. . .miss the target. They veer off course; they peter out midair. We miscalculate. Maybe we couldn't really see the target in the first place.

Proverbs 20:24 expresses this "unknowableness" in life—the fact that we can't fathom everything that unfolds in our lives because we aren't the one at the controls. Some translations, like the New International Version, highlight the mystery. Some, like the New Living Translation, seem resigned: "The LORD directs our steps, so why try to understand everything along the way?" Others, like The Message, point to God's providence: "The very steps we take come from GOD; otherwise how would we know where we're going?" Yet no matter what the translation, the conclusion is the same. Map and maneuver all you want, but God is Lord over every step. (See also Proverbs 16:9 and Proverbs 19:21.) Now, that reality could bother you, or it could be a cause for praise and for peace.

Trust God with your eternal destiny. *And* trust Him with each step you take along the way.

Lord, thank You for directing my steps. I place each plan,
each goal, each dream in Your hands. Amen.

"I Confess!"

*Whoever conceals their sins does not prosper, but the
one who confesses and renounces them finds mercy.
Blessed is the one who always trembles before God,
but whoever hardens their heart falls into trouble.*

PROVERBS 28:13–14 NIV

L ife is humming along, then you realize you've sinned. You have a couple of options to deal with your wrongdoing.

Option 1: stuff it in a drawer. Yes, you could ignore that sin. You could pretend you didn't do it or that it wasn't that bad. You could think of reasons why it wasn't your fault. You might even be able to convince yourself that what you've done is not a sin at all. . .except God isn't fooled: "If you say, 'But we didn't know about this,' won't He who weighs hearts consider it? Won't He who protects your life know? Won't He repay a person according to his work?" (Proverbs 24:12 HCSB). The answer is "Of course!" God is aware of everything—our excuses, our sins, our hearts. It's wasted effort to hide ourselves or our actions from Him.

So, there's option 2: bring your wrongdoings out into the open. Confessing sin to a holy God may make us feel rotten. But we can praise God because as we bare our hearts to Him, we *will* find not just His forgiveness and mercy but His blessing too.

*God, soften my heart so that I will confess
and turn from sin right away. Amen.*

Role Model

She is clothed with strength and dignity, and she laughs without fear of the future. When she speaks, her words are wise.
PROVERBS 31:25–26 NLT

Ah, the Proverbs 31 woman. She's got brawn—but she's also got brains! She's savvy, a jill-of-all-trades. She sure has things figured out. Next to her, we might have more in common with Agur of Proverbs 30. He gave himself a big fat F in wisdom: "I am weary and worn out, O God. I am too stupid to be human, and I lack common sense. I have not mastered human wisdom, nor do I know the Holy One" (Proverbs 30:1–3 NLT). But Agur knew enough to understand that godly insight comes from God alone. "Who but God goes up to heaven and comes back down?" Agur asked (v. 4 NLT). "Every word of God proves true; he is a shield to those who take refuge in him" (v. 5 ESV).

Therein lies the woman's secret to success. Each of her good qualities hinges on one: "a woman *who fears the LORD* is to be praised" (Proverbs 31:30 NIV, emphasis added). With that as her starting point, the rest falls into place. And only when God reigns in *our* lives will we move past confusion to the kind of confidence the Proverbs 31 gal wears so well.

Lord, may I be God-fearing above all else. I want my life to be praiseworthy and full of praise! Amen.

Polar Opposites

*To every thing there is a season, and a
time to every purpose under the heaven.*
ECCLESIASTES 3:1 KJV

Ecclesiastes 3:1 introduces an often-repeated passage of scripture. The lyrical chain of verses depicts the dual sides of life—the positive and negative that define our days. Perhaps you've witnessed, or even experienced, some of these opposites: "a time to give birth and a time to die. . .a time to weep and a time to laugh; a time to mourn and a time to dance. . .a time to search and a time to count as lost. . .a time to love and a time to hate; a time for war and a time for peace" (vv. 2, 4, 6, 8 HCSB).

Perhaps you tend to zoom in on the negative. You read Solomon's words, "What do people really get for all their hard work? I have seen the burden God has placed on us all" (Ecclesiastes 3:9–10 NLT), and your heart adds, *Ain't it the truth!*

Yes, it's the truth, but don't call it quits there. We may not be able to escape the bad, yet we *can* cling to the good. We can hold on to the assurance that "God has made everything beautiful for its own time." *And* we can hold on to the God-given promise of a perfect time to come: "He has planted eternity in the human heart" (Ecclesiastes 3:11 NLT).

God, help me hold tightly to the good. Amen.

Vanity of Vanities

"Absolute futility," says the Teacher. "Everything is futile."
Ecclesiastes 12:8 hcsb

❧❧❧

E verything is futile." What a downer. Much of Ecclesiastes is about the ways this life is pointless. Solomon ("the Teacher") observed the goings-on of the world, and he tested various pursuits. In the end, he concluded all of it was vanity, like chasing after the wind. "It's all smoke, nothing but smoke" (12:8 msg).

Considering his less than glowing review, Solomon's response isn't the downer you might expect. "I recommend having fun, because there is nothing better for people in this world than to eat, drink, and enjoy life. That way they will experience some happiness along with all the hard work God gives them under the sun" (8:15 nlt). Again Solomon urges, "Seize life! Eat bread with gusto, drink wine with a robust heart. Oh yes—God takes pleasure in your pleasure! . . . Each day is God's gift. It's all you get in exchange for the hard work of staying alive. Make the most of each one!" (9:7, 9–10 msg).

What an upside-downer! Even though life won't change—it will still be messy and messed up—we can flip our reaction to life. Rather than bemoaning all that's wrong, we can rejoice and be glad in the days that our Lord has made (Psalm 118:24).

Lord, life may be imperfect, but it is a gift.
Help me enjoy it every day—starting today! Amen.

𝓛.𝓞.𝓥.𝓔.

Love flashes like fire, the brightest kind of flame.
Many waters cannot quench love, nor can rivers drown it.
SONG OF SOLOMON 8:6–7 NLT

❧❧❧

The Song of Solomon is a love story, a poetic recounting of the deep love between Solomon and his bride, of the joys of romance and marriage. But maybe this love story doesn't thrill you. Maybe it does the opposite. What if you're married, but happily ever after didn't follow "I do"? What if in your married life the trials outweigh the triumphs by far? What if death has taken your beloved? Or what if you're single and still waiting for the "one"? What if you've made mistakes, if you've awakened love too early, and you're afraid that a love story like the Song of Songs can never be yours? What if. . .love has let you down?

Truth is, even the deepest, most joyous human love will let us down if we don't let Love Himself love us first. Our souls won't be satisfied nor our desires met until we find satisfaction in Him and He becomes our highest desire. No true love can complete us—only the One with the truest love of all. But praise God! He's reaching out with that love. Will you reach out too?

> *Lord, Your love is greater than any other, and You've*
> *given it to me! Earthly love may disappoint me,*
> *but I can rejoice and rest in Your love forever. Amen.*

Bright White

"Come now, let's settle this," says the LORD. "Though your sins are like scarlet, I will make them as white as snow. Though they are red like crimson, I will make them as white as wool."

ISAIAH 1:18 NLT

᠁

T he book of Isaiah opens on a low note. God's people had gone astray. They were like a nation of unruly kids—even animals knew better! So Isaiah laid it all out there:

Listen, heavens, and pay attention, earth, for the LORD has spoken: "I have raised children and brought them up, but they have rebelled against Me. The ox knows its owner. . .but Israel does not know; My people do not understand" Oh sinful nation, people weighed down with iniquity, brood of evildoers, depraved children! They have abandoned the LORD; they have despised the Holy One of Israel; they have turned their backs on Him. (Isaiah 1:2–4 HCSB)

Yet in the low note, God threw out a lifeline. He offered redemption. The Israelites were ailing from head to heels, piled high with sin, but God would revive them and remove their sin. All they had to do was obey. All they had to do was turn from sin to Him.

No person is so sinful, no life so stained with sin that God cannot wash them clean. The Redeemer throws out a lifeline and says, "Come now, let's settle this."

Lord, we praise You for taking away sin.
To You we owe eternal thank-Yous. Amen.

Woe!

Woe to those who call evil good and good evil.
ISAIAH 5:20 ESV

Of the twenty-three verses at the end of Isaiah 5, six begin with *woe*. They're warnings to the sinful of Judah, the "wild grapes" in God's vineyard—those who were greedy, those who were drunk, those who were flippant, those who were deceptive, those who were prideful, and those who were unjust—because eventually the wicked would be cut down to size: "So people will be brought low and everyone humbled" (Isaiah 5:15 NIV).

Now compare the woes in chapter 5 to Isaiah's "woe" in chapter 6. After seeing a vision of the Lord, the prophet said, "Woe is me for I am ruined because I am a man of unclean lips. . .and because my eyes have seen the King, the LORD of Hosts" (Isaiah 6:5 HCSB). "Woe is me" is right! None of us unrighteous humans are worthy to stand before a righteous God. Seeing God's holiness made Isaiah's sinfulness stick out—like a glaring neon sign. He couldn't ignore it. But Isaiah's despair over his sin, instead of delight in it, led to confession—and forgiveness!

Bringing *ourselves* low as we admit our sin is, well, humbling. But bowed before our Lord is exactly where we need to be for Him to lift us up.

You, Lord, exalt the humble. Because of You,
my "woe is me" has turned into praise. Amen.

Jesus

*For unto us a child is born, unto us a son is given: and
the government shall be upon his shoulder: and his name
shall be called Wonderful, Counsellor, The mighty God,
The everlasting Father, The Prince of Peace.*

ISAIAH 9:6 KJV

Troubled times lay ahead. An Assyrian invasion and a Babylonian captivity would leave gloom in their wake. But Isaiah also prophesied dawn on the horizon: "That time of darkness and despair will not go on forever. . . . There will be a time in the future when Galilee of the Gentiles. . .will be filled with glory. The people who walk in darkness will see a great light" (Isaiah 9:1–2 NLT). What was that light? A child would be born, bringing with Him the brightest ray of hope ever! God's people could look beyond the hardship to the coming Messiah.

These days, we might fear that troubled times lie ahead. Our world is aching, and there's already abundant gloom. But Isaiah's words promise dawn on the horizon. The Messiah is coming back! He's coming back to put things right for good and for certain: "His government and its peace will never end. He will rule with fairness and justice. . .for all eternity. The passionate commitment of the LORD of Heaven's Armies will make this happen!" (Isaiah 9:7 NLT). Look beyond any hardship to the returning King.

Jesus, You are the Light of the World and of my life! Amen.

Our Salvation

*"See, God has come to save me. I will trust in him
and not be afraid. The LORD GOD is my strength
and my song; he has given me victory."*

ISAIAH 12:2 NLT

I saiah 12 anticipates a time of praise that will arrive on the heels of pain. Isaiah wrote, "You will say in *that day*: 'I will give thanks to you, O LORD, for though you were angry with me, your anger turned away, that you might comfort me. Behold, God is my salvation; I will trust, and will not be afraid; for the LORD GOD is my strength and my song, and he has become my salvation'" (vv. 1–2 ESV, emphasis added). "That day" is the day of Israel's regathering following the tribulation. That day, the Jews will call Christ "King" and worship Him. Interestingly, a portion of their praise is an echo from the past. The words "the Lord is my strength and my song, and he has become my salvation" (Exodus 15:2 ESV) were sung after Israel crossed the Red Sea. God did not forsake His people then, and He will not forsake the remnant in the end times.

God will not forsake you either. What kind of Red Sea blocks your path? What tribulation is too intense for you to withstand? Trust in God and don't be afraid. Because the One who is your strength and song gives victory!

*Lord God, I praise You! I know You won't
forsake me—not now, not ever. Amen.*

Strike to Heal

And the LORD will strike Egypt,
striking and healing.
ISAIAH 19:22 ESV

It's one oracle of doom after another as Isaiah works his way through the nations God would judge. But don't lose track of God's heart in all that destruction because God's aim is restoration.

Take Egypt. God reduced Egypt to a glimmer of its former glory, crushing her gods, her Nile, her princes. Yet God's striking is paired with healing. "GOD will wound Egypt, first hit and then heal." Why? So that "Egypt will come back to GOD, and GOD will listen to their prayers" (Isaiah 19:22 MSG).

Our Lord is a merciful God, and even now He is orchestrating events to achieve His ends, which are peace and blessing! God's Word promises harmony in the most conflict-ridden places. "There will be a highway from Egypt to Assyria," Isaiah says; "Assyria will go to Egypt, Egypt to Assyria" (Isaiah 19:23 HCSB), and the two nations will worship together. One day, God will bless equally people once split by enmity. Can you imagine? "Israel will take its place alongside Egypt and Assyria, sharing the blessing from the center. GOD-of-the-Angel-Armies, who blessed Israel, will generously bless them all: 'Blessed be Egypt, my people! . . . Blessed be Assyria, work of my hands! . . . Blessed be Israel, my heritage!' " (Isaiah 19:24–25 MSG).

Praise the God who strikes to heal.

You mend this broken world, Lord. Hallelujah!

Absolute Power

Who has purposed this. . . ? The LORD of
hosts has purposed it. . . . He has stretched out
his hand over the sea; he has shaken the kingdoms.
ISAIAH 23:8–9, 11 ESV

A mong Isaiah's prophesies is a message to a palace official in Jerusalem, a man named Shebna. Shebna was arrogant. He looked after himself when he should have been looking after the people. But God knew how to put the lofty man in his place. "Who do you think you are, and what are you doing here. . . ?" went the message. "For the LORD is about to hurl you away, mighty man. He is going to grab you, crumple you into a ball, and toss you away" (Isaiah 22:16–18 NLT).

Out with the bad! And in with the good. God replaced Shebna with Eliakim, whom He called "my servant" (v. 20) and described in terms reminiscent of Christ: "I will give him the key to the house of David . . . . When he opens doors, no one will be able to close them; when he closes doors, no one will be able to open them" (Isaiah 22:22 NLT; see Revelation 3:7).

However troubling leadership may be, you can be sure that our Sovereign Lord is still holding the reins. He's in control! Of leaders. Of nations. And nothing can thwart His purposes.

I rest easy in Your will, Lord. How great You are! Amen.

Goodbye, Death

*O Lord, you are my God; I will exalt you; I will
praise your name, for you have done wonderful
things, plans formed of old, faithful and sure.*
Isaiah 25:1 esv

Young or old. Man or woman. Across classes, continents. . .you
name it, death touches us. Since that day in the garden of Eden
when death entered the world, death hasn't left. It has spread far and
wide—everywhere, in fact, because everyone sins, and the two (death
and sin) go hand in hand. Sin's stiff payment is death, and death costs
us dearly. We feel it deep down at the funeral. We could fear it down
deep all our days.

But. . .

God has a remedy for death: life through Him. God will surely
punish sinners—reading about His wrath can be grim!—but God will
just as surely pardon those who believe in His Son. He has had a grip
on death always, and He will get rid of death before long. Depend upon
it. Praise Him for it:

*He will destroy death forever. The Lord God will wipe away the
tears from every face. . .for the Lord has spoken. On that day it
will be said, "Look, this is our God; we have waited for Him, and
He has saved us. This is the Lord; we have waited for Him. Let
us rejoice and be glad in His salvation." (Isaiah 25:8–9 hcsb)*

God, I can't praise You enough for eternal life! Amen.

Looking Up

Woe to those who go down to Egypt for help, who rely on horses, who trust in the multitude of their chariots and in the great strength of their horsemen, but do not look to the Holy One of Israel or seek help from the LORD.

ISAIAH 31:1 NIV

The Assyrian army had been invading and expanding its kingdom borders long before Isaiah was born. When a young man, he saw the Assyrians topple Israel and Samaria. As an old man, he was witnessing the fall of Judah and the exile of many.

Imagine the desperation that was setting in. Who could they turn to when the ravaging army was approaching? Judah was desperate. Isaiah, a prophet in Judah, offered his God-inspired counsel. Though Egypt was strong militarily, going to that country for help was not the answer. Isaiah advised God's people to rely not on another country's superior strength or speed but on the Lord. Above all else, they were to trust in Him, and He would deliver.

Psalm 121 says, "I lift up my eyes to the mountains—where does my help come from? My help comes from the LORD, the Maker of heaven and earth." When tough situations arise, remember to "seek help from the LORD" (Isaiah 31:1). He will deliver you.

Dear Lord, keep my eyes looking up to seek You not just in times of trouble, but always. For You are my help and salvation.

Key to Happiness

He will be the sure foundation for your times, a rich store
of salvation and wisdom and knowledge; the fear
of the Lord is the key to this treasure.

Isaiah 33:6 niv

During the days of Isaiah, things were downright scary in Jerusalem. The Assyrian army was ravaging everything in sight, threatening Jerusalem's very existence. But Isaiah was the voice of calm, revealing God's words to His people, assuring them that God would save them.

The words of Isaiah resonated with the people then as they do now. The key, as Isaiah tells us, is to fear the Lord. In this case, the word *fear* does not mean to be afraid but rather to have respect and reverence. This is the same way we "fear" our parents or those in authority.

What is "this treasure" of which Isaiah speaks? Unlike a chest overflowing with gold and jewels, Isaiah refers to a treasure far more valuable. This treasure offers safety, peace of mind, knowledge, and wisdom. As Proverbs 8:11 tells us, "Wisdom is more precious than rubies, and nothing you desire can compare with her."

Remember to let God be your foundation, and you will certainly reap the bounty of His treasure.

Dear Lord, help me to trust in You, to respect You, and
to be secure in the knowledge that my confidence lies
in You. Help me seek the treasure You offer, the true
treasure of salvation, wisdom, and knowledge.

The One and Only

"Now, LORD our God, deliver us from his hand, so that all the kingdoms of the earth may know that you, LORD, are the only God."
ISAIAH 37:20 NIV

Things had gone from bad to worse for King Hezekiah in Judah. His future, as well as Judah's, looked bleak. Assyrian forces were poised to invade and conquer, and there seemed to be no way out. When Hezekiah's advisors were visited by Rabshakeh, an envoy of the king of Assyria, he repeatedly tried to discourage their faith in the one true God. Hezekiah, undaunted, once again sought God's counsel through Isaiah.

Isaiah gave his king words of comfort and security. God will deliver His people. Not one of the false gods worshiped by many, but the one *true* God. For, as God had told Moses, "You shall have no other gods before me" (Exodus 20:3).

"Other gods" come in many forms. In the days of Isaiah, surrounding areas, including Assyria, believed in a variety of other gods. Today, those other gods some people worship can be money, status, or valuable possessions. While it's okay to enjoy these material blessings, they're not to be an object of your devotion. Remember, worship is reserved for the one true God. He has your back, and He will never fail you.

Dear Lord, help me keep my eyes on the one true prize—You. For it's You who will deliver me from evil and give me hope for the future.

No Fear

"So do not fear, for I am with you; do not be dismayed,
for I am your God. I will strengthen you and help you;
I will uphold you with my righteous right hand."

ISAIAH 41:10 NIV

F ear is one of the biggest stressors in our lives today, as it has been since Adam and Eve (Genesis 3:10). And not one of us is immune from fear. In the world, the nation, even in our own neighborhoods, people are inundated by reports of dangerous threats, situations, and occurrences. It seems inevitable that we would be fearful. Yet, in Isaiah 41:10, we are reassured that God is here for us, to protect, strengthen, and uphold us. And although God doesn't deny that bad things may happen to us, He does promise to get us through them.

In Psalm 27, David agrees with Isaiah, writing, "The LORD is my light and my salvation—whom shall I fear? The LORD is the stronghold of my life—of whom shall I be afraid?"

Live your life with the reassurance that God has things under control. Although you may never understand why things happen, you can trust that, as Christians, God will always be there for you, to lift you up when you fall.

Sister, have faith. Know that God has you safely in the palm of His hand.

Dear Lord, I pray You will protect me as promised.
Because You're with me, I will not fear.

Forgiven

"I, even I, am he who blots out your transgressions,
for my own sake, and remembers your sins no more."
ISAIAH 43:25 NIV

I f you have children, you soon realize it's your job to discipline them. When they misbehave and you correct them, some kind of punishment may be involved. You do these things not to be mean but to teach them right from wrong. Once their bad behavior is identified, the children have owned up to their misdeeds, and their punishment endured, you move on. You forget the bad behavior. You do not hold a grudge or hold their misbehavior and misdeeds over their heads. You, in effect, simply "forgive and forget."

Throughout your children's lives, this process continues; then one day, your offspring find themselves repeating the process as they raise their own kids.

Our relationship with God, our Father in heaven, is no different. As His imperfect children, we are apt to sin, to stray from His Word through our deeds. That's human nature. But it's *God's* nature to forgive us through His infinite love. We have but to acknowledge our failings and sincerely ask for His forgiveness, and our loving Father instantaneously forgives us.

God never holds a grudge. Why should you?

Dear Lord, I humbly come before You to ask forgiveness for my
shortcomings. I know You are a loving Father and will graciously
forget my misdeeds and forgive me. In Jesus' name, amen.

I'll Be There

"Even to your old age and gray hairs I am he, I am
he who will sustain you. I have made you and I will
carry you; I will sustain you and I will rescue you."

ISAIAH 46:4 NIV

No doubt you have looked in the mirror day after day, year after year, and noted the changes that come with the passage of time. Much to our chagrin, age brings with it some not-so-subtle differences of which you may not be a fan. Perhaps a few wrinkles emerge, or gray hairs, or less energy. Father Time does indeed make his mark.

Regardless of these physical changes, God promises He will always be there to support us and carry us through the hard times. Remember the beautiful poem "Footprints in the Sand" by Mary Stevenson? In the memorable last lines, God reminds us: "The years when you have seen only one set of footprints, my child, is when I carried you."

Through the journey of life, even through old age, God reminds you He will always be there for you. Your job is to believe Him.

Lord in heaven, I am comforted to know that You are forever
there to save me, sustain me, and carry me through the most
difficult times in my life. I thank You and am uplifted by Your grace.

Celebrate

Shout for joy, you heavens; rejoice, you earth;
burst into song, you mountains! For the LORD comforts
his people and will have compassion on his afflicted ones.
ISAIAH 49:13 NIV

H ave you ever been so elated that you literally shouted for joy? Perhaps your sports team won a championship or your child was part of a theater or musical performance. You applauded wildly and perhaps let out a "woo-hoo!" Maybe you were so happy that you felt like singing. It is most definitely a joyful noise, indeed.

In Psalm 100:1–2, we learn to "Shout for joy to the LORD, all the earth. Worship the LORD with gladness; come before him with joyful songs." When we sing hymns of praise in church, we certainly feel the joy that the music inspires.

In Isaiah 49:13, you are reminded that the Lord is always there for you. But who are the "afflicted ones" to whom it refers? They are everyone. They are human beings. They include you. God promises that He will comfort you and that He will always have compassion for you. In other words, He has your back. So, raise your voice in praise of Him, burst into song, and know that He is with you always.

Lord, I celebrate Your love, I praise You and the enduring
strength You offer me, and I thank You for the unconditional
compassion You shower on me, Your afflicted one.

Good News

How beautiful on the mountains are the feet of those who
bring good news, who proclaim peace, who bring good tidings,
who proclaim salvation, who say to Zion, "Your God reigns!"
ISAIAH 52:7 NIV

You have most likely seen the Christmas classic cartoon *A Charlie Brown Christmas*. In one of the most famous scenes of that delightful holiday offering, Linus explains the true meaning of Christmas, quoting Luke 2:9–11 (KJV):

And, lo, the angel of the Lord came upon them, and the glory of
the Lord shone round about them: and they were sore afraid.
And the angel said unto them, Fear not: for, behold, I bring you
good tidings of great joy, which shall be to all people. For unto
you is born this day in the city of David a Savior, which is Christ
the Lord.

The "good tidings" of which Linus speaks are precisely what are prophesied in Isaiah's scripture. The feet that bring such wonderful news, the messenger who delivers it, can be nothing but beautiful. For the news of our promised salvation is the greatest message ever delivered. There is truly a hope for all. God is good!

Dear Lord, I rejoice in this promise of salvation. I thank You for Your
beautiful messengers of this Good News and for this proclamation
of peace. Help me to spread this message of hope to all around me.

Revival

*For this is what the high and exalted One says—he who
lives forever, whose name is holy: "I live in a high and holy place,
but also with the one who is contrite and lowly in spirit, to revive
the spirit of the lowly and to revive the heart of the contrite."*

ISAIAH 57:15 NIV

As a child, you likely heard the words "God is everywhere." That's
not an easy concept to understand. Our human brains struggle
to comprehend it. Yet, according to these words from Isaiah, God is
exalted, living in heaven, but also comforting the lowly in spirit here
on earth. The only thing He requires of us is that we be contrite. We
need only be remorseful for our sins and God will offer revival of both
our spirit and heart. It's that simple.

In Proverbs 22:4, this sentiment is stated clearly: "Humility is the
fear of the LORD; its wages are riches and honor and life." Easier said
than done. In a world where greatness is sometimes defined on the
basis of athletic prowess, acting talent, or musical ability, it is hard to
remember that worship should be reserved for the one true, almighty
God and no other.

*Lord, grant me the ability to live my very best life
according to Your Word and to remember that no matter
how great my achievements, they pale in comparison to
You. Help me to remain contrite and humble.*

Green Thumb

For as the soil makes the sprout come up and a garden
causes seeds to grow, so the Sovereign LORD will make
righteousness and praise spring up before all nations.
ISAIAH 61:11 NIV

I f you have ever tried your hand at gardening, you know there are a lot of factors that contribute to a successful harvest. You must pick a spot that is just right. The condition of the soil, the content of rocks, the amount of sun, and the access to water are just some of many factors you must consider. Clearly, it is important to create an environment that makes it favorable for a seed to thrive.

What you can*not* do is *make* that seed grow. You, as a mere mortal, cannot magically reach into that seed and extract that plant. Your power is limited to external factors, to earthly conditions. God alone controls the growth.

Just as plants are a part of your garden, you are a part of God's garden. So, create in yourself the perfect environment to cultivate God's blessings. Prepare yourself to be as good a vessel as you possibly can. God has planted the seed in you. Now it's up to you to help it along.

God is the master gardener. Allow yourself to blossom under His hand and with His help.

Dear God, You are the grower of all good things.
Help me to prepare a proper environment within myself
to receive Your blessings. Let my heart be a vessel
worthy of Your promises of love and eternal life.

Work of Art

Yet you, LORD, are our Father. We are the clay,
you are the potter; we are all the work of your hand.
ISAIAH 64:8 NIV

The great sculptor Michelangelo once said, "The true work of art is but a shadow of the divine perfection." Even a master like Michelangelo acknowledged that no matter how talented an artist might be, God is the only one capable of perfection. Everything else in this world is flawed.

Each person is as the earthly clay, put together by the one true God, the potter of perfection. God has created each individual by the work of His hand, designed in His own image. Although He has blessed each person with different gifts and attributes, each human being has this in common: God our creator is the quintessential master artist.

Next time you look in the mirror and aren't happy with what you see, remember that God does not make junk. He makes nothing cheap. For God, the master potter, created each person just the way He saw fit. You are a work of art. You are here for a reason. You were made for this time. And you have a purpose.

Dear Father in heaven, thank You for my life. Thank you for
creating me out of Your divine clay, for molding me into the
person You wanted me to be. I pray that I can live my life
in accordance with Your great plan for me.

Favorite Child

*"Before I formed you in the womb I knew you, before you were
born I set you apart; I appointed you as a prophet to the nations."*
JEREMIAH 1:5 NIV

E xpectant parents often wonder what their future bundle of joy will look like. Whom will he most resemble? Will the baby have hair? How much will he weigh? There are so many questions. Though both parents had a part in the creation of this new little being, they are clueless as to exactly what kind of person their offspring will become.

This was not the case with God when He called Jeremiah, who was already a young man. God wanted Jeremiah to know how vital he was. He had Jeremiah earmarked as special long before he was even born. God called him to play an important role in His plan.

God the Father knows you as well. You too are one of His blessed children. He knew you long before you were born and knows you now. He calls to you and has you earmarked to play a role in His plan. You just need to be receptive to His call, to listen intently for His instruction, to know, believe, and trust that you are vital to His plan.

*Dear Lord, help me remember that I am special to You. Open my
ears to Your voice. I, Your faithful and loving child, am here to
serve You, to answer Your call, to spread Your Word.*

Metallurgy

*"I have made you a tester of metals and my people
the ore, that you may observe and test their ways."*
JEREMIAH 6:27 NIV

These days, it seems we're surrounded by nothing but bad news. Headlines leave us saddened or angered or both. Social media can be cruel, weighed heavily in gossip, and tinged by a lack of compassion. Taking everything at face value can be overwhelming.

This was also true in Jeremiah's day. God gave Jeremiah the task of assessing those around him, the inhabitants of Judah and Jerusalem. They were out of control, worshipping false gods. God, speaking through Jeremiah, says, "They are all hardened rebels, going about to slander. They are bronze and iron; they all act corruptly" (Jeremiah 6:28).

Take God's advice in Jeremiah 6:27 to heart. Test those around you to discern the character of people speaking negatively. Just as the metallurgist assesses the quality of metals, so you can assess the quality of your fellow humans. Only allow people of value into your life, those who will uplift you and tell the truth.

Proverbs 25:4 says, "Remove the dross from the silver, and a silversmith can produce a vessel." By removing the junk from your own life, you too can create your own treasure-filled world.

*Dear Lord, please help me to root out the negativity from
my life. By allowing only honorable and faithful people into
my world, I know You will reward me with a better life.*

Bragging Rights

*"But let the one who boasts boast about this: that they
have the understanding to know me, that I am the LORD,
who exercises kindness, justice and righteousness on earth,
for in these I delight," declares the LORD.*

JEREMIAH 9:24 NIV

The tendency to brag is inherently human. Most people like to toot their own horn when they feel they have done something great. They enjoy the limelight. They revel in all the praise. However, Galatians 1:5 makes it pretty clear to whom the praise should go: "To whom be glory for ever and ever! Amen."

It is comforting to read the God-inspired words of Jeremiah, wherein God reminds you and all His children that He is loving, caring, and delights in justice and righteousness. So, if you feel the tendency to boast rising up within you, consider that your greatest claim to fame should be that you know the Lord your God, that you understand and fear Him. When you do, giving Him all the credit, He, in turn, will delight in you and your adherence to His Word.

Woman, by all means, brag God up! Boast about all the great things *He* has done!

*Dear Lord, let my lips brag of no one but You. Help me sing
Your praises day and night. Remind me that You delight
in my understanding and my knowledge of You. In You I
can boast confidently, knowing that You delight in me.*

Winning the Race

"If you have raced with men on foot and they have worn you out,
how can you compete with horses? If you stumble in safe country,
how will you manage in the thickets by the Jordan?"

JEREMIAH 12:5 NIV

Some people tend to make a mountain out of a molehill. If you yourself follow that credo, unable or unwilling to deal with a minor obstacle, how then will you deal with something major? A better idea is to put things into perspective, to remind yourself that a minor inconvenience, though a nuisance, is not something that should derail your journey through life.

God makes that message clear in Jeremiah 12. He tells His people that if they don't have the stamina to race men, how will they compete with horses? If they stumble on a safe road, how will they ever make it through thickets? God would have you learn to pace yourself in any race. To take things slow and steady. Remember this is how the tortoise won the proverbial race against the hare. By pacing yourself, you save energy for the larger problems in life. In other words, don't sweat the small stuff.

Dear Lord, help me pace myself in this relay of life. Help me
recognize the difference between small inconveniences and
severe situations. Help me to remember that You are with
me through the small stuff as well as the large because You
are my salvation in all ways and for all days.

High Hopes

Do any of the worthless idols of the nations bring rain? Do the
skies themselves send down showers? No, it is you, Lord our God.
Therefore our hope is in you, for you are the one who does all this.
JEREMIAH 14:22 NIV

I t's always a joy to watch children frolic in summer showers. Sometimes they pretend to do a rain dance, wanting to keep the precipitation coming down. While it's fun to watch them take such joy in their dance, everyone knows the children do not actually control the rain. Only God can, just as He controls the snow and the sunshine, the wind and the hail. God alone has the power to sustain and maintain the universe. He alone is your hope.

In Psalm 31:24, David reminds us, "Be strong and take heart, all you who hope in the LORD." There's that word again: *hope*. It implies trust, an expectation of the fulfillment of God's promise to His children on earth.

Today and every day, be courageous and strong, trusting in God's pledge of hope for your future. He's in your corner, and with Him, *you can do anything.* For "with God all things are possible" (Matthew 19:26).

Dear Lord, I trust that You will bring both rain and
sunshine into my life. My hope is in You, Lord,
maker of all things and deliverer of salvation.

Serenity

"They will be like a tree planted by the water that sends out its roots by the stream. It does not fear when heat comes; its leaves are always green. It has no worries in a year of drought and never fails to bear fruit."

JEREMIAH 17:8 NIV

J eremiah paints a beautiful picture with his words. He describes what life is like for those whose trust is in the Lord, those who have full confidence in Him. This idyllic scene brings comfort and hope to the reader. It is a message of peace and serenity. A tree planted by water will never thirst; it will never fear excessive heat because it remains hydrated. No matter what, it will always bear fruit and thrive.

You will be like that tree if you trust in the Lord fully, knowing He will always care for you and meet your needs. Thus, you need not stress.

Psalm 1:3 contains similar words to those of Jeremiah 17:8, saying that they who delight and meditate on God's law are "like a tree planted by streams of water, which yields its fruit in season and whose leaf does not wither—whatever they do prospers."

Fully trust in God, live in His Word, and then revel in His peace. Ah. . .that's better.

Dear Lord, take me to that place of peace where I trust in You with full confidence. With You, I have no reason to fear.

Rescued

*Sing to the LORD! Give praise to the LORD! He rescues
the life of the needy from the hands of the wicked.*
JEREMIAH 20:13 NIV

There is a good reason why you feel happy when you sing. Singing brings joy to your spirit. It even releases endorphins, which make you feel good physically. Music is powerful stuff. An upbeat song can do so much to improve your mood. Therefore, it is no surprise that Jeremiah recommends you sing to the Lord. What better way to give praise to a generous and merciful God? He who rescues the needy will rescue you as well. So, by all means, sing songs of praise to the Lord!

Psalm 98:4 reminds you to "Shout for joy to the Lord, all the earth, burst into jubilant song with music." Here, the word *jubilant* gives you additional instruction. The word implies not only joy but also triumph. Sing to the Lord in joy and in confidence that He will always deliver you from your troubles.

With God and song, you *will* persevere, you *will* be triumphant!

*Dear Lord, I thank You for Your mercy and grace.
You rescue the needy from the perils of the wicked, and You
give me so many reasons to sing Your praises. Through You,
I experience joy. To You, I raise my voice in jubilant song.*

Heart to Heart

*"I will give them a heart to know me, that I am the LORD.
They will be my people, and I will be their God, for they
will return to me with all their heart."*

JEREMIAH 24:7 NIV

You have probably said the words "I love you with all my heart" when talking to a beloved family member. Yet what does that mean, exactly? And what prompted you to add those last four words—"with all my heart"—to an already endearing phrase? They take the concept of love to a whole new level. Those words reveal that you love that person not only on a human-to-human level but on a spiritual level, with everything you have. And your heart, which gives you life and is the core of your being, is the embodiment of that deep, deep level of love.

In Proverbs 4:23, you are warned, "Above all else, guard your heart, for everything you do flows from it." Woman, there is nothing more important than your heart and your love, so guard that heart. And love your God. Know Him with your whole heart, returning to Him today and every day.

*Dear Lord, I thank You every day for the gift of my life,
for the heart You have given me, and for the ability to love
You and know You with that whole heart. Thank You for
being my God, the One who loves and cares for me.*

Shouting from the Rooftops

*"This is what the LORD says: Stand in the courtyard of the
LORD's house and speak to all the people of the towns of
Judah who come to worship in the house of the LORD.
Tell them everything I command you; do not omit a word."*

JEREMIAH 26:2 NIV

J eremiah delivered this message from God to the people of Judah in desperate times. It was shortly before the invasion of Babylonian forces and during a time when the majority of people had lost their connection to the one true God. False idols and deplorable lifestyles had become commonplace. Yet God never gave up in trying to reach His people.

The subject of Jeremiah's message is timeless, for God tells His people (including us) to stand in the courtyard, the very center, the hub of the area, and speak to all who come to worship. Speak up, share the Good News! Shout it from the rooftops; repeat it to all who will listen.

And what is that Good News? Well, it's all about Jesus and the fact that He is the way, the truth, and the life. That no one comes to the Father except through Him (John 14:6). It can't get any clearer than that! Take joy in knowing that through God's Son, you have the promise of eternal life.

*Dear Lord, help me share Your message of hope
and salvation to all I can, and help me always
remember Your saving promise to me.*

Best Laid Plans

*"For I know the plans I have for you," declares the
LORD, "plans to prosper you and not to harm you,
plans to give you hope and a future."*
JEREMIAH 29:11 NIV

No matter how well you prepare or make specific plans in your life, no matter how elaborate your projects or proposals, sometimes they just don't come to fruition. You planned it. You prepared for it. You did everything you thought was right. But it seems that the story of your life suddenly encountered a plot twist.

Paul Simon, in his song "Slip Sliding Away," seems to have an accurate assessment of this situation. He sings, in part, that "God only knows. God makes his plan. The information's unavailable to the mortal man." And "to the mortal *wo*man," we might add.

In Jeremiah's letter to the surviving elders of the exile in Babylon, he assures them that God indeed has a plan and that they should take comfort in knowing His promise of salvation will be fulfilled.

Remember, God has plans for you too: "Many are the plans in a person's heart, but it is the LORD's purpose that prevails" (Proverbs 19:21).

*Dear Lord, Your will, not mine, be done in my life.
Help me to remember that I do not need to understand
Your plans but only to accept them. I can rest assured
that You have my future securely planned for me.*

Godly Planetarium

*This is what the LORD says, he who appoints the sun to
shine by day, who decrees the moon and stars to shine
by night, who stirs up the sea, so that its waves roar—
the LORD Almighty is his name.*

JEREMIAH 31:35 NIV

I n today's scripture, you're reminded rather eloquently of God's power and His command over all things. These words accompany His promise to regrow the ancient cities of Judah and Jerusalem, which were destroyed by the people's own faithlessness. Through God's infinite compassion, His people are saved.

Did you ever sit on the beach and marvel at the massive oceanic expanse before you? Probably one of the most beautiful earthly sights is a sunrise over a sea. The roar of the waves as they crash on the beach; the sound of the sea gulls as they fly low overhead, searching for a morning bite of crab; the colors of the sun peeking over the horizon; all are a part of God's morning masterpiece. He appoints the sun to rise each day and later to set, bringing with it darkness and slowly but surely beautiful twinkling stars to dot the sky.

*Dear Lord, my God Almighty, thank You for Your grace,
for the beauty that You have created here on earth.
Help me to value it and treasure it and to always bear
in mind that it was You who created it.*

Can You Hear Me Now?

*"Call to me and I will answer you and tell you great
and unsearchable things you do not know."*
JEREMIAH 33:3 NIV

Although Jeremiah was imprisoned in a courtyard of King Zedekiah of Judah, God never abandoned him. His message of comfort and hope came to Jeremiah at a time when he needed it. Imprisoned and alone, he was still relaying God's messages to the unreceptive ears of the people he was trying to help.

Did you ever feel all alone while facing a daunting task or a bleak outlook? Remember, there is Someone there at your side to hear your pleas. God is clear in His message to Jeremiah and to all of us: we need only to call on God and trust in Him. He will fill us with awe and comfort.

Psalm 50:15 has a similar message of hope from God: "And call on me in the day of trouble; I will deliver you, and you will honor me."

Call on God. He will answer you. He will support you, comfort you, and direct you. You have but to make that toll-free call. No telephone—neither cell nor landline—needed.

*Dear Lord, help me to come to You in times of trouble. Help me
to remember that You will answer me and tell me great and
wonderful things. Help me also reach out to You in times
of bounty and give You thanks for the joy it brings.*

Tough Love

"Whoever stays in this city will die by the sword,
famine or plague, but whoever goes over to the Babylonians
will live. They will escape with their lives; they will live."
JEREMIAH 38:2 NIV

Jeremiah led a difficult life in his role as God's messenger to Jerusalem and Judah. The armies of Babylon were attacking, taking prisoners. For King Zedekiah, there was no escape. Zedekiah resisted the message from Jeremiah to willingly deliver himself into the hands of his enemy, Babylon. It was counterintuitive. To survive, why would he surrender to his adversary? Yet that was what God instructed.

During difficult times, you too may be inclined to resist a strategy when your gut tells you to go another way. Yet you know God knows best. Don't resist His plan. Although you may not recognize His as the best route, it may all make sense eventually.

Consider an executive woman with a high-powered job who has no time for herself. Because she must support her family, she may feel trapped. Then a life-changing heart attack hits, and she is forced to give up her career. With the pressure gone, she begins to focus on things such as family, passions, church, and volunteering. God's plan for her was drastically different from her ambitions. Yet God saved her from herself by bringing her to *Him*self.

Lord, sometimes I resist Your plan, especially in tough times.
Help me let go of my plan and commit to Yours each and every day.

The Rescuer

"But I will rescue you on that day, declares the LORD;
you will not be given into the hands of those you fear."
JEREMIAH 39:17 NIV

As the voice of God, Jeremiah endured many hardships while living in a land besieged by Babylonians. Thrown into a pit and left to die, Jeremiah's life was saved by a brave man named Ebed-Melech. God repaid the courage of this man with the promise of protection from those he feared, those who would take him prisoner.

Just as God promised to protect Ebed-Melech, He promised to protect Joshua. In Deuteronomy 3:22, God reminds him, "Do not be afraid of them; the LORD your God himself will fight for you."

Fear is something against which everyone struggles. And there will be many situations in which each of us will have to face our fear. Yet all we need to do is remember God's Word telling His people to rest assured, to not be afraid.

The Lord your God *will* rescue you on your hardest days. He *will not* deliver you into the hands of your darkest fears but *will* bring you into the light and protection of His presence.

Dear Lord, the Word You gave me through Your Son
Jesus Christ tell me that You will deliver me from evil.
I pray You will take away my fears and in my darkest
day will rescue me from the depths of despair.

Unconditional Obedience

"Whether it is favorable or unfavorable, we will obey the
LORD our God, to whom we are sending you, so that it
will go well with us, for we will obey the LORD our God."

JEREMIAH 42:6 NIV

Desperate times call for desperate measures. In the aftermath of the invasions by Babylonian forces, the surviving Israelites sought out Jeremiah's help. Desperate, they realized the only path available to them was to heed God's instructions through Jeremiah, His messenger. They were finally resigned to the fact that they must obey God's words, whether or not they liked what He had to say.

Sometimes the right course in your life may seem counterintuitive. That's when you need to let go and let God. Once you renounce what you feel you should do and do what you realize God wants you to do, your situation will improve and peace will be restored to your soul. Within God's plan lies your correct course. Although His course may appear difficult, in the end your pledge of obedience will be the best choice you can make to lay the foundation for the best course you can take.

Dear Lord, I ask that You help me to be Your obedient servant, to trust
in Your supreme plan for me, and to rest assured that Your will is
the best course for me. Though I may not be happy with the path
You have laid out for me, Lord, Your will, not mine, be done.

Chin Up

"Do not be afraid, Jacob my servant; do not be dismayed, Israel.
I will surely save you out of a distant place, your descendants
from the land of their exile. Jacob will again have peace
and security, and no one will make him afraid."

JEREMIAH 46:27 NIV

P eace. A part of many church services involves people wishing peace to those around them. "Peace be with you" is the phrase used by the clergy. The people's response is "And also with you." At this point, the congregants greet their fellow churchgoers with a handshake, a wave, or a hug to wish them peace.

In today's passage, God reassures the surviving Israelites that they will be safe. These exiles, now living in a strange place, away from their homeland, having lost everything, were certainly alone and afraid. But God was there to reassure them that He would restore peace and security once again.

God holds out that same promise to you today. He wants you to know that you are safe and sound in His hands. All you need to do to tap into that peace is to "let be and be still, and know (recognize and understand) that I am God. I will be exalted among the nations! I will be exalted in the earth!" (Psalm 46:10 AMPC).

Dear Lord, grant me Your peace, the peace You promised Your
people many years ago and that You continue to promise
to me today. Help me to trust in You always.

Divine Discipline

"Yet I will restore the fortunes of Moab in days to come,"
declares the LORD. Here ends the judgment on Moab.
JEREMIAH 48:47 NIV

There was no doubt about it. The people of Moab were sinners. Despite many warnings from God through the prophet Jeremiah, they continued to live in their sinful ways and disobey God. As a loving Father to His children, God had no choice but to follow through with the punishment He had laid out for the cities of Moab.

As any good parent of children knows, it's difficult to discipline them. But always the parent has the best interest of the child at heart.

In today's reading, God's "child" Moab had become self-destructive and sinful. And although it's difficult to read Jeremiah 48's description of the punishment God is about to unleash upon the disobedient children of Moab, at the end we see the glimmer of hope. He promises to have mercy one day soon and will forgive Moab's sins.

This hope for Moab can be a hope for all. Yes, you, as a member of humankind, are by nature flawed. And yet, when you fall, God is there to pick you up and get you back on His track.

Dear Lord, I come to You to ask for Your mercy when I
fall short. Get me back on track when I'm tempted or weak.
Restore Your love, and plant Your guiding light in my heart.

Guilt-Free

"In those days, at that time," declares the Lord, "search will be made for Israel's guilt but there will be none, and for the sins of Judah, but none will be found, for I will forgive the remnant I spare."

Jeremiah 50:20 niv

✎

People experience guilt for many reasons. Some have guilt from years ago. Others pick up a fresh load of guilt on a daily basis. The problem is that guilt is a powerful thing and can be debilitating. But take heart! God wants you to live guilt-free because He forgives you.

To the survivors of Israel and Judah, God declares there will be no guilt and no regret. The people are to look forward not back. Yesterday is done, and if you strayed from God's path, ask His divine forgiveness and move on. He will gladly grant it. Once forgiven, forget it. Don't let guilt be a weight that drags you down into the depths of regret. If God forgives you, why not forgive yourself?

Each day, God gives you a new page to write the next chapter of your life. So, learn from your mistakes, but don't get lost in them. Just as God gifted Israel and Judah with a guilt-free life, He will do the same for you.

Dear Lord, I am grateful for Your forgiveness when I stray. Thank You for Your presence in my life. Help me avoid sin. Grant me wisdom to ask for Your forgiveness when I fail.

Rumor Has It

*"Do not lose heart or be afraid when rumors are heard in
the land; one rumor comes this year, another the next,
rumors of violence in the land and of ruler against ruler."*

JEREMIAH 51:46 NIV

M ost people have been a victim of the rumor mill. Unsubstantiated information tends to spread like wildfire. What's worse, as it spreads, it tends to get more colorful and less factual. This is not a new phenomenon—throughout the history of humankind, rumors have been born and spread.

The captives in Babylon were no exception to being affected by rumors. Through Jeremiah, God offered His people a warning. Knowing the rumor mill would be working overtime to try to instill fear in them, God proactively reassured His people. His telling them not to lose heart nor be afraid prevented widespread panic.

Today, in these troubled times, it's good to remember God's preemptive words, counseling His people not to lose heart or be afraid. You, as one of His chosen people, can rise above the rumors that run rampant each day via social media, radio, television, and newspapers.

Although some would like you to panic, remember God has given and continues to give you the inside scoop.

*Dear Lord, thank You for directing me away from rumors
and thus preventing me from being afraid. Help me steer
clear of unsubstantiated sources of information and
heed only information that contains Your truth.*

Overwhelmed

What can I say for you? With what can I compare you, Daughter Jerusalem? To what can I liken you, that I may comfort you, Virgin Daughter Zion? Your wound is as deep as the sea. Who can heal you?
LAMENTATIONS 2:13 NIV

E veryone experiences tough times, days when things seem bleak and there appears to be no way to escape despair. In those times, many may seek to commiserate with friends or family and take some solace in the fact that others are worse off. While this is small consolation, it *is* consolation nonetheless. Yet as well-meaning as those friends or family members are, their advice does not solve your problems.

The accounts related in the book of Lamentations make it clear the people of Jerusalem were going through tough times. However, their struggle would not last forever. God alone was the solution to their problems. God alone was able to heal their afflictions.

God alone can help you too. Allow Him to uplift you right now with these words: "I will restore you to health and heal your wounds" (Jeremiah 30:17).

Dear Lord, sometimes I feel overwhelmed by hardship and can see no way out. Please open my eyes to see You and my ears to hear You. I trust that You will heal me and restore peace in my life. I have faith, Lord, that no matter how bad things look, I truly am blessed and am grateful for Your presence in my life.

Deep Within the Pit

But I called on your name, LORD, from deep within the pit.
You heard me when I cried, "Listen to my pleading! Hear my cry
for help!" Yes, you came when I called; you told me, "Do not fear."
LAMENTATIONS 3:55–57 NLT

Maybe you've heard the old expression "He has to hit rock bottom before he'll come to God." It's true! Many people won't turn their eyes to Jesus until they're in such a deep, dark place that they have no other choice.

The book of Lamentations focuses on the people of God in deep torment, lamenting to the Lord about their troubles. Some situations were so painful, some pits were so deep, God's children may have felt they'd never escape them.

Perhaps you can relate to the people of God who'd hit rock bottom, as revealed in today's verses. Yet hope remains, for these verses also show that God hears our cries, no matter how low we've fallen. His response to us, even while we're sinking deep in our sin? "Do not fear!"

Isn't that the most gracious thing you could say to a person who's buried in a pit, terrified she will stay there forever? God, the rescuer, comes to save even the ones most hopeless. What a wonderful Father!

Father, You've rescued me more times than I could count.
How I praise You for snatching me out of the pit! Amen.

The Spirit Speaks

*"Stand up, son of man," said the voice. "I want to speak
with you." The Spirit came into me as he spoke, and he
set me on my feet. I listened carefully to his words.*

EZEKIEL 2:1–2 NLT

So many people treat prayer as a one-way conversation. They look at it as a way to pour out a litany of concerns or complaints to God, then end the chat and walk away. As long as some of their requests are answered, the petitioners feel better.

That's good to a point, but remember, *the Lord wants your time with Him to be a two-way street.* He wants your ears to be as open as your mouth. It's one thing to pour out your troubles; another to wait for God's response.

Ezekiel found himself in this situation. A strange voice spoke to him, and it didn't take long to realize it was the Holy Spirit. Whether he heard the words in an audible voice or felt the impression of the words on his heart, we'll never know. But we do know for sure that the Spirit was speaking.

The Bible says God is the same yesterday, today, and forever. If He could speak to Ezekiel back then, He can and will speak to you today.

What is He speaking to your heart today?

*Thank You for the reminder that You're still
speaking, Lord! My ears are wide open. Amen.*

Purify Your Dwelling

Proclaim this message from the Sovereign LORD against the mountains of Israel. This is what the Sovereign LORD says to the mountains and hills and to the ravines and valleys: I am about to bring war upon you, and I will smash your pagan shrines.

Ezekiel 6:3 nlt

Remember back in the old days when women would spring clean their houses? They would bring the rugs outside and hang them on the line, then beat the dust out of them. Everything inside would be scrubbed squeaky clean. Winter items were tucked away and lighter, springtime items emerged.

Perhaps you're one who loves to deep clean. If so, you would never clean your whole house and then dump a pile of trash on your living room floor, would you? You'd be tripping over it—and dealing with the stench—all day long!

Something similar happened with the Israelites. The Lord wasn't content to see His people dwelling among unclean things. It was time to get rid of those pagan shrines. (That stinky trash had to go!)

Purifying your dwelling means getting rid of anything that could bring infestation. For the Israelites, it meant getting rid of the shrines around them. What does it mean for you? Is there anything the Lord needs to sweep out of your spiritual house today?

Lord, I give you permission to deep clean.
Purify my heart, I pray. Amen.

His Glory Fills the Temple

And the glory of the LORD went up from the cherub
to the threshold of the house, and the house was
filled with the cloud, and the court was filled with
the brightness of the glory of the LORD.
Ezekiel 10:4 esv

I f you've ever pondered the logistics of heaven, you can only imagine how majestic it will be. Rivers of living water. Streets of gold. Mansions of splendor. It defies explanation. No set designer in Hollywood could ever do it justice.

There, with the Lord on His throne, billions of believers gathered around, surrounded by cherubim and seraphim, we will cry out, "Holy, holy, holy is the Lord God Almighty." We will spend eternity in the presence of God.

The Bible gives us glimpses into what that will be like. In the book of Ezekiel, the glory of God filled the temple like a cloud, causing a curious glow to radiate across the courtyard.

Can you picture it now? Does your imagination stretch that far? Can you feel the weight of God's glory enveloping you like a cloud? Are your eyes blinded with His magnificence?

Oh, what an exquisite foretaste of what is to come!

I love to spend time in Your presence, Lord. I can't wait until
I'm able to do that for all eternity. What a day it will be,
when I witness it all firsthand for the first time. Amen.

False Prophets Among Us

Then this message came to me from the Lord:
"Son of man, prophesy against the false prophets
of Israel who are inventing their own prophecies.
Say to them, 'Listen to the word of the Lord.' "

Ezekiel 13:1–2 nlt

W e are living in precarious times, when people who claim to speak for God really don't. Many are quite vocal with their so-called God-opinions. They shout them on street corners and slam-dunk their friends on social media.

This is nothing new, of course. There have always been false prophets, all the way back to Ezekiel's time.

The Lord feels strongly about people who assert themselves as prophets when, in fact, they speak only for themselves or their agenda. Nothing good will come of their message, so guard yourself.

Eyes wide open, woman of God! Make sure you don't fall into any traps. Steer clear of those who claim to speak for God but otherwise bring chaos and division. The enemy is very cunning and keen on luring you away with silver-tongued devils. Don't fall into that trap.

Thank You for opening my eyes, Father. I know that not
everyone who claims to speak for You actually does.
May I follow hard and fast after only You, Lord. Amen.

A Shelter from the Storm

*"This is what the Sovereign LORD says: I will take a branch from
the top of a tall cedar, and I will plant it on the top of Israel's
highest mountain. It will become a majestic cedar, sending
forth its branches and producing seed. Birds of every sort will
nest in it, finding shelter in the shade of its branches."*

EZEKIEL 17:22–23 NLT

What a lovely passage from the book of Ezekiel. It paints a brilliant picture, with images of birds finding shelter in the branches of a majestic cedar. Clearly, God has always cared about serving as our shelter during a storm.

Perhaps you've experienced that firsthand. God has given you rest (and not just on days like today, Labor Day), but even in the middle of the storms you've faced.

Think of a time when God spread Himself out over your situation in much the same way the branches of that cedar tree were spread to welcome the birds. He's not a discriminator. The passage assures us that "birds of every sort" are welcome.

What sort of bird are you? Are you ready to fly into God's arms today for some much-needed rest?

*Lord, You are my shelter not just in times of storm but every day.
How I love You for welcoming me into Your arms. Amen.*

Second Chances

"But if wicked people turn away from all their sins and begin to obey my decrees and do what is just and right, they will surely live and not die. All their past sins will be forgotten, and they will live because of the righteous things they have done."

Ezekiel 18:21–22 nlt

God has always been in the business of giving second chances, from Old Testament times until now. He has requirements for good living, of course, but for those who choose Him over their mistakes of yesterday, all sins (and that truly means *all* sins) will be forgotten.

In Psalm 103:12, we learn that God casts our sin as far as the east is from the west. That's a great distance. Picture your mistakes and misdeeds flying all the way from Texas to China, from India to Chile! He wants us to have that visual so that we won't be held back by our past. It's so far behind us that we can't even see it anymore.

Have you turned away from the things that are separating you from God? If not, this is the perfect day to do so. Turn. . .and live!

Father, I choose to turn from my past to face You with confidence. I accept Your offer of a second chance, Lord! Amen.

Purified by Fire

"Just as silver, copper, iron, lead, and tin are melted down in a furnace, I will melt you down in the heat of my fury."
EZEKIEL 22:20 NLT

God has always been in the purification business. Just as a silversmith takes the precious metal and places it into the fire, the Lord performs a similar service on us. He has a way of driving out all the things that shouldn't be in our lives—bad attitudes, temper, gossip, and so on.

Why do you suppose God is looking for pure gold or pure silver? We're human, after all. He doesn't expect perfection, but He's looking for people who are willing to be changed—really changed—by His Spirit.

Are there areas of your life that need to be melted down in the furnace? Have you picked up some habits that you've clung to unnecessarily? If so, are you willing to let them go today? Get alone with God. Ask Him to purify your heart, even if it hurts a little to let go of the "pets" you've allowed in your life. They need to go in Jesus' name!

Father, the words "Purify my heart!" ring from my lips today. May nothing remain in me that displeases You, Lord. Amen.

He Said It. That Settles It.

*"I, the LORD, have spoken! The time has come, and I
won't hold back. I will not change my mind, and I will
have no pity on you. You will be judged on the basis of all
your wicked actions, says the Sovereign LORD."*
Ezekiel 24:14 NLT

Have you ever had a friend who said she would do something, but you knew she probably wouldn't follow through? Maybe, when you were a kid, one of your parents was like that. His or her remark "I'll spend time with you on Saturday" was really just a way to get you to stop nagging. You knew that parent wasn't really going to do anything special with you on Saturday.

When God says He's going to do something, He follows through. You can take it to the bank. We see this in Isaiah 55:11, as well, where God says: "It is the same with my word. I send it out, and it always produces fruit. It will accomplish all I want it to, and it will prosper everywhere I send it."

Your God is a god of His Word. And He wants you to be a woman of *your* word too. If you say you're going to do it. . .do it.

*Lord, I want to be a woman of my word. If I say it,
that settles it! I'll do what I said I would do; I'll go where
I said I would go. Thank You for Your help in this! Amen.*

Boasting's End

The word of the LORD came to me: "Now you, son of man,
raise a lamentation over Tyre, and say to Tyre, who dwells
at the entrances to the sea, merchant of the peoples to many
coastlands, thus says the Lord GOD: O Tyre, you have said,
'I am perfect in beauty.' Your borders are in the heart of the
seas; your builders made perfect your beauty."

EZEKIEL 27:1–4 ESV

T he major cities of old felt they had a lot to boast about. The same is true today. People from various regions feel they are more prestigious because of where they live. But God isn't a fan of boasting.

If you've spent any time in the presence of a prideful person, one who loves singing his own praises, you know it can be tiring. He believes his own press and acts as if he's better than everyone else. Time usually proves these types of people wrong, of course. The prideful fall just as quickly as the meek, but they cause more damage as they fall (if only to themselves).

If you have to put up with a boaster, God bless you! If you notice you're tooting your own horn, consider setting it down so someone else can pick it up for a change. Or, better yet, use it to draw attention to someone else worth complimenting.

I don't want to be a boaster or a show-off, Lord.
Please help me refrain from singing my own praises. Amen.

God's Intervention

"I will strengthen the arms of the king of Babylon, while the arms of Pharaoh fall useless to his sides. And when I put my sword in the hand of Babylon's king and he brings it against the land of Egypt, Egypt will know that I am the LORD."

EZEKIEL 30:25 NLT

❧❧❧

I t's interesting to think that God actually intervened in battles of old, yet that was definitely the case here. You don't often hear Babylon spoken of in a positive manner, but in this case the Lord decided to strengthen the arms of the Babylonian king and to put Pharaoh in his place. God, and only God, controlled the outcome of the battle.

God controls the outcome of your battles too. That should come as quite a relief if you're facing an enemy right now. God not only intervenes in the situations that come against you, He actually fights on your behalf—in both the natural and supernatural realms.

What battles are you facing? Pray and ask the Lord to intervene. He's far better with a sword in hand than you will ever be!

Father, I'm so grateful I don't have to fight my battles alone. You are my defender, my protector, the one who intervenes on my behalf. Come to me now, Lord. Put a circle of fire around me. Amen.

The Problem with Prospering

"This great tree towered high, higher than all the other
trees around it. It prospered and grew long thick branches
because of all the water at its roots. The birds nested in its
branches, and in its shade all the wild animals gave birth.
All the great nations of the world lived in its shadow."
EZEKIEL 31:5–6 NLT

Oh, how we love to stand head and shoulders above the crowd, reveling in our successes. We spread wide our proverbial branches, overshadowing friends at parties with stories of our latest, greatest adventures. Hubby's new job promotion. Our big, beautiful home. Our recent trip overseas. How well the kids are doing in college. Our expensive hairstyle. Our latest wardrobe purchases.

It's not a bad thing to prosper. There's nothing wrong with taking pride in your beautiful things or your job promotions. But take a closer look at what you're sharing with others. Are you deliberately choosing to share only the best parts? Are you filtering the picture, wiping out the negative and leaving only the positive?

Maybe it's time to share a glimpse into the real you—the not-so-perfect, not-so-prosperous moments. God can use your humility to reach those who aren't as fortunate.

Lord, I'm proud of my accomplishments and I'm grateful for all
You've provided for me, but I don't ever want to be seen as a show-off.
Help me share only what will bring glory to You, Father. Amen.

Take Action

*"You are very entertaining to them, like someone who sings love
songs with a beautiful voice or plays fine music on an instrument.
They hear what you say, but they don't act on it!"*

Ezekiel 33:32 nlt

I f you've ever had friends (or, worse yet, children) who didn't take
you seriously, perhaps you have an inkling of what God feels like at
times. He speaks. . .but we don't always pay close attention or act on
His words. This was often the case in ancient Israel (as in Ezekiel's time),
but it's equally as true today.

God still speaks through His Word or to your heart in a still, small
voice. He speaks through friends or even through life's circumstances.
He speaks through the pastor's message on Sunday (which we find
entertaining or even convicting at times). He's always speaking, and
although we're decent listeners, we don't always act on what He says.
We're like our own children, hearing a parental unit say, "Go clean your
room!" but then refusing to budge from our spot on the sofa. How much
easier life would be if we always listened and obeyed.

Today, think about the last message God laid on your heart. Did
you spring into action? If not, what are some steps you can take today
to begin the process?

*Lord, thank You for speaking. May I be a doer not just
a hearer. I want to please Your heart, Father. Amen.*

He Makes Provision for You

"But the mountains of Israel will produce heavy crops of fruit
for my people—for they will be coming home again soon!
See, I care about you, and I will pay attention to you.
Your ground will be plowed and your crops planted."

EZEKIEL 36:8–9 NLT

It's fascinating to see how God always made provision for His people in Old Testament times. He fed them manna in the desert, quail from the heavens, and provided heavy crops of fruit when they reached the Promised Land.

Why did God so often prove Himself through food and daily provisions? Because the Israelites saw the meeting of their daily needs as a sign of love and care from their Creator.

Would you, as a parent, hold back daily provision from your child? No! On the contrary, you would do anything you could to make sure that child had everything he needed—food, clothing, shelter, water—all of the basic necessities of life.

God wants to meet your needs too. So, whatever you're lacking, whatever you're afraid you'll have to do without, lift that need to the Lord and wait with expectation for His provision.

Father, I'm Your child, and I know I can trust You to provide the things I need. I'll never go without as long as You are in control.

Rise Again

Then he said to me, "Speak a prophetic message to these
bones and say, 'Dry bones, listen to the word of the LORD!
This is what the Sovereign LORD says: Look! I am going
to put breath into you and make you live again!' "
 EZEKIEL 37:4–5 NLT

W ow, what a picture of the change God can bring! If He can take dry, dead bones and bring them to life again, what can He do with you? If He can put breath into dead things and watch them rise to life, what can He do with your dreams?

So many times, we give up too soon. We get right to the brink of a miracle and stop believing. We lose heart. We lose faith.

Don't give up! There are things you've been praying for that might be just around the corner. There are dreams that have died but are meant to be resurrected. There are bones lying dead in a heap that God wants to bring to life again.

No matter what dreams you've buried, it's not too late. Even now, God is longing to breathe life into your situation. Will you give it to Him?

Lord, I'll admit, I often give up when things don't move at the pace I'm
hoping for. But today I'm grateful for the reminder that You've come to
breathe life into dry bones. I give my dreams to You afresh. Amen.

Set Apart

"When the priests leave the sanctuary, they must not go directly to the outer courtyard. They must first take off the clothes they wore while ministering, because these clothes are holy. They must put on other clothes before entering the parts of the building complex open to the public."

EZEKIEL 42:14 NLT

In the inner sanctuary of the Tabernacle was a designated room known as the Holy of Holies or "the most holy place." Here, in this set-apart place, the high priest would enter dressed in special robes to make an offering of atonement on behalf of the people. God would then roll back their sins for another year.

When the priest came out of the Holy of Holies—as he stepped out of the overpowering presence of God—he was instructed to remove his priestly garments and clothe himself like the rest of the people. The set-apart clothing was required no more until the following year.

It's fascinating to think that the Lord cared about what the priests wore in His presence. Perhaps this act of preparing to be in God's presence is a lesson for us today, that we can—and should—prepare our hearts (dress ourselves) before spending time with Him. Today, think of some ways that you can begin to prepare your heart for your next encounter with God.

Father, I love to be in Your presence. Thank You for preparing my heart even now. Amen.

Rushing Waters

Suddenly, the glory of the God of Israel appeared from the east.
The sound of his coming was like the roar of rushing waters,
and the whole landscape shone with his glory.

Ezekiel 43:2 NLT

I f you've ever been in a truly powerful worship service, you have a foretaste of what's to come in heaven. There the presence of God will be so strong that we can only fall on our faces and cry, "Holy, holy, holy!" Wow!

There's no need to wait until you're in heaven to experience God's presence. Even now, people are engaging with the Lord in powerful, magnificent worship services. Others are huddled in their prayer closets, pouring their hearts out to Him and experiencing His presence in new, fresh ways.

Can you envision being so overwhelmed by the magnitude of God's presence that it feels (and sounds) as if a mighty roaring river is about to sweep over you? That's what it's like to be caught up with Him. You're swept away—away from your troubles, your broken heart, your rocky relationships. In those moments, as those holy waters sweep over you, you're washed afresh with His power, His joy, His holiness.

God wants you to meet Him at this river, to dive in, to enjoy all that He has to offer.

Lord, I long for Your presence even now. I don't want to have to wait for heaven. May I experience Your glory right here, right now. Amen.

A Portion for the Lord

"When you divide the land among the tribes of Israel,
you must set aside a section for the LORD as his holy portion."
EZEKIEL 45:1 NLT

The Israelites traveled for years to reach the Promised Land. When they arrived, each of the twelve tribes was assigned a section of the countryside. But there was an additional section, one you rarely hear about. A portion of the Holy Land was set apart for the Lord. It was the Israelites' offering back to Him.

From Old Testament times until now, God has longed for His kids to be givers. Have you ever thought about why? After all, the Lord has everything He could ever need. He doesn't require *our* nickels and dimes. So. . .what's He after? Our hearts. And He knows they're directly linked to our pocketbooks. Snag one and you've got the other.

Perhaps you've heard the saying "You can't outgive God." That mind-set starts with acknowledging that everything you have is His anyway. The food on your table, your job, that car you drive. . .all those things belong to God. So, today, look into your heart. Thank God for all His giving. Then mimic Him by giving back the first portion to Him as your act of worship to the One who makes sure you have all you'll need and more.

You meet my every need, Lord! I gladly offer back to You
a portion of what You've so generously given me. Amen.

A River of Healing

He asked me, "Have you been watching, son of man?"
Then he led me back along the riverbank. When I
returned, I was surprised by the sight of many trees
growing on both sides of the river.
EZEKIEL 47:6–7 NLT

If you've ever been through a drought, you know the kind of damage it can do—to your grass, your crops, even your attitude. When the land around you dries up, it can even cause your soul to get dry and cracked.

Picture a river running through that field of dried grass. The moment the water spills over its banks and onto the parched, dry land, everything changes. The river brings life! Before long, trees are growing, life is returning.

Jesus is the river of life! He's come to split the dry, parched areas of your life wide open and to pour His living water over it all so that life might return.

What dried-out areas can you turn over to God today? Picture Him soaking those areas with holy water. How amazing, to watch them spring to life once more!

You're a miracle worker, Lord! You take my parched life
and saturate it with Your holy presence, bringing life
anew. I praise You, Father! Amen.

God's Elevation Plan

*Then the king appointed Daniel to a high position and gave
him many valuable gifts. He made Daniel ruler over the whole
province of Babylon, as well as chief over all his wise men.
At Daniel's request, the king appointed Shadrach, Meshach,
and Abednego to be in charge of all the affairs of the province
of Babylon, while Daniel remained in the king's court.*

DANIEL 2:48–49 NLT

❦

D aniel's journey was filled with unexpected twists and turns. First,
he was taken into captivity in Babylon as a boy. Next, Daniel was
appointed as ruler over the whole province of Babylon (and chief over all
the king's wise men). Wow! That's quite a jump from kidnapped young
nobleman to man in charge.

The key to Daniel's elevation was found in his obedience to God.

Perhaps you don't like to hear that obedience is a requirement for
elevation. Maybe you feel like you've been overlooked for a promotion or you can't understand why a coworker got the raise you should
have received. Perhaps you wonder why you can't catch a break when
others can.

It's time for a little self-examination. Are there areas of your life,
perhaps, where you've slipped out of obedience and into selfishness? Do
you need to bring that area of your life to the Lord to ask His forgiveness?

Obey. . .and watch God move.

*Lord, it's not always easy to obey,
but I want to bring joy to Your heart.*

The Fiery Furnace

*But suddenly, Nebuchadnezzar jumped up in amazement
and exclaimed to his advisers, "Didn't we tie up three men
and throw them into the furnace?" "Yes, Your Majesty,
we certainly did," they replied. "Look!" Nebuchadnezzar
shouted. "I see four men, unbound, walking around in the
fire unharmed! And the fourth looks like a god!"*

Daniel 3:24–25 nlt

When Shadrach, Meshach, and Abednego refused to bow down to
King Nebuchadnezzar's image, they knew they were probably
going to die at the king's hands. Regardless, they could not ignore their
consciences. They could not—would not—bow down to an idol.

Because of their courage and faithfulness, God spared them from
death. They emerged from the fiery furnace without so much as the
smell of smoke on them.

Perhaps you've been through a few fiery furnace experiences in
your life too. You've paid a heavy price for choosing your faith over the
lifestyle you once knew. But God is faithful. You have emerged without
a hair singed. And just like those three Hebrew boys were not alone,
you have not been alone either.

*I've never been alone in the fiery trials, Lord. You've been right there
beside me, protecting, defending, and saving. I'm so grateful. Amen.*

The Handwriting on the Wall

*Suddenly, they saw the fingers of a human hand writing on the plaster
wall of the king's palace, near the lampstand. The king himself saw
the hand as it wrote, and his face turned pale with fright. His knees
knocked together in fear and his legs gave way beneath him.*

DANIEL 5:5–6 NLT

P icture this. You're having an ordinary day when suddenly a human
hand appears on the wall of your home. The fingers begin to move.
They write a message on the wall, one that requires an interpretation.

How would you respond? Likely you would turn white like
Belshazzar did!

God will do anything necessary to get His intended's attention.
When He's got a message to deliver, He does it in unforgettable ways.

Balaam got his message through a donkey (Numbers 22). The young
virgin girl, Mary, received hers through the angel Gabriel (Luke 1).
God spoke to Moses in a burning bush (Exodus 3). He spoke to Joseph
through a dream (Genesis 37).

Think of the different ways God has gotten your attention. Perhaps
He spoke through a friend. Maybe He conveyed His message through
circumstances. He's got messages to convey. Messages to and for you.
Make sure your eyes and ears are wide open.

*Lord, I don't want to make this hard on You. No handwriting
on the wall is necessary. I'm listening, Father. Convey
Your message to my heart, I pray. Amen.*

An Angelic Visitation

As Gabriel approached the place where I was standing,
I became so terrified that I fell with my face to the ground.
"Son of man," he said, "you must understand that the events
you have seen in your vision relate to the time of the end."
DANIEL 8:17 NLT

M ary wasn't the only one who received a message from the angel Gabriel. Daniel received a visit, as well (Daniel 8). How stunned he must have been when Gabriel showed up.

Angels are mentioned in the Bible repeatedly, from creation (where Satan and his minions fell from grace) all the way to the book of Revelation. Many of those heavenly creatures are called by name, and some are given the title of archangel.

So, who are these angels? What role do they play in your life? According to scripture, they are sent to protect, to intervene, to carry out tasks on God's behalf.

Can you think of a time in your life where you thought, perhaps, an angel had cushioned your fall or protected you? Perhaps you won't know until you get to heaven, where you will spend eternity alongside these majestic creatures!

Are there really angels all around me, Lord?
Thank You for sending them to guard and protect. Amen.

A Vision of the Future

*In the third year of the reign of King Cyrus of Persia,
Daniel (also known as Belteshazzar) had another vision.
He understood that the vision concerned events certain to
happen in the future—times of war and great hardship.*

DANIEL 10:1 NLT

Daniel was given several glimpses into the future. He saw things that probably perplexed and even terrified him. (There's nothing like having the veil peeled back for a peek at what's coming.)

Maybe there have been times in your life when you've wished you could see into the future. Will you get that job you've been hoping for? Will you live in a fine house? Will your children grow up happy and healthy? How many grandchildren and great-grandchildren will you have? Whether you're propelled by worry or joy, there are things you'd like to know.

The future is filled with unknown variables, but it's best you find out as you go along in life. There are probably things you couldn't bear to see now, so asking for a glimpse beyond the present time isn't to your advantage. Because, as He did the manna, God gives you what you need for each day, no more, no less.

Instead of worrying about the future, give it to the Lord. All your days are His, after all.

*Father, I don't want to see into the future. Instead, I choose
to trust You with whatever is coming. For I know You'll
be with me, no matter what lies ahead. Amen.*

The Lord's Unfailing Love

"But then I will win her back once again. I will lead her
into the desert and speak tenderly to her there. I will
return her vineyards to her and transform the Valley of
Trouble into a gateway of hope. She will give herself to
me there, as she did long ago when she was young,
when I freed her from her captivity in Egypt."

HOSEA 2:14–15 NLT

Oh, how God loves Israel! He has chased her, caught her, lost her, chased her again. Over and over He's proven His love to her.

That same love that propelled God to chase after His beloved Israel also propels Him to chase after you. No matter how far you wander, no matter how stubborn you get, He won't give up on you. You're His daughter, His beloved. He adores you, even on the days when you're grumpy, bloated, and just want to pull the covers over your head.

Isn't the image of God speaking tenderly to you, the one He loves, so precious? He's not standing next to you, berating you or beating you over the head for your mistakes. Quite the opposite, in fact! His words are laced with love. And because you know you're loved, it's so easy to slip your hand into His for a happily-ever-after.

You love me, Lord! I hear those sweet words of encouragement
and forgiveness, even on the hard days. And I choose to
respond with love for You, my precious Father. Amen.

Pressing on to Know Him

"Oh, that we might know the Lord! Let us press on to
know him. He will respond to us as surely as the arrival
of dawn or the coming of rains in early spring."
Hosea 6:3 nlt

Getting to know someone takes time. It doesn't happen in one chance encounter, despite what the romance novels say. The more time you spend together, the more you learn about the other person's personality, quirks, feelings, and so on. If you neglect to take the time, if you jump with haste into a situation, you might end up paying a heavy price.

Getting to know the Lord is no different. It takes time to understand how He speaks, how much He loves you, and how He guides you into fuller relationship with Him. This is time well spent because your relationship with the Creator of the universe will change the course of your life.

Press in to know God. Take the time. Linger in His presence. Listen to the messages He's whispering in your ear. This Friend of all friends will never betray you. He's incapable of bringing you harm. He will be the finest friend you've ever known and one who will stick with you till the end—and beyond.

What an amazing friend You are!
Oh, how I long to know You even more, Lord!

Bring Your Confessions

Bring your confessions, and return to the LORD.
Say to him, "Forgive all our sins and graciously
receive us, so that we may offer you our praises."
HOSEA 14:2 NLT

H ave you ever met someone who didn't appear to have a conscience? Maybe he hurt someone but simply didn't care about the pain he caused. Maybe she stole money from an employer but didn't think twice about it. Perhaps he drove while intoxicated and caused serious bodily harm to a passenger but refused to take responsibility for it.

God longs to forgive all sin. In fact, Jesus died to cover the cost of all sins. But if a person refuses to acknowledge her wrong, if she blows it off or acts like she's not at fault, how can God be expected to forgive?

This is why the Bible is clear that we must bring our confessions to the Lord. And those confessions *have* to be sincere. Nothing glib. Nothing nonchalant. Come with a penitent heart, ready to confess your sin so that you can be completely forgiven.

Lord, today I confess my sins. It's not easy to say, "I did wrong,"
but I want and need Your forgiveness, Father. So, I come,
ready to do business with You once and for all. Amen.

He Will Pour Out His Spirit

*"Then, after doing all those things, I will pour out
my Spirit upon all people. Your sons and daughters
will prophesy. Your old men will dream dreams,
and your young men will see visions."*

Joel 2:28 nlt

All around you, people are in direct rebellion to God. They raise their fists against those who love the Lord. They seek to quiet those who want to share their faith.

Perhaps you've experienced oppression at the hands of unbelievers. It's not always easy to stay calm when you come under persecution. Many Christians wonder what the world will be like when their children or grandchildren are old. Will they be allowed to live out their faith at all?

Here's some great news, found in the book of Joel. In the last days, God promises to pour out His Spirit on all mankind. If it's true that we're in the last days even now, then we have to believe that this promise from Joel is happening even now.

Look around you! God is on the move. All kinds of amazing, supernatural things are taking place. Lives are being healed. Relationships are being restored. People are coming to the Lord in record numbers.

Yes, persecution will come. But the Lord is already providing a supernatural outlet for His children. Look up!

*Lord, I won't be afraid. Instead, I choose to be excited
to be alive during this pivotal point in Church history.
Thank You for pouring out Your Spirit, Lord! Amen.*

Walking in Agreement

Can two people walk together without agreeing on the direction?
AMOS 3:3 NLT

I f you've ever watched oxen yoked together in a field, you've seen what it's like to walk in agreement. If one decides to go one way, and the other decides to go another, they're in a world of trouble. Both will come to a stop and the task (plowing the field) will go undone.

God wants us to walk in agreement with those we're in relationships with. This is true of spouses, children, parents, friends, and so on. The Lord isn't asking us for uniformity. He created us with distinct, different personalities, after all. Primarily, God is warning against division in the body of Christ. If we're going to impact this world, if we're going to win others to Him, then we have to work as one. We have to be equally yoked.

Unbelievers are watching. When they see Christians squabbling, fighting among themselves, they look at the situation, shake their heads, and say things like, "That's why I'll never go to church." These people have a point. It's time for the body of Christ to walk in unity, to lay down division, and give up selfishness and pride.

How are your relationships with fellow believers? Maybe it's time to strengthen your bonds so that, together, you are more effective.

Thank You for the reminder that I need to walk in
unity with my brothers and sisters, Lord. Amen.

Her People Will Return

*"But Jerusalem will become a refuge for those who escape;
it will be a holy place. And the people of Israel will
come back to reclaim their inheritance."*

OBADIAH 17 NLT

The Jewish people have always longed to be at rest in their homeland, Israel. From Old Testament times until now, prophets have spoken of a period when this would actually come to pass. They promised that God's chosen people, the Jews, would not only return to Jerusalem but would never again be displaced.

For thousands of years this seemed impossible. Then, in the 1940s, a stirring began. In 1948 the official establishment of Israel took place and holocaust survivors, along with Jewish refugees from Arab nations, began to flood the country. From that time until now, biblical prophecies have unfolded right and left.

Even now, God is on the move in Israel. People still flock to its borders to find refuge. Believers come from all over the world to visit, to experience the undeniable holiness they find there.

Israel will play a key role in end-time prophecies, and it will be fascinating to see how much of that we will witness in our lifetime. But what a privilege, to be part of a generation that got to see the return of God's people to their homeland.

*God, my eyes are on this precious nation, Israel.
My heart is with Jerusalem and all who love her. Amen.*

Get Up and Go

The LORD gave this message to Jonah son of Amittai:
"Get up and go to the great city of Nineveh. Announce my
judgment against it because I have seen how wicked its
people are." But Jonah got up and went in the opposite
direction to get away from the LORD.

JONAH 1:1–3 NLT

W hat Jonah had heard from God couldn't have been any clearer: "Get up and go!" But God's instructions caused Jonah to go in the opposite direction. God wanted him to focus on the things above, not on earthly comforts below.

It took a series of events, including the Lord allowing Jonah to be swallowed by and trapped inside a great fish, to get the prophet's attention. Jonah, humbled by this fishy circumstance, finally obeyed the Lord. Afterward, Jonah expressed his frustration to God for sending him to speak to "more than 120,000 people living in spiritual darkness" (Jonah 4:11).

Has God asked you, His precious daughter, to say something bold or do something that seems nearly impossible? Chances are the answer is yes. As you continue to read God's Word, consider it your mind's training manual. Soaking in scripture will prompt you to *want* to obey God and focus on the upside of this life. As you do, you will find yourself praising Him more than putting Him down.

God, wherever You lead me, I want to follow You!
Give me the courage and conviction to get up and go.

Promised Peace

*Israel will be abandoned until the time when she who is
in labor bears a son, and the rest of his brothers return to
join the Israelites. He will stand and shepherd his flock in
the strength of the LORD, in the majesty of the name of
the LORD his God. And they will live securely, for then his
greatness will reach to the ends of the earth.*

MICAH 5:3–4 NIV

This is one of the many predictions of the coming Messiah, the King, who would rule and reign over His chosen people. While there would be great turmoil during the time of His birth, Jesus would bring peace in the midst of it. His birth would be the beginning of a time of advancement and protection for those who believed in Him. Unlike the kings who had come and gone before Him, the Messiah would rule differently.

Your life right now might be filled with many challenges. Though it might be different from those who had waited for and needed Jesus thousands of years ago, your need for a Messiah and the promised peace that comes with Him is just as important.

Open up your hands and heart to Jesus today. Tell Him what is troubling you. Invite Him, your Lord and miracle worker, to be your promised peace.

*Jesus, I need Your deliverance right now. Thank You for filling
me with Your Holy Spirit's provision of power and peace.*

Cartwheels of Joy

Though the cherry trees don't blossom and the strawberries don't ripen, though the apples are worm-eaten and the wheat fields stunted, though the sheep pens are sheepless and the cattle barns empty, I'm singing joyful praise to God. I'm turning cartwheels of joy to my Savior God. Counting on God's Rule to prevail, I take heart and gain strength. I run like a deer. I feel like I'm king of the mountain!
Habakkuk 3:17–19 msg

The book of Nahum is a great reminder of the place God wants to have in your life. As the Message translation puts it, "God is serious business" (Nahum 1:2). The book of Nahum, as well as that of Habakkuk, reminds us of God's glory over His faithful ones as well as His perspective on what will happen if a person lives in disobedience to Him.

The prophet Habakkuk's prayer speaks volumes to and about the God you serve. You have a God who sees and hears all things that might come against you in the flesh and spirit. You have a God who has deliverance and joy in mind for you.

Take some time today to recount all the instances where God was there for you. What happened? How did God break through for you? Now pretend you're a kid again. Do some cartwheels. Skip around your home like a deer. Lift your heart with laughter. Sing praises to God.

Lord, You are an awesome God!
May my joy come from You!

A Place of Peace

" 'The silver is mine, and the gold is mine, declares the
LORD of hosts. The latter glory of this house shall be
greater than the former, says the LORD of hosts. And in
this place I will give peace, declares the LORD of hosts.' "

HAGGAI 2:8–9 ESV

G od owns it all.
In today's text, one of the many examples of what God owns is gold and silver. Yet the bottom line reveals that *everything you possess is His*. The same is true of your gifts, talents, accomplishments, and blessings. All glory for all things can only be accredited to Him.

While God spoke through many prophets during Old Testament times and did much through their obedience—and by His grace much was done even in their *dis*obedience, lack of faith, and repentance—there was something even better coming from the long-awaited Messiah. And that something was peace.

Think back to when you accepted Jesus into your life. What was your life like then? Did you have the kind of peace you have now? Today, can you acknowledge God for who He is in your life and all He has given you? Take some time to find a place of peace and thank Him.

Lord, thank You for being my Prince of Peace. Thank You for
all You've given me: this life, this breath, this time, this calm.
I love You, Lord. You are and always will be my all in all.

Turn Toward God

Therefore say thou unto them, Thus saith the LORD
of hosts; Turn ye unto me, saith the LORD of hosts,
and I will turn unto you, saith the LORD of hosts.
ZECHARIAH 1:3 KJV

T he word *repentance* means to turn away from that which has been hindering a right relationship with God, asking for forgiveness, and turning back to Him. It is, in essence, looking up instead of looking down. It's freedom instead of bondage. As one turns back to God and His ways, God might seem closer and more real than ever before. Yet His grace can be overwhelming at times.

Those living during Old Testament times had to adhere to many religious rituals. They had to go through a long, tedious process to experience peace, cleanliness, and good standing with God.

For you, dear sister in Christ, yesterday might have been like any other day. Or perhaps it wasn't. Maybe you almost lost your temper, thought about saying or doing something that would go against what you knew was right. What was the end result? Did you lose your cool or not? If you did, guess what? There's an opportunity to turn back to God. All you need to do is talk to Him.

Father, I look up to You to fill my mind, mouth, and heart
with Your goodness. When I make a mistake, help me be
humble and turn to You for forgiveness. Then show me
how to make things right. . .in Your sight.

Jewels of a Crown

And the Lord their God will save them on that day as the flock of His people, for they shall be as the [precious] jewels of a crown, lifted high over and shining glitteringly upon His land.

ZECHARIAH 9:16 AMPC

❦

The promised Messiah was coming. Nobody knew exactly when, but they knew because He was prophesied about numerous times. With His kingdom would come abundant joy and blessings. *And* the Lord's children would be highly regarded, like jewels of a crown.

Over two thousand years later, you now know the other side of the story. You can grasp—with faith—what people back then wanted, needed, and waited so desperately for. Yet, do you truly live as though you are considered precious in God's eyes? Do you believe that you, who are a part of His church, have been delivered from the burdens of sin and death? Or are you still living among your own false beliefs and rituals?

Today, think about what Zechariah heard from the Lord and communicated to His people. God doesn't want you to live in your own "Old Testament" way of life: the past. God wants you to live in the "New Testament" Gospel message: a new creation, as precious as a gem in His jewel-filled crown!

Lord, thank You for thinking of me as Your precious jewel. Help me to believe it from the inside out so that I will shine brightly for You.

Yahweh Is Our God

"I will put this third through the fire; I will refine them as silver is refined and test them as gold is tested. They will call on My name, and I will answer them. I will say: They are My people, and they will say: Yahweh is our God."

Zechariah 13:9 HCSB

The Old Testament has embedded within it constant reminders that God was in charge. What He wanted wasn't so much a whole lot of rituals and cleansing of sins but for His people to be fully one with Him. Like a captain sailing a ship, God wanted the hearts, minds, and souls of every person to be on board with Him.

For some this meant they would walk through seasons of testing in order to bring seasons of testimony. They would be refined like silver and tested like gold. God wanted them to be in dialogue with Him by calling out to Him. In return, He promised He would answer them, those set apart to be holy, different, uniquely chosen for God's special work (Deuteronomy 14:2).

When you just want to rail at God, remember who He was for those in the Old and New Testaments. Though you might feel like you're going through the refiner's fire, stay steady in Him. For on the other side of it, He'll confirm once more that He is truly your God.

God, lift my eyes to remember You are in control as I lift my voice in praise of You.

The Tithe Test

*"Bring all the tithes into the storehouse so there will be
enough food in my Temple. If you do," says the LORD of
Heaven's Armies, "I will open the windows of heaven for you.
I will pour out a blessing so great you won't have enough
room to take it in! Try it! Put me to the test!"*

MALACHI 3:10 NLT

A s the Old Testament ends, the book of Malachi reminds readers to, once again, take God seriously. While what was to come in the New Testament would free believers from many of the repetitive rituals for the atonement of sins, there are still a few principles from the Old Testament that apply to the New.

One such principle was with the tithe, an amount often considered a tenth of what a person produced or earned. Speaking through Malachi, God says He'd been cheated out of tithes and offerings. He now wanted true repentance from the people. He wanted them to test His faithfulness to them by giving their tithes—even though they were long overdue—and watching what He'd do next.

Are there areas in your life that you are holding back from God, not giving Him the first fruits? Ask God to show you where in your life that might be happening. Then step out in faith, give back to Him, and watch what happens next.

*Lord, I want to receive all of Your abundant blessings.
Help me step out in faith and give generously.*

The Family Line

Thus there were fourteen generations in all from
Abraham to David, fourteen from David to the exile to
Babylon, and fourteen from the exile to the Messiah.
MATTHEW 1:17 NIV

N umerous names. The birth of Jesus. The Magi find and visit the long-awaited Messiah. The escape to Egypt, and then the return to Nazareth. John the Baptist prepares for Jesus' ministry and baptizes Him. Then, Jesus is tested in the wilderness and shortly after begins to preach, appoints His first disciples, and heals the sick.

A lot of the details of Jesus' early life get covered in the first four chapters of the book of Matthew. So much to consider during the early life of the King. And here's something to think about as you read today's text: *you* are very much a part of this story. Why was it so important for you to read all of the Old Testament? To see how all those generations of prophets and leaders who obeyed God's call on their life were progenitors of Jesus. They paved the way for Jesus' ministry. Even though they didn't get to meet Jesus on this earth, they prepared for His presence among us.

You are a part of Jesus' family line. When you accepted Him into your life, you became an adopted daughter and an heir to all God's promises. How awesome is that, sister in Christ?

Lord, thank You for allowing me to be a
part of Your family and Your master plan.

Strive for Contentment

"You're blessed when you're content with just who you are—
no more, no less. That's the moment you find yourselves
proud owners of everything that can't be bought."
MATTHEW 5:5 MSG

I n Matthew 5–7, Jesus gave His Sermon on the Mount. He had a lot to say about what it meant to be truly blessed and be salt-and-light witnesses. He explained how He came down from heaven to complete the law of God. Jesus spoke of how those who are guilty of murder, insults, and anger were all subject to similar judgment; the importance of neither committing adultery nor getting a divorce; and the value of keeping your word. Jesus also talked about loving your neighbors; doing good for God and others; and how to pray, worship, and live with integrity.

So, where do you start to live all of this out in your own life? If you're living for God and not the world, you'll find yourself content with who you are and what you have, for none of what Jesus talks about can be bought or earned.

As a present-day Jesus follower, you too are to strive for contentment in life. When you do, God's peace will overflow within and without. And much of what Jesus shared in these chapters will be a natural way of life.

Lord, help me to seek You and not the things of this world.
When I'm looking up to You, contentment reigns inside and out.

Take a Time-Out

And they went and woke him, saying, "Save us, Lord;
we are perishing." And he said to them, "Why are you
afraid, O you of little faith?" Then he rose and rebuked
the winds and the sea, and there was a great calm.
MATTHEW 8:25–26 ESV

During Jesus' ministry, He healed many people and performed miracles. Yet today's readings make it clear that putting faith, hope, and trust in Jesus most likely won't make life any easier. But having a relationship with Him can help provide healing, peace, inspiration, wisdom, and direction in an often chaotic and callous world.

The disciples sitting in the boat with Jesus had calamity all around them. A storm had surged at sea, and they were anxious about what to do. Like children who awaken their parents during a middle-of-the-night thunderstorm, the disciples woke up Jesus because they believed He had the authority and power to calm the water. And they were right. When Jesus rebuked the winds and the sea, those elements of nature obeyed. Like misbehaving children on the verge of receiving a time-out, the winds and waves ceased.

Take some time out today to be with God. Share with Him the areas in your life that need healing and peace. Then follow His guidance, assured He *will* calm your storms within and without.

Lord, help me carve time out of my day to be
with You. I long for Your miraculous touch.

Accepting the Call of Ministry

Come unto me, all ye that labour and are heavy laden, and I
will give you rest. Take my yoke upon you, and learn of me;
for I am meek and lowly in heart: and ye shall find rest unto
your souls. For my yoke is easy, and my burden is light.

MATTHEW 11:28–30 KJV

In Matthew 10, Jesus commissioned the twelve disciples. His instructions on how they were to conduct themselves in ministry meant they were going to have to live and lead a different way of life. Their acceptance of the ministry to which Jesus had called them was going to take all their strength and energy. That's why Jesus emphasized the importance of their depending on Him for all things, including much needed rest.

When you accept the call of ministry and service on your life, there will be times that you too will need rest from the demands and responsibilities that threaten to wear you out. Needing to rest doesn't mean it's time to quit serving the Lord. It's simply hitting the PAUSE button.

Are you feeling worn down? Or are you trudging your way through ministry? If so, hit that PAUSE button. Take time to rest. Evaluate what God has placed before you. Then ask for a new, fresh vision.

Jesus, thank You for placing a ministry in my life
so I can serve You and others, spreading Your
Good News and building up Your kingdom.

God's Family

*For whoever does the will of My Father in heaven
is My brother and sister and mother!*
MATTHEW 12:50 AMPC

A s Jesus continued to teach during His ministry, He started to speak in parables, stories that had spiritual meaning and principles that were sometimes challenging to understand. He also made it clear that those who do His will are considered to be a part of His family.

So much of what Jesus spoke about didn't make a lot of sense to people. Why? Because it seemed counterintuitive, going against what many believed was right.

As a daughter of Jesus, there may be things you say or do that conflict with what other people think is okay or that just don't make any sense at all to those closest to you. You might find yourself wanting to explain things or prove your value. *But the truth is you are already very valuable to God.* When you accepted Him into your life and asked Him to forgive you of your sins, you made a permanent residence with God for eternity!

So, remember who you are, and in light of that identity in Christ, don't let *anything* get you down. Instead keep your eyes fixed upward, and watch Jesus embrace and remedy not only you but your circumstances as well.

*Lord, when I feel misunderstood, help me remember You have
already experienced what I'm going through. Give me perspective
on how to be at peace with this life You've given me.*

Gains and Losses

*Jesus said to His disciples, "If anyone wants to come
with Me, he must deny himself, take up his cross, and
follow Me. For whoever wants to save his life will lose it,
but whoever loses his life because of Me will find it."*
MATTHEW 16:24–25 HCSB

Have you ever withheld something from yourself that seemed very good and on the surface okay to indulge in? Or have you ever had to let go of something with the hope that someday you would get something even better in return? Or have you, as a daughter in Christ, ever experienced extreme loss or trauma?

The Christian pathway isn't an easy road to travel. That is made very evident by the story of John the Baptist's beheading. All the miracles and healings Jesus performed solidifies the fact that this is a fallen, broken, challenging world to live in, one that needs the healing touch and presence of a savior. And last but definitely not least, the eventual whipping, beating, and crucifixion of Jesus can also remind you how cruel this world can be.

Yet there is hope, hope that when you withhold things in your life that seem good, when you let go of certain dreams or expectations and run to the cross, you *will* find a life filled with peace and blessings, just the way God intended.

*Lord, help me lose my life and turn
it over to You so that I may find it in You.*

The Greatest

Then he said, "I tell you the truth, unless you turn from your sins and become like little children, you will never get into the Kingdom of Heaven. So anyone who becomes as humble as this little child is the greatest in the Kingdom of Heaven."

MATTHEW 18:3–4 NLT

Jesus used the illustration of little children several times in His teachings. Why? Probably because children are innocent. They don't allow logic, reasoning, and intuition to get in the way of accepting Jesus into their life. Kids don't have years upon years of built-up pride, experience, and accolades to push God aside as being the supreme master and authority. They've accepted Jesus for who He is, and, in turn, Jesus called them the greatest in the kingdom.

Although you might not be a baby, toddler, youth, preteen, or teenager, you are still a child in God's eyes. No matter what your age, you are His beloved and redeemed daughter as well as His friend. When you find yourself at your wits' end, begrudging God, maybe it's time to interact with a child. Play with her, love her, joke around and color with her. Soon, as your spirit changes, you'll realize you're having fun again. Approach God in prayer, just as a child would, and enter into His kingdom.

*Lord, the busyness and stresses of the day sometimes consume me.
Help me become as innocent as a child, embracing You,
loving You, running to You with no strings attached.*

Underdog Grace

"So the last will be first, and the first will be last."
MATTHEW 20:16 NIV

※

M any of Jesus' parables didn't make a lot of sense to a lot of people. But to those who had the ears to hear and the eyes to see, Jesus' words gave breath and life to them.

Such is the case with the parable of workers in the vineyard. Throughout the story, grace and compassion are evident. People who were considered underdogs, less than, and looked down upon looked up to God, and He saw them as His very own.

Matthew 20:26–28 says, "Whoever wants to become great among you must be your servant, and whoever wants to be first must be your slave—just as the Son of Man did not come to be served, but to serve, and to give his life as a ransom for many."

Today, consider areas in your life where you've been considered an underdog but got to experience God's grace. Think about other people in your life, underdogs to whom you can extend this same gentle love and compassion. Then, the next time you find yourself overlooking someone, look up to God. Ask Him to show you how to act and what to say as a way to serve and express God's love poured out.

Jesus, I'm not always the best at loving others
the way You did. Help me to be more like You.

What's Most Important

Jesus said, " 'Love the Lord your God with all your passion and prayer and intelligence.' This is the most important, the first on any list. But there is a second to set alongside it: 'Love others as well as you love yourself.' These two commands are pegs; everything in God's Law and the Prophets hangs from them."

Matthew 22:37–40 msg

A Pharisee asked Jesus which command in God's law was the greatest. Jesus said His followers are to love God with all they've got (Deuteronomy 6:4–5). He added they are also to love others as they love themselves (Leviticus 19:18). These two commands were considered the foundation of God's law for all believers for they're the bedrock to a good life with Jesus.

When you take your eyes—as well as your heart, soul, mind, and energy—off Jesus, you miss what's truly most important in this life and the next. When you turn your love toward material things, you may not only lose your passion for God but lose your compassion and empathy for other people, those who need or count on your love. When you lose your love of self, you may find it difficult to love others.

Today, consider these "most important" commandments. How do you score when it comes to loving God, yourself, and others?

Lord, I confess that some days You aren't my top priority. Help me to stay focused on loving You, then others, as I do myself.

Talent Show

*"For to everyone who has will more be given,
and he will have an abundance. But from the one
who has not, even what he has will be taken away."*
MATTHEW 25:29 ESV

In today's readings, Jesus shared the parable of the talents. This story illustrated the importance of using the gifts, talents, resources, and abilities God has given you, for His glory, purposes, and service. If you don't use them, what has been given to you will be taken away. Sister in Christ, there's no sense letting something very unique and special about you sit dormant because of fear, lack of experience, or any other reason.

If you have a child in your life who is very close and special to you, chances are you have witnessed that child wanting to show you her talent, recently learned skill, or ability to do something—even if she has yet to fully master it. To her, it's an opportunity to show others something she's excited about, passionate about, or even proud of.

As an adult daughter in Christ, utilizing your talents and abilities isn't necessarily about entering the next talent show. But it does mean using your gifts and abilities because God knows and wants you—His masterpiece—to show your potential! So, get up, get going, and live for His glory!

*Lord, sometimes I don't want to use my time, talents,
and resources because I'm afraid or uncomfortable.
Give me the courage to step out in faith.*

Leave a Legacy

*Verily I say unto you, Wheresoever this gospel shall be
preached in the whole world, there shall also this, that this
woman hath done, be told for a memorial of her.*

MATTHEW 26:13 KJV

W hen Jesus was in Bethany, he visited the home of Simon, a man who'd previously had leprosy. While Jesus was eating, a woman with an alabaster jar approached Him and did what others thought unthinkable, perhaps even outrageous. Inside this jar was expensive perfume that she proceeded to pour on Jesus' head. The disciples witnessing this were shocked because that jar with perfume could have been sold for a high price and the money given to the poor.

Jesus provided the disciples with perspective. The poor would always be among them, but what this woman did helped prepare Jesus for burial. Furthermore, her actions showed how much she honored and believed in her King. Her anointing of Jesus, regardless of the personal cost, was a sacrifice this nameless woman was willing to make. What she did would be remembered and discussed for generations to come.

As a precious woman of God, you too can leave a legacy of faith. Whether it's how you serve people, treat others, or use your time, talents, and resources, be a woman who doesn't hold back. Be generous, forgiving, and gracious; and others, including God, will notice.

*Jesus, help me leave a legacy of faith,
regardless of the personal cost.*

Go and Tell

*So they left the tomb hastily with fear and great joy and
ran to tell the disciples. And as they went, behold, Jesus
met them and said, Hail (greetings)! And they went up to
Him and clasped His feet and worshiped Him.*

MATTHEW 28:8–9 AMPC

After Jesus' crucifixion, He was laid in a tomb that'd been cut out of a rock. Later, an angel of the Lord came and moved the stone covering the entrance to the tomb. The men guarding the tomb shook with fear. Mary Magdalene and the other Mary, who'd arrived on the scene, also showed great apprehension. However, the angel told them, "Do not be afraid. . . . Go quickly and tell his disciples: 'He has risen from the dead and is going ahead of you into Galilee' " (Matthew 28:5–7 NIV). The women, "commissioned" by the angel to spread the Good News, went and did as the angel had said.

As soon as Jesus and His followers met in Galilee, He told them to go and make disciples of all nations, baptizing them and teaching them God's commands. He also reminded them to trust that God would always be with them.

It's interesting that the very first thing Jesus did after His resurrection was to commission His disciples, imploring them to tell others the Good News. As a woman of God, who will you tell about Jesus today?

*Lord, even if I feel afraid, help me be willing
to go and tell others about You.*

Follow Him

"Follow Me," Jesus told them, "and I will make you fish for people!"
Immediately they left their nets and followed Him.
MARK 1:17–18 HCSB

F or some, following Jesus required a lot of sacrifice. It meant leaving behind their homes, possessions, trades, professions, and family members for the sake of God's call on their life.

When you accepted Jesus into your life, chances are you shared this news with others. Were some people excited for you? Did they encourage you? Or did you feel like some of them rejected you, distanced themselves from you, or mocked you and criticized your newfound faith?

What has following Jesus been like for you over the years? Was there anything you've had to give up or let go of? Did you ever come to a point where you realized you were on the wrong path and had to completely change direction?

While the cost of following Jesus can be great, there's nothing better than believing in and trusting Him. Life is more thrilling, more abundant, more worthwhile when you surrender your life to your Creator.

Lord, I recommit to following You and Your ways. Although
others around me are not living for You, I know I must. Help me
stay fixed and focused on the call You have placed on my life,
and give me the courage to continue in my faith walk.

In Good Company

Then Jesus told them, "A prophet is honored everywhere except in
his own hometown and among his relatives and his own family."
MARK 6:4 NLT

Jesus returned to His hometown of Nazareth. He taught in the synagogue, where many were amazed by His wisdom and ability to perform miracles. As soon as those people heard where Jesus was from—their own town—they were quick to discredit and reject Him. In fact, these people were "deeply offended and refused to believe in Him" (Mark 6:3).

Have you ever experienced something similar? Perhaps you went back home and were able to share with others about Jesus, but they simply looked at you with suspicion, then turned away. Maybe you picked up the phone and reached out to an old friend. As you caught up, you shared your faith, and the phone went silent.

If, because of your faith, you have ever experienced the cold shoulder from those closest to you, you're in good company. Jesus understands. Yet the fact that you stood up and decided to follow Him and then went to tell others is very important.

Keep looking up to Jesus for wisdom and guidance about how to share His Good News. Don't worry if you get rejected every now and then. The Lord sees what you're doing and will reward you in due time.

Lord, I've told those I care for about You. Even though I felt
their rejection and disapproval afterward, I pray that my
words planted seeds of love and faith in their hearts.

What Comes Out

*Again Jesus called the crowd to him and said, "Listen to
me, everyone, and understand this. Nothing outside a
person can defile them by going into them. Rather, it is
what comes out of a person that defiles them."*

MARK 7:14–16 NIV

The Pharisees and some of the teachers of the law saw Jesus' disciples eating with unwashed hands. To these religious leaders, eating with unwashed hands was considered an act of defilement. So, they asked Jesus why He allowed His followers to eat this way, a way that went against the traditions of the elders.

Wanting to set the record straight, Jesus told the Pharisees and teachers of the law that the traditions they were getting so caught up in weren't important. Focusing on the commandments of God was.

For you, there might be certain traditions you grew up with that are sometimes hard to navigate as an adult. Some of them might not even make any sense. On the other hand, there might be some meaningful traditions you truly love and want to continue to practice. Whatever the case, bring your customs before God in prayer. Ask Him which are most important, worthwhile, and honoring to Him. Then practice those traditions, all the while remembering that the most important thing is focusing on God alone.

*Lord, thank You for setting me free from unnecessary beliefs,
patterns of behavior, and rituals that don't make a lot of sense.
In all that I say and do, may I focus on You alone.*

Follow Jesus

"On your way," said Jesus. "Your faith has saved and
healed you." In that very instant he recovered
his sight and followed Jesus down the road.

MARK 10:52 MSG

Jesus spent time in Jericho and was leaving town with His disciples. On His way, a blind beggar named Bartimaeus cried out to Him. The beggar needed God's grace and mercy for he was unable to see. So, Jesus called the man over and asked him what he wanted. Bartimaeus replied, "I want to see" (Mark 10:51). Jesus said, "On your way. . .Your faith has saved and healed you" (Mark 10:52). His sight restored, Bartimaeus "followed Jesus down the road."

As you consider all of the ways in which life can bring you down— i.e., a health issue, loss of a job, loss of a friend or family member, seeing a child suffer, etc.—it may take a lot of effort to look up to God, to cry out for His unmerited favor and mercy, to throw off whatever may be hindering you, to run after the Lord, and to put your most fervent and heartfelt desire into words.

So, sister, today, even if it physically or emotionally hurts, pick your head up. Literally cry out to God for what you need most. Then, by faith, whether you receive an instant healing or complete silence, choose to follow Jesus.

Lord, in every season You, Your Word,
Your touch are all I need.

Give Generously

And he called his disciples to him and said to them, "Truly, I say to you, this poor widow has put in more than all those who are contributing to the offering box. For they all contributed out of their abundance, but she out of her poverty has put in everything she had, all she had to live on."

MARK 12:43–44 ESV

Imagine what it must have been like to witness rich people putting large sums of money into the offering box. Then comes a poor widow who places two copper coins, an amount equivalent to a penny but that, in that day and age, amounted to a day's wages for a laborer.

A mere penny? We might think the widow didn't put in enough. But to Jesus she had put in everything. He explained to the disciples that even though her offering didn't seem like much, she'd placed in more than all the others. They contributed out of their abundance, but she put in everything she had.

Imagine what it would be like to give that generously. Whether it's your time, talents, or resources, you too can play a role in giving God your all. Instead of feeling frustrated the next time the offering plate comes your way, consider how to give joyfully above and beyond what you normally give. Then watch as God gives it back to you abundantly.

Lord, help me follow the example of the poor widow who gave everything she had for Your kingdom work.

Sufficient Sovereignty

And he said, Abba, Father, all things are possible unto
thee; take away this cup from me: nevertheless not
what I will, but what thou wilt.

MARK 14:36 KJV

When Jesus prayed in Gethsemane, He prayed a prayer that sounded troubled and a prayer that is also universal. A prayer that what He was about to go through on the cross could pass from Him. Jesus was willing to go through it if it was His Father's will. The Son of God was willing to endure it, knowing all that had been prophesied about Him and His path and fully aware there was a greater glory on the other side.

As a woman of God, chances are you too have dealt with some challenging situations. More than likely, you know firsthand what it's like to witness or endure suffering. Maybe you can relate to what Jesus prayed and have found yourself praying similar words.

No matter where your faith journey is today, trust God. Look up instead of down. Be willing to do whatever He asks of you, even if it looks or feels like it might temporarily hurt. God has good things in store for you. He'll resurrect your current suffering to reveal His sufficient sovereignty.

Lord, give me the eyes to see that whatever I'm going through
right now will have a good outcome in the days, weeks, months,
and years ahead. Keep my head up and my eyes focused on You.

Be Filled

And it occurred that when Elizabeth heard Mary's greeting, the baby leaped in her womb, and Elizabeth was filled with and controlled by the Holy Spirit.

LUKE 1:41 AMPC

E lizabeth and Zechariah were far along in their years when the news that they would give birth to a son came their way. An angel of the Lord, Gabriel, approached Zechariah to share the news that this boy, who they were to name John, would make a way for the promised Messiah. Gabriel told Zechariah his son should never touch wine or any other alcoholic drink because he would be filled with the Holy Spirit.

Later in the story, Mary comes to visit her cousin Elizabeth. As soon as Elizabeth hears Mary's greeting, the baby inside of her womb leaps. She too is then filled with and controlled by the Holy Spirit.

The Holy Spirit's an important part of God's plan and purpose. What seemed impossible—for an elderly couple to conceive and give birth to a son in their later years—was a miracle.

God wants to do miracles inside of you! Is there something you have been railing at God about? Something you wish would come to pass but seems so impossible? Put the begrudging attitude, the doubts, and the what-ifs aside, and invite the power of the Holy Spirit to live and reign within you.

Lord, I need a special touch of Your Holy Spirit's power in my life. Transform me today. Work miracles in and through my life.

In Her Heart

Then He went down with them and came to Nazareth
and was obedient to them. His mother kept all these
things in her heart. And Jesus increased in wisdom and
stature, and in favor with God and with people.
Luke 2:51–52 hcsb

The stories that led up to the genealogy of Christ and the beginning of His ministry were important reminders to Mary that He was God's one and only chosen Son. It's evident that she wanted to be obedient and faithful to God's call to bring Him into the world and raise Him according to God's plan. Yet as a human mom, Mary wanted what was best for Jesus too.

You too may have influence in a younger person's life. Maybe you are a grandmother, a mom, an auntie, a sister, a mentor, a kids' Sunday school teacher, a youth minister, or a Bible study leader. Whatever your relationship or role, invite God into each specific association you have with a younger person. Pray for every individual you get to interact with. Ask God to show you how to keep leading with the best of intentions as well as be more attuned to the Lord's will.

Lord, I want what is best for those I care about. I want
to see them flourish into the godly men and women
You desire them to be. Help me hold these precious
relationships in my heart and be inspired by their lives.

Sent Out

But he replied, "I must preach the Good News of the Kingdom of God in other towns, too, because that is why I was sent."
Luke 4:43 nlt

Jesus was rejected when preaching in His boyhood hometown of Nazareth. Yet that didn't stop Him from continuing to cast out demons and heal people in other towns. Jesus was committed to "preach the Good News of the Kingdom of God" for He knew that's why God had sent Him.

Yet in Nazareth, Jesus' hometown, the people were furious at the words He said, so they mobbed Him and tried to force Him to the edge of the hill on which the town was built, intending to push Him off the cliff! Thankfully, Jesus was able to pass through the crowd and went on His way.

You too have been called by God to do some amazing things for the faith. Sometimes you might receive great opposition. But keep stepping out in faith. Don't give up. Remember you were called for a divine purpose, which is to live for Christ. More specifically, God has given you a ministry to focus on. When the pressure is on and it feels like no one is supporting you, remember *God* loves and supports you!

Lord, when I feel downcast, unsupported, or looked down upon because of my faith, may You quickly open new doors of ministry for me. Give me the strength to do what You've called me to do.

Beatitude Attitude

*"Blessed are you when people hate you, when they
exclude you and insult you and reject your name
as evil, because of the Son of Man."*

LUKE 6:22 NIV

J esus preached a series of blessings known as the beatitudes. These blessings provided perspective to those in the faith, a viewpoint on how to live in such a way that the challenges and cruelties of this world would not taint a relationship with God.

This life isn't easy. There may be times when you want to throw in the towel. Yet your faith can be a catalyst to break through and make changes in your life or in the lives of others, if you are able to endure some of the curve balls that come your way.

Sometimes you might experience seasons of being financially deprived. Sometimes you might know what it's like to not have enough to eat. Sometimes circumstances may figuratively or literally bring you to tears. Sometimes you might experience a cold shoulder because of who and what you believe in. If—or when—these things happen, look to God. Remember the beatitude attitude He desires you to have. Know He will see you through whatever your circumstances are and will bless you because of it. That's His promise!

*Lord, when my attitude gets the best of me, help me to remember
the blessings You have in mind for me. Help me look up to You
instead of down and to rest in Your promises all around.*

Seize the Day

Jesus said, "No procrastination. No backward looks. You can't
put God's kingdom off till tomorrow. Seize the day."
LUKE 9:62 MSG

Jesus wanted people to follow Him not their traditions. And as they followed Him, believers didn't have to be one of the twelve disciples to be able to do the will of God. In fact, one of the disciples saw someone cast out a demon using Jesus' name, and they stopped him because he wasn't a part of their group. But Jesus told them, "Don't stop him. If he's not an enemy, he's an ally" (Luke 9:50).

Later, someone said they wanted to follow Jesus but first wanted to get home to bury his father. Jesus said, "First things first. Your business is life, not death. And life is urgent: Announce God's kingdom!" (Luke 9:60).

Today, on Halloween, there are many people who are attending to their own traditions and celebrations. But on this day, you are called to be different. This is a great opportunity to share your faith with friends and neighbors and those who knock at your door. Think about some creative ways to be a witness for the Gospel, because it's what you're called to do.

Jesus, help me seize this day. May Your light shine through me
into this dark world. When people come to my door, may my
actions and character be enough to show something is different
about me. And that difference is You—in me. Amen.

Anxiety or Priority

Martha, Martha, you are anxious and troubled about
many things; there is need of only one or but a few things.
Mary has chosen the good portion [that which is to her
advantage], which shall not be taken away from her.
LUKE 10:41–42 AMPC

Three siblings—Mary, Martha, and Lazarus—lived together in Martha's house in Bethany. When Jesus entered the village, Martha invited Him into her home, then began preparing supper for the crowd. As she did so, she noticed her sister, Mary, had sat down at Jesus' feet, listening to the words that fell from His mouth. "But Martha [overly occupied and too busy] was distracted with much serving" (Luke 10:40). So, she asked Jesus to tell her sister, Mary, to get up and help her.

Yet instead of telling Mary to help her sister, Martha, Jesus told her, "Martha, Martha, you are worried and upset about many things, but one thing is necessary. Mary has made the right choice, and it will not be taken away from her" (Luke 10:41-42 HCSB). In other words, Martha had opted for being anxious about many things instead of focusing on one main thing: making Jesus, His presence, and His teachings her highest priority.

Today, choose to focus on making Jesus your highest priority instead of living a worldly life rife with high anxiety.

Jesus, I choose to make You my priority in this life.
As I sit at Your feet, Lord, speak to me. I'm listening.

Your Day to Choose

And [Jesus] said to His disciples, Therefore I tell you,
do not be anxious and troubled [with cares] about your
life, as to what you will [have to] eat; or about your body,
as to what you will [have to] wear. For life is more than
food, and the body [more] than clothes.

LUKE 12:22–23 AMPC

Do you often find yourself anxious, overwrought, and worried? If so, Jesus offers you a cure.

In His Word, Jesus makes it clear you're not to be troubled about anything in your life, neither as to what you'll eat nor what you'll wear. Instead, you're to trust God to provide for you, just as the birds trust Him for their food. Besides, Jesus says, your worrying will get you nowhere. It only subtracts, not adds, to your life.

Yet not worrying can be difficult if you were raised with the conviction that you need to be able to take care of yourself. Thus, it can take some time to let go so that you can let God. But it can be done. How? By choosing to seek the Lord and His kingdom above all things and before all people. That means looking to God and His Word in the beginning of the day, before your feet even touch the ground.

Lord, above all other things and people in my life, I choose to trust
and seek You. I know that as I do, You will supply all I need.

Open-Arm Policy

So he got up and came to his [own] father. But while
he was still a long way off, his father saw him and was
moved with pity and tenderness [for him]; and he ran
and embraced him and kissed him [fervently].
LUKE 15:20 AMPC

In our eagerness to pave our own way, to start our life, and to find our own purpose and direction, we may, at times, find ourselves heading in the wrong direction or making bad choices, choices that God wouldn't make for us. That's what happened to a rich man's youngest boy in Jesus' parable of the Prodigal Son.

Son number 2 asked his dad for his inheritance early. With riches in hand, the son went off and had a great time. Until the money ran out. While feeding hogs for a farmer so he could eat, the young man, who "could not satisfy his hunger" (Luke 15:16), went back to his father, thinking he'd fare better working for him.

While the son rehearsed the speech he'd give to his dad, his dad saw him. Moved with compassion, the father ran to his son, kissed him, and celebrated his return.

When you make a mistake, God does the same for you. It's His open-arm policy.

Help me to stay on the right path with You, Lord, but to
remember that if I do veer off, Your arms will always be
open for me, welcoming me home with love and compassion.

God or Mammon?

No servant is able to serve two masters; for either he
will hate the one and love the other, or he will stand by
and be devoted to the one and despise the other. You
cannot serve God and mammon (riches, or anything in
which you trust and on which you rely).

Luke 16:13 ampc

In today's scripture, God is making it perfectly clear who you're to trust in and rely on: Him. Alone. No one else. Ever. Why? Because one woman cannot serve two different bosses: you either serve God or you serve mammon, or anything else to which you've given over the reins of your life.

Very early on in our story with God, our forebearers were so insecure they made themselves a golden calf while Moses was up on a mountain, hanging out with the Lord. And Aaron, a leader of the Israelites and Moses' brother, helped the people commit this egregious act! God tipped off Moses to what was happening down below. In His anger, God decided to destroy them. But Moses interceded on the people's behalf, and so God stayed His hand.

Today, consider who or what you may be serving. Who is your true master—the almighty God or the almighty dollar?

You, Lord, are my only true Master. Help me reflect
that in my life, my words, and my actions. Amen.

Endless Possibilities

*[Jesus] told them a parable to the effect that they ought always
to pray and not to turn coward (faint, lose heart, and give up). . . .
What is impossible with men is possible with God.*
LUKE 18:1, 27 AMPC

Life is full of challenges, especially for those of us who find ourselves the least in society. Yet Jesus shines a ray of hope into our lives by telling us to keep on praying. Don't get scared, frustrated, or weak and give up. What is possible with people is possible with God!

Jesus then tells a story to illustrate His point. Once there was a judge who feared neither God nor man or woman. But this poor widow, looking for justice, kept on coming to him, demanding he not just protect and defend her but give her justice. Finally, because of her persistence, the judge gave in to her demands and gave her what she'd desired.

Your God will do all that and more when you come to Him and present your case. You may have to pray more than once, but you are to never give up. Remember, what is impossible with *wo*men is more than possible with God!

*With You in my life, Lord, I know all things are possible.
Even for me! Thus, I will never give up. I will never
surrender for You, my God, can do anything!*

Stay Calm and Carry On

*When you hear of wars and insurrections (disturbances,
disorder, and confusion), do not become alarmed and
panic-stricken and terrified; for all this must take place
first, but the end will not [come] immediately.*

LUKE 21:9 AMPC

These days it seems to get harder and harder for believers to watch or listen to the news. Each news story about wars, murder, torture, terror, mass shootings, etc., seems to cut the heart over and over again. And if it feels that way for normal believers, imagine what it does to believers who have especially tender hearts.

No matter what kind of heart you have, Jesus tells you that when you hear all the bad news about wars and other acts of violence that humans inflict upon other humans, you are not to freak out and become terrified. These things are going to happen as the end of this age comes closer and closer. Yet, once again, Jesus asks you to be patient and on your guard during these times. Don't let "your hearts be overburdened and depressed" (Luke 21:34). Don't get fixated on the worries or on the business of life. Instead, get focused on God. Then no matter when or where the end time does come, you'll be ready.

*Lord, help me stay calm and carry on no matter what's going
on in this world. Help me simply trust that You see all,
know all, and are with me. In Jesus' name, amen.*

Hearts Greatly Moved

*And they said to one another, Were not our hearts greatly moved and
burning within us while He was talking with us on the road and as
He opened and explained to us [the sense of] the Scriptures?*

LUKE 24:32 AMPC

Sometimes it can be difficult to understand what God is trying to tell you in His Word. That's why there's such a great market for different translations and study editions of Bibles. Yet even then, it can still be difficult to fathom what God is saying. But when you do, when a passage you've read at least fifty times suddenly becomes clear, it's amazing how your heart is moved!

That's what two disciples walking to Emmaus experienced after Jesus' death and resurrection. They were talking about what'd happened when they were joined by a stranger. Unbeknownst to them, that stranger was Jesus! He began explaining to them how all the recent events had been foretold in the scriptures. Then, when they invited Him in for a meal and He blessed then broke the bread, they realized the stranger was Jesus—and He vanished!

That same Jesus who walked with those two disciples on their way to Emmaus is walking with you right now. And He's ready to reveal Himself in the scriptures so you too can understand who He is. So, woman, open your Bible and pray for Jesus to open your eyes.

*Show me, Jesus, what You would have me
know and understand in this moment.*

The Heart Whisperer

He did not need anyone to bear witness concerning man [needed no evidence from anyone about men], for He Himself knew what was in human nature. [He could read men's hearts.]

JOHN 2:25 AMPC

No matter what you're feeling or when, Jesus knows what's happening deep within you. That's because He can read your heart. By the time this supernatural feat had been recorded about Jesus, His reading of hearts had already been witnessed.

It happened like this. . . . John the Baptist had announced Jesus was the Son of God. The next day, Jesus invited Philip to follow Him. Philip then told Nathanael about Jesus of Nazareth, describing Him as "the One Moses wrote about in the Law" (John 1:45 HCSB). Then when Jesus saw Nathanael coming toward Him, He said, "Here is a true Israelite; no deceit is in him" (John 1:47 HCSB). When Nathanael asked how Jesus knew him, Jesus said, "Before Philip called you. . .I saw you" (John 1:48 HCSB).

If Jesus knows you and what's in your heart, you can be sure He knows others and what's in their hearts. So, trust Jesus, your Heart Whisperer, to lead you down the right path, the sure route to lush meadows and still waters.

Lord, You who know all, help me navigate the maze of people in my life by searching their hearts—as well as my own!

Letting Go

*He said to him, Do you want to become well? [Are you
really in earnest about getting well?] The invalid answered,
Sir, I have nobody when the water is moving to put me into
the pool; but while I am trying to come [into it] myself,
somebody else steps down ahead of me.*

JOHN 5:6–7 AMPC

When Jesus stopped at the pool at Bethesda, He saw many sick
people waiting for an angel to move the water. Because "the first
one who got in after the water was stirred up recovered from whatever
ailment he had" (John 5:4 HCSB).

Seeing there a man who'd been unable to walk for thirty-eight
years, Jesus asked him, "Do you truly desire to get well?" But instead of
answering Jesus' question, the man complained how no one would help
him into the water. So, Jesus simply told him to get up, pick up his mat,
and walk. At that very moment, the man was healed and did just that!

Sometimes, our illnesses become such a part of us that we have
trouble letting them go and putting them—and ourselves—into God's
hands. If you have a problem or illness you've been holding on to,
choose to turn it and yourself over to God. Decide here and now that it's
more important to let go than to sing a constant refrain of woe.

*Today, Lord, I choose to let go of my hurts, infirmities,
and troubles so I can better serve You and others.*

Are You Willing?

Jesus said to them, It is I; be not afraid! [I AM; stop being frightened!] Then they were quite willing and glad for Him to come into the boat. And now the boat went at once to the land they had steered toward. [And immediately they reached the shore toward which they had been slowly making their way.]

JOHN 6:20–21 AMPC

After a day of preaching to and then feeding five thousand men (not including women and children), Jesus went up the mountain to spend some time alone with Father God. That evening, the disciples took a boat across the sea of Galilee to Capernaum. The sun had already set and still Jesus hadn't rejoined them.

When the sea became rough because of a violent wind, the disciples struggled to fight against it. After having rowed three or four miles, the men looked up and saw Jesus walking on the water! As He got closer to their boat, they became terrified. But Jesus told them, "It's only Me—the I AM. Stop your panicking." Once they were willing to let Jesus into their boat, the disciples "immediately. . .reached the shore toward which they had been slowly making their way"!

Once you stop your fears from rising up and welcome Jesus into your life, you too will find yourself soon reaching that destination toward which you've been striving. Are you willing?

I refuse to live in fear anymore.
I invite You, Lord, into my heart and life.

The Entrance of God's Word

*You plan to kill Me, because My word has no entrance
(makes no progress, does not find any place) in you. . . .
I assure you, most solemnly I tell you, if anyone observes My
teaching [lives in accordance with My message, keeps My
word], he will by no means ever see and experience death.*

JOHN 8:37, 51 AMPC

Jesus, the Word, the Son of God in the flesh, came to give people life. Yet when He walked this earth, the Word He brought could not get through to some, including God's chosen ones. And for those who do not accept or abide by God's good Word, before them was not only a life fraught with evil but an eventual and inevitable death. Yet for those people who not only accept but live a life aligned with Jesus' message, they will *never ever* see death!

What kind of impression has God's Word made upon you? In what ways do you follow Jesus' teachings? How well do you keep His Word—in church and out? No matter what you need or desire, you can find the truth in God's message, a message that not only remedies but feeds and strengthens your heart, body, mind, spirit, and soul—today and every day of your life.

*I don't want to be dead to Your Word, Lord. So please,
show and tell me what You want me to see, hear,
and know. Make me a veteran of the Word.*

Because Jesus Is, You Will. . .

I assure you, most solemnly I tell you,
that I Myself am the Door for the sheep.
John 10:7 ampc

✎

J ust as God revealed Himself to Moses, identifying Himself as the "I Am" (Exodus 3:14), Jesus revealed Himself to His followers as the I am (John 4:26; 6:20; 13:19). Yet Jesus goes even further to describe Himself, saying He is the bread of life (John 6:35, 41, 48, 51); the light of the world (John 8:12); the door of the sheep (John 10:7, 9); the resurrection and the life (John 11:25); the good shepherd (John 10:11, 14); the way, the truth, and the life (John 14:6); and the true vine (John 15:1, 5)! Thus:

Because Jesus is the bread of life, you will never be hungry or thirsty.

Because Jesus is the light of the world, you'll never get lost in the darkness.

Because Jesus is the door of the sheep, you will be safe from predators.

Because Jesus is the resurrection and the life, you will never die.

Because Jesus is the good shepherd, you will never get lost.

Because Jesus is the way, the truth, and the life, you will find your path through the truth and knowledge of God.

Because Jesus is the true vine, you can attach yourself to Him, allowing His life to flow in and through you.

Thank You, Lord, for being who You are and
allowing me to find all I need within You. Amen.

Love

I give you a new commandment: that you should love one another.
Just as I have loved you, so you too should love one another.
By this shall all [men] know that you are My disciples, if you love
one another [if you keep on showing love among yourselves].

JOHN 13:34–35 AMPC

Love. That's the main thing Jesus wants us to do: love each other just like He loved us before we were even born, while we were still sinners, enemies of God, by dying for us on the cross (Romans 5:8). That is amazing love.

Love lies at the heart of Jesus' greatest commandments: "Love the Lord your God with all your heart and with all your soul and with all your mind (intellect). . . . You shall love your neighbor as [you do] yourself" (Matthew 22:37, 39).

Love. May that treasure lie at the very core of your being. May this precious love, springing from your creator, God, who is Love personified (1 John 4:8), flow from Him and be continually dispersed through you to others. How else will others know and understand who God is if you, one of His adherents, do not reflect that same love to all—even those who are difficult to love?

Today, start and end your day with the greatest treasure and resource you have. Love.

I want to reflect You in this world, Lord.
Help me be known as a person of love.

Everlasting Peace

Peace I leave with you; My [own] peace I now give and bequeath to you. Not as the world gives do I give to you. Do not let your hearts be troubled, neither let them be afraid. [Stop allowing yourselves to be agitated and disturbed; and do not permit yourselves to be fearful and intimidated and cowardly and unsettled.]
JOHN 14:27 AMPC

D o you want to be free of worry and fear? Want to live a life filled with peace and calm? Jesus holds the answer!

Yes, Jesus has left His peace with you. And this peace, *His* peace, is not the kind of peace the world holds. His is a supernatural peace. And it is found in the presence and strength of God and His Word. *But,* you may be asking, *How can this be? How can I access this amazing and unsurpassed peace Jesus talks about?* By calling on the Comforter, aka the "Counselor, Helper, Intercessor, Advocate, Strengthener, Standby" (John 14:26). You know, the Holy Spirit, the one God sent down in Jesus' name to teach you and remind you of things Jesus has already told you in His Word (John 14:26).

Today, stop allowing yourself to be frightened and freaked out. Instead, seek God's presence and receive His peace.

Here I am, Lord, before You. Bless me,
pour upon me, Your everlasting peace.

Jesus' Prayer for You

Neither for these alone do I pray [it is not for their sake only that I make this request], but also for all those who will ever come to believe in (trust in, cling to, rely on) Me through their word and teaching, that they all may be one, [just] as You, Father, are in Me and I in You.

JOHN 17:20–21 AMPC

If ever you have a day where you just can't drag your lower lip up off the floor, remember how much Jesus loves you and how far His love reaches across the ages. Most of all, remember how He prayed for you—one of "all those who will ever come to believe"—thousands of years ago.

Through the hearing of God's Word, the power of Jesus' prayer, and the teachings of believers who walked the road you're now on, you are one with other believers. So today, let go of all that discourages, disheartens, disturbs, and destroys. Tap into the power, prayers, promises, and presence of God the Father, Jesus the Son, and the Spirit of Comfort. And acknowledge that the same love God had for His one and only Son is the same love God has for you.

Jesus, I'm honored that You prayed for me all those years ago and that Your Father loves me just as He loves You. In the power of that prayer I rise. In the power of that love I live. Amen.

Live in Expectation

Jesus came, though they were behind closed doors,
and stood among them and said, Peace to you! . . .
Jesus said to him, Because you have seen Me, Thomas,
do you now believe (trust, have faith)?
JOHN 20:26, 29 AMPC

By the time the disciples were hiding behind closed doors, Jesus had already been crucified, died, was buried, and had risen again. He'd already been seen by Mary Magdalene, as well as some of the other male and female disciples. The only one who had yet to encounter Him was Thomas. That's when Jesus appeared in the disciples' upper room, blessing them with His peace and convincing Thomas that He was alive! Then, Jesus blessed you, saying, "Blessed and happy and to be envied are those who have never seen Me and yet have believed and adhered to and trusted and relied on Me" (John 20:29).

Before His ascension, Jesus showed up once more in an unexpected time and place. It happened when the disciples went fishing. All night they'd caught nothing. Then a stranger (who was actually Jesus) from the shore told them to "Cast the net on the right side of the boat and you will find [some]. So they cast the net, and. . .hauled the net to land, full of large fish, 153 of them" (John 21:6, 11).

Expect Jesus where and when you least expect Him.

Lord, I live in expectation of Your
presence in my life! Come, Jesus! Come!

Joy in Jesus

*I saw the Lord constantly before me, for He is at my right
hand that I may not be shaken or overthrown or cast
down [from my secure and happy state]. . . . You have
made known to me the ways of life; You will enrapture me
[diffusing my soul with joy] with and in Your presence.*

ACTS 2:25, 28 AMPC

❧❧❧

Death is no match for the God to whom you belong, to the Son of
God you serve. And because you believe in God, death is no match
for you either. But the good news does not end there.

If you keep God constantly before you, keeping Him close, right
by your side, you will never be shaken up. Nothing can defeat you or
bring you down. Thus, all that's left for you to do is rejoice! You can say,
"I'm glad from the inside out, ecstatic; I've pitched my tent in the land
of hope. I know you'll never dump me in Hades; I'll never even smell
the stench of death. You've got my feet on the life-path, with your face
shining sun-joy all around" (Acts 2:25–28 MSG).

Today, stay close to Jesus. When you do, He'll stay close to You.
And with Him constantly before you, beside you, and within you, you
too will find the joy He alone can bring today and forevermore.

*With You right beside me, Lord, my joy, peace,
and contentment know no bounds!*

One More Proof

If this doctrine or purpose or undertaking or movement is of human origin, it will fail (be overthrown and come to nothing); but if it is of God, you will not be able to stop or overthrow or destroy them; you might even be found fighting against God!

ACTS 5:38–39 AMPC

The apostles were busy healing the sick and driving out demons. As a result, the number of believers in Jesus kept growing. So, the high priest and his cohorts (the Sadducees) arrested the apostles and had them thrown in jail.

Yet not even bars could contain Jesus' believers. "During the night an angel of the Lord opened the prison doors and, leading them out, said, Go, take your stand in the temple courts and declare to the people the whole doctrine concerning this Life" (Acts 5:19–20). And the apostles did just that.

Meanwhile, the Sadducees convened a meeting and asked for the apostles to be brought before them. But, amazingly enough, when the temple guards got to the prison, the jailers were still standing in front of the doors. Yet no one was found inside!

Any plan of human origin will dissolve. But any plan of God's will never be stopped. Live your life knowing the power of that truth and Your God.

Knowing no plan or purpose of Yours can ever be thwarted boosts my faith a hundredfold, Lord. To You I lift my voice in praise!

Presence and Prosperity

*And the patriarchs [Jacob's sons], boiling with envy and
hatred and anger, sold Joseph into slavery in Egypt;
but God was with him, and delivered him from all his
distressing afflictions and won him goodwill and favor
and wisdom and understanding in the sight of Pharaoh.*

ACTS 7:9–10 AMPC

❧

E ven those closest to us can prove themselves unfaithful by either their action or inaction. Yet even then, God can use ne'er-do-wells to fulfill His purposes in the lives of those He loves and supports.

Joseph was once a favored son, put to work but also pampered more than his ten older brothers. Their resentment of their father Jacob's partiality to Joseph, their boiling over with envy, hatred, and anger is what led them to sell one of their own flesh and blood. Yet even though Joseph was sold into slavery, unjustly accused of rape, and put into prison, he continued to rise in the ranks of and prosper in his environment. Because. . .God. . .was. . .with. . .him. And in the end, Joseph won the day, not only reuniting with his brothers and father but saving their lives and those of their children.

Just as God was with and delivered Joseph, God is with and will deliver you.

*In You alone I trust, Lord. Be with me today and
every day, for in Your presence, I prosper.*

Blessed in Obedience

And the Lord said to him, Get up and go to the street called
Straight and ask at the house of Judas for a man of Tarsus
named Saul, for behold, he is praying [there]. And he has
seen in a vision a man named Ananias enter and lay his
hands on him so that he might regain his sight.

ACTS 9:11–12 AMPC

Saul (who later became Paul) had been persecuting Christians until Jesus caught up to him on the road to Damascus, reprimanded him from heaven, and then blinded him with His light. Saul was next led by the hand into Damascus. For three days, Saul was unable to see physically, but he did have a vision that a man named Ananias would lay hands upon him, restoring his sight.

And that's just what God told Ananias to do, to go and lay his hands on this man who'd been persecuting Jesus' followers. Although Ananias expressed his reservations, his fears of helping the bloodthirsty Saul, God told him to go anyway. And so Ananias went. In the end, God blessed both men *and* the Church by giving it a new apostle.

Even though God may give you a dangerous task to fulfill, when you obey Him, you can be sure He'll give you the means and courage to do it, and a blessing besides.

Lord, give me the means and courage to do what
You have called me to do. In Jesus' name, amen.

The Power of Persistent Prayer

*So Peter was kept in prison, but fervent prayer for him was
persistently made to God by the church (assembly). . . . When
he, at a glance, became aware of this [comprehending all
the elements of the case], he went to the house of Mary the
mother of John, whose surname was Mark, where a large
number were assembled together and were praying.*

ACTS 12:5, 12 AMPC

A fter killing the disciple James, King Herod saw how much it pleased the Jews. So, he went even further and had Peter arrested, put in prison, and guarded by four soldiers. Yet while Peter was in prison, the Church was fervently praying for him.

Because of their prayers, the very night before Herod was going to bring Peter out to be executed, an angel appeared, woke Peter up, and told him to get up. As Peter rose, his chains simply fell off his hands! After Peter got dressed, the angel led him straight out of the prison and down the street. Next thing Peter knew, the angel had gone. Having come to himself, Peter headed straight to Mary's house, told them he was free, then left.

When your future seems unfair, uncertain, and impossible, take your case and pleas before God. Prayer has the power to alert angels, change the landscape, and free imprisoned souls.

*Help me, Lord, become a persistent prayer
for You and those You love. Amen.*

Shake It Off

*But [the apostles] shook off the dust from their feet against them
and went to Iconium. And the disciples were continually filled
[throughout their souls] with joy and the Holy Spirit.*

ACTS 13:51–52 AMPC

When Jesus first sent out His disciples two by two, He told them to lodge in and bless with peace those places where the Gospel message was eagerly received. But wherever Jesus' message was not accepted, the disciples were to shake the dust from their feet as they left.

In today's reading, we see Paul and Barnabas in Antioch, preaching and teaching about Jesus. But the leading Jews incited some devout women and prominent men to turn on the two men, forcing them to leave the city. As Paul and Barnabas did so, they shook the dust off their feet and went on to the next city. Yet the apostles didn't get discouraged. Instead, they let the people's negative reaction slide off, then simply moved on, filled with elation and the Spirit.

Look back on your own life. Consider times when others didn't want to hear your message or made trouble for you because of it. Then ask God to help you obey Jesus' command to shake off the negative and look to Him for the positive.

*Sometimes, Lord, I allow the negativity of others to
stagnate me. Help me shake off the rejection of others and
move on with a smile on my face and a psalm in my heart.*

In God's Care

*Believe in the Lord Jesus Christ [give yourself up to Him,
take yourself out of your own keeping and entrust yourself
into His keeping] and you will be saved, [and this applies
both to] you and your household as well.*

ACTS 16:31 AMPC

After Paul exorcised a spirit of divination from a slave girl, her owners, realizing their cash cow had dried up, dragged both Paul and Silas before the magistrates in the marketplace. There the apostles were attacked by the crowd, beaten with rods, and thrown into prison.

At midnight, Paul and Silas were praying and singing hymns while the other prisoners listened. Suddenly the earth shook, the jail doors opened, and everyone's bonds came unfastened. When the jailer woke and saw what had happened, he assumed the prisoners had escaped. Just as he was about to kill himself with his sword, Paul told him everyone was still present and accounted for. It was then the jailer believed in Jesus and was saved, along with his entire household.

Belief in Christ is what allowed Paul and Silas to pray and praise instead of cry and complain. It's also what allows human souls to walk through the door of heaven.

Today and every day, give God charge over you and your life. Trust Him to take care of you. And you too will find yourself looking at the upside of life.

I hand myself over to You, Lord. Keep me in Your care.

Speaking Out

*The Lord said to Paul in a vision, Have no fear, but speak
and do not keep silent; for I am with you, and no man shall
assault you to harm you. . . . And God did unusual and
extraordinary miracles by the hands of Paul.*

ACTS 18:9–10; 19:11 AMPC

P aul, a tentmaker by trade and a preacher by choice, had had an
extraordinary number of God experiences, visions, and miracles
since his conversion. Sometimes, the audience was more than receptive
to God's message. At other times, his listeners were indifferent. At the
worst of times, God's Good News incited riots.

Paul must have been feeling a bit discouraged, for the Lord made a
point of speaking to him, encouraging the apostle to be brave and not
remain silent. Why risk speaking for the Lord when crowds of people
might become violent? Because God would be with Paul. He would allow
no one to harm him. And Paul took the Lord at His word. That was the
reason God was able to do "unusual and extraordinary miracles by the
hands of Paul."

God is speaking to you today, using the same words He spoke to
Paul. So, woman, fear nothing. Speak what God would have you say, for
He is with you, encouraging you, loving you, leading you, protecting you.

*Lord, thank You for giving me the courage to do what You
would have me do. Because of You, I find my voice and life!*

What Matters Most

*"What matters most to me is to finish what God started: the job
the Master Jesus gave me. . . . Now I'm turning you over to God,
our marvelous God whose gracious Word can make you into
what he wants you to be and give you everything you could
possibly need in this community of holy friends."*

ACTS 20:24, 32 MSG

As Paul was saying goodbye to the elders of the Church in Ephesus, he told them what mattered most to him: finishing what God had started. Paul was determined to complete the job that his Master, Jesus, had given him. He was determined to go to Jerusalem, not knowing what exactly lay ahead of him. "I do know that it won't be any picnic, for the Holy Spirit has let me know repeatedly and clearly that there are hard times and imprisonment ahead" (Acts 20:23).

Today, on this day of Thanksgiving, take heart knowing that God is in control. That all you need to do is finish what God started by completing the task Jesus has given you. Then turn yourself over to God, marveling at His power and thanking Him for His strength, protection, and love. Know that God's Word can and will mold you into exactly who He wants you to be and that He'll provide you with all you need to get there from here.

*Oh Lord, You're what matters most in my life.
For that and all things, I thank You.*

Take—and Spread—Courage!

*And [that same] following night the Lord stood beside
Paul and said, Take courage, Paul, for as you have borne
faithful witness concerning Me at Jerusalem, so you
must also bear witness at Rome.*

ACTS 23:11 AMPC

When the apostle Paul was brought before the Sanhedrin, things turned ugly. So ugly that a Roman commander feared Paul might be torn apart. So, the commander had Paul brought into the soldiers' barracks for his own protection.

That same night, Jesus came to Paul once again. He stood beside him and told him to be brave and continue to be His witness. The very next day, forty incensed Jews plotted to kill Paul, vowing to neither eat nor drink until their dirty deed was done.

Yet God knows all, sees all, and controls all. He made sure Paul's nephew heard about the plot to kill his uncle. The young man first let Paul know. Paul then sent the nephew to the commander, and the commander took things in hand from there to ensure Paul's safety.

Once God speaks courage into someone's ears, it has a domino effect and begins spreading to others. Today, allow God to speak courage into your ears. As you feel that courage strengthening you, spread it to the next person you meet!

*Today, Lord, I take the courage You so willingly offer. Help me,
Lord, to spread that same mettle to everyone I meet today.*

On Standby

*There stood by my side an angel of the God to Whom I belong
and Whom I serve and worship, and he said, Do not be frightened,
Paul! It is necessary for you to stand before Caesar; and behold,
God has given you all those who are sailing with you.*

ACTS 27:23–24 AMPC

P aul was handed over with some other prisoners and put on a ship
to Italy, but inclement weather threw the ship into dire straits. As
the storm kept raging, the hungry men began to lose all hope. That's
when Paul stood up and restored it.

Paul told the men an angel had stood by him and told him to not
be frightened. (Just like the Lord had stood by Paul and told him to
take courage [Acts 23:11].) He told Paul that God's plans would not
be thwarted and that God would not just protect Paul but all the men
with him.

Because Paul had given himself completely to God, he could
speak and act with calm assurance. He could then pass this God-given
confidence to his companions, telling them, "Keep up your courage, men,
for I have faith (complete confidence) in God that it will be exactly as it
was told me" (Acts 27:25).

Live your life with calm assurance knowing the Lord and His angels
are on standby, ready to come when you call.

Lord, thank You for being with me on every stage of my voyage.

As You Are

*It is through Him that we have received grace (God's
unmerited favor) and [our] apostleship to promote
obedience to the faith and make disciples for His name's
sake. . .and this includes you, called of Jesus Christ and
invited [as you are] to belong to Him.*

ROMANS 1:5–6 AMPC

There's nothing you can do to earn God's grace. It's a free gift He gives to you, wanting nothing but love and obedience in return. Yet even then you may feel as if you're falling short. But not to worry. You have and are called by and invited to belong to Jesus Christ—*just "as you are"!* In other words, God had you at "hello."

When a woman gets pregnant, people might say she and her husband are "expecting." And that's true. They're expecting a child. Yet they do not know who that child will look like or how he or she will behave. And even when that child does appear, even when it's birthed or adopted into a (hopefully) loving family, how it will someday "turn out" is a mystery to everyone but God!

Just like that expected child, you too are no mystery to God. He has called you, invited you, to take this life journey with Him—*just "as you are."* So, stop striving and begin thriving. God's got you. Your job is to simply "get" Him.

Thank You, Lord, for wanting and accepting me just as I am.

A Mighty Word-Keeper

*No unbelief or distrust made him waver (doubtingly question)
concerning the promise of God, but he grew strong and was
empowered by faith as he gave praise and glory to God, fully
satisfied and assured that God was able and mighty to keep
His word and to do what He had promised.*

ROMANS 4:20–21 AMPC

N eed some strength and power? Perhaps some assurance? Look no
further than to your God!

Abraham had it right. No thing, no person, no circumstance kept
him from doubting God's Word. Because he was fully assured God would
keep His promises, his faith and strength continued to grow. The God
in whom he believed, the God who gave life to the dead, also "speaks of
the nonexistent things that [He has foretold and promised] as if they
[already] existed" (Romans 4:17)!

What do you think your life would look like if you had the faith of
Abraham? How would your life change if you were fully assured that God
would keep the Word He's spoken to you and to you alone? What would
happen if you remembered, moment by moment, that God is true to
His promises to you, to each and every guarantee recorded in the Bible?

Today, tomorrow, and every day, believe like Abraham, and watch
God work through His Word.

*Mighty Word-Keeper, it's in Your Word alone that
I believe and in Your promises only that I trust.*

Beyond Doubt

We are assured and know that [God being a partner in their labor] all things work together and are [fitting into a plan] for good to and for those who love God and are called according to [His] design and purpose.

ROMANS 8:28 AMPC

~~~~

When we're in that moment of time in which some disaster has struck—one in which our faith is tested because of the illness, death, separation, abuse, etc., of ourselves or ones we love—it can be hard to remember all will work for our good. This seems to be the case even though the Bible gives us example after example of how our heartaches can eventually lead to our happiness or how our disappointment can turn into deliverance.

To keep the faith in times of trouble, you need only recall the stories of Joseph, Hannah, and Elijah of the Old Testament or Elizabeth, Mary, and Paul of the New. For each of these believers were "sure that neither death nor life, nor angels nor rulers, nor things present nor things to come, nor powers, nor height nor depth, nor anything else in all creation, will be able to separate us from the love of God in Christ Jesus our Lord" (Romans 8:37–39 ESV).

Go beyond doubt and become a believer, God-fitted to do amazing things.

I believe, beyond a doubt, that You, Lord, will work all things for my good and Your purpose.

Transformed

Do not conform to the pattern of this world, but be
transformed by the renewing of your mind. Then you
will be able to test and approve what God's will is—
his good, pleasing and perfect will.
ROMANS 12:2 NIV

Think back to your high school days. You likely did your best to fit in, to be accepted. After all, it's normal human behavior to go along with the crowd, especially in the teen years. The problem is that peer pressure and fears of being excluded or bullied prompt behavior that's perhaps not the best.

Today's scripture encourages believers to avoid conforming to the pressures of the world and its myriad of temptations. To steer away from the advertising world that urges you to buy fashionable high-priced products; restaurants that encourage you to eat far too much; the entertainment industry that offers more violence and less quality in its productions.

In Peter's letter to the Romans, he states conformity is not the answer. Instead, you are to turn your entire being over to God and let His will and way re-create you.

Sister, do not conform to the ways of this world. Don't let this society mold you into something you don't want to be. Rather, pray to God and let Him transform you according to His almighty plan.

Dear Lord, help me to stay strong, to transform and not
conform, and to come to You with a new mind-set.

Build Me Up

*Let us therefore make every effort to do what
leads to peace and to mutual edification.*
ROMANS 14:19 NIV

E ach year, churches and Christian organizations from all over send teams of teenagers and their chaperones to the poorest regions in Appalachia. The purpose is to make the homes, which are crumbling around the families residing within them, warmer, safer, and drier. Each group tag-teams other groups over seventeen weeks to rebuild and strengthen these houses for grateful homeowners. While working on rebuilding these homes physically, the Appalachia teams end up uplifting families spiritually as well.

The good news is that you don't have to travel to Appalachia to bring Paul's words to life. You can just do your best to bring peace and uplift to those around you. For example, if someone is in need, offer a helping hand. Or hold a door for a senior citizen. Allow a car to enter your lane of traffic during rush hour. Compliment those with whom you come in contact. Find something positive to say to a friend, family member, or stranger. As you lift up those around you, those people may then be more inclined to lift up someone else. What a wonderful way to put in motion a potentially never-ending wave of blessings and peace.

*Lord, build me up that I may in turn build up those
I meet. Make me be a blessing to others and help me
to bring peace wherever possible.*

Wise Guy

*Do not deceive yourselves. If any of you think you
are wise by the standards of this age, you should
become "fools" so that you may become wise.*

1 CORINTHIANS 3:18 NIV

S ome say wisdom comes with age. This is based on the idea that, as you go through life, encountering experiences, you come away with more knowledge as to how to better confront certain situations. Hopefully, as you become more and more enlightened, you can use this information to help others facing similar circumstances. The question is, as time goes on and you (theoretically) become wiser, what kind of wisdom have you gained?

Worldly wisdom, while important for our day-to-day survival, is not the most important kind of wisdom to seek. It's the heavenly wisdom you should be going after. For "the wisdom that comes from heaven is first of all pure; then peace-loving, considerate, submissive, full of mercy and good fruit, impartial and sincere" (James 3:17).

Thus, it makes no difference if you have a string of letters following your name or you never finished high school. For true wisdom, heavenly wisdom, God's wisdom, is found in His Word.

So, be a wise guy. Seek wisdom.

*Dear Lord, true wisdom comes only from You. I pray You will
help me to acquire Your wisdom through Your Word and
to remember that earthly wisdom pales in comparison.*

Eye on the Prize

Do you not know that in a race all the runners run, but only
one gets the prize? Run in such a way as to get the prize.
1 CORINTHIANS 9:24 NIV

❧❧❧

I f you have ever taken part in a sporting competition, you know it's necessary to train extensively in preparation. The harder you train, the better your chances of taking that coveted trophy.

So, you begin to live a regimented lifestyle dictated by the rules of your particular discipline. You start to work hard to achieve your goal, doing extensive research and studying all aspects of your chosen sport. In the process, the effects of all your sacrifices and hard work will be long-lasting, and the glory of winning that top prize will be yours to cherish for years to come.

Imagine what it would take to train for the quest of gaining the greatest prize ever—a heavenly reward, offered by your heavenly Father, one that will last forever. All you need to do to win it is adhere to His training regimen. The only playbook you need to read and study is the Holy Bible. And your only requirement to enter the challenge is to believe.

Dear Lord, help me prepare for the greatest race
for the greatest prize imaginable, Your holy reward
in heaven, a trophy that will endure forever.

The Greatest

And now these three remain: faith, hope and love.
But the greatest of these is love.
1 CORINTHIANS 13:13 NIV

I f you've been to a wedding, you have likely heard these beautiful words from 1 Corinthians. While all three of these attributes—faith, hope, and love—are important, God tells us to value love above all. Love is selfless, gives with no expectation of anything in return, is unconditional, and never dies.

Of course, the greatness of love does not minimize the importance of having faith and hope but rather puts the three in perspective. While faith is the essential belief in that which you cannot see and hope is the desire for a certain thing to happen, it is love whose existence surpasses them all. Divine love or *agape* is God's love for humankind and humankind's love for God. It is love in its purest form, knows no boundaries, is powerful, and is the highest kind of love.

God commands us to love one another as He has loved us (John 15:12). So, open your heart and allow God's love to pour into you so you can share His love with those around you. From this day forward, make it your aim to "trust steadily in God, hope unswervingly, love extravagantly" (1 Corinthians 13:13 MSG).

Dear Lord, thank You for these encouraging words,
Your unconditional love, and the faith and hope they offer me.
Uplift me always with Your love, which I treasure above all.

Confused?

For God is not a God of disorder but of peace—
as in all the congregations of the Lord's people.
1 Corinthians 14:33 niv

✤

"God is not a God of disorder." Yet there is so much dissension within different religious denominations, even within churches. One would think that groups that worship together based on the same teachings would be in harmony. But then one would be wrong.

Your God is a god of peace. God does not encourage disorder, dissension, or confusion. Instead, He promotes peace. Jesus too was a person of peace. Like Father, like Son.

Today's verse encourages you to take God's path, to seek peaceful solutions. When faced with a difficult situation, consider asking yourself, "WWJD. What would Jesus do?" More than a catchy slogan emblazoned on bracelets or T-shirts, WWJD is a reminder to all believers that Jesus, whom they are to emulate, almost always opted for the peaceful path. And just as Jesus was led by His Father in all His actions, so will God lead you in all His actions, including in the ways of peace.

Remember, peace, complete tranquility and serenity, has been promised to believers. And it's that peace, "the peace of God, which transcends all understanding" that "will guard your hearts and your minds in Christ Jesus" (Philippians 4:7).

Dear Lord, please make me an instrument of Your peace.
Help me to be a calming voice of reason in disorder
and to encourage Your peace to all I encounter.

Shine On!

For God, who said, "Let light shine out of darkness,"
made his light shine in our hearts to give us the light of the
knowledge of God's glory displayed in the face of Christ.
2 CORINTHIANS 4:6 NIV

D id you ever sit outside, enjoying the sunlight, and find yourself feeling more peaceful and serene? Light has that effect on us all. That's why in the winter months, when there is a decrease in the sunlight's power and duration, a small percentage of people become anxious and depressed.

Yet the light of God is even *more* powerful than that of the sun. Just as He created, sustains, and brings you physical light, God has created, sustains, and can bring you spiritual light, if only you'd open your eyes to it. This "light" is the knowledge of God, which He has given us all through His Word. And with it comes the peace that this knowledge brings.

As you bask in God's awesome light, remember that it's not to be hidden under a blanket or hoarded from the crowd but shared with others and spread to all you encounter. So put God's light in a prominent place, perhaps upon a pedestal, for all to see. And you'll be doing your part to illuminate all.

Dear Lord, let Your divine light shine upon and through me. Allow it
to bring me Your peace. Help me to share Your light with those around
me. For through Your light, Lord, I find the illumination I need.

Cleanliness

*Therefore, since we have these promises, dear friends,
let us purify ourselves from everything that contaminates
body and spirit, perfecting holiness out of reverence for God.*
2 CORINTHIANS 7:1 NIV

"Your body is a temple" (1 Corinthians 6:19 ESV). And today's verse encourages you to keep that temple and your spirit pure.

Chances are you try to live in accordance with God's will. Although it's sometimes difficult in this world, you do your best to maintain a healthy spirit by studying God's words, attempting to do His works, and going to Him in prayer.

Meanwhile, as God helps guide and nourish your spirit, it's up to you to keep your body healthy. When it comes to your body, moderation in all things is key, though at other times complete abstinence may be your best solution.

You'll no doubt feel better having tweaked your lifestyle to help your body and spirit maintain their purity, but this is just the beginning. For as you and other believers, with a pure body and spirit, combine to make up the temple of the living God, He promises to dwell among you. In fact, God has made a vow to "welcome you, and. . .be a father to you" (2 Corinthians 6:17–18 ESV).

*Father God, help me focus on my spiritual and
physical health, to surround myself with those
things that will bolster my reverence for You.*

Strength Training

*That is why, for Christ's sake, I delight in weaknesses,
in insults, in hardships, in persecutions, in difficulties.
For when I am weak, then I am strong.*
2 CORINTHIANS 12:10 NIV

You may have heard that those who are sightless have heightened abilities in their other senses. A blind person may have extraordinarily good hearing as well as a sharpened sense of smell, taste, and touch. You could say a sightless person's strength comes through his or her weakness.

The apostle Paul endured a lot of suffering through his own vulnerability and weakness. Yet he never questioned God as to why he suffered. Rather, he asked for the strength to continue. Despite or perhaps because of Paul's weakness, God made him His humble and faithful servant. He granted Paul the ability and confidence to overcome the adversities he endured.

God may not take away your hardships or afflictions, but He does give you the strength to deal with them, to endure your struggles. Through perseverance, you too will find victory. In your weakness, you too will become strong in Christ.

*Dear Lord, I pray for Your strength. I know I am weak;
I know I have faults and troubles. Yet I also know You
will bolster me through the rough times and bless me
with the grace to persevere and to triumph.*

Lean on Me

Carry each other's burdens, and in this
way you will fulfill the law of Christ.
GALATIANS 6:2 NIV

❧❧❧

There is a great song by Bill Withers called "Lean on Me." The chorus starts "Lean on me, when you're not strong" and goes on to describe mutual and unconditional support between friends. It is a wonderful depiction of today's verse by Paul, which instructs each of us to bear one another's burdens. When shared, burdens seem lighter and become a fulfillment of Christ's law.

What's the "law of Christ"? It's found in Jesus' response to a scribe's question, "Of all the commandments, which is the most important?" (Mark 12:28). Jesus said, first and foremost, " 'Love the Lord your God with all your heart and with all your soul and with all your mind and with all your strength.' The second is this: 'Love your neighbor as yourself' " (Mark 12:30–31).

God knows you will have burdens in this world. But by leaning on others, you can sustain and carry each other, just as God sustains and carries all.

Today, lean on God—and others—when you're not strong.

Dear Lord, I ask Your help to sustain me as I do my best
to sustain those around me. By carrying the burdens of
others, I will do my best to fulfill Your commandment.

Grace

For it is by grace you have been saved, through faith—
and this is not from yourselves, it is the gift of God—
not by works, so that no one can boast.
Ephesians 2:8–9 niv

H ave you ever given what you thought would be a perfect gift to someone? Maybe your present was in that person's favorite color, bore her specific sports team logo, or was in her exact size? Maybe it was all three! And having chosen the perfect gift, you're quite pleased with yourself.

In Ephesians, there's a particular gift given to you by God, one that makes all others pale in comparison. It's the gift of salvation.

You can rejoice in the fact that God has saved you not because of anything you have done but through your faith alone. Yes, it's that simple. God's greatest gift is offered to you free of charge. Because this gift was not of your doing, you cannot boast or brag. You are just the joyful beneficiary for eternity.

So have faith, that amazing confidence in what you hope for and assurance in what you do not see (Hebrews 11:1). And leave the boasting to God, the perfect Giver of the perfect gift.

Dear Lord, thank You for Your incredible gift of salvation, given not because of anything I have said or done but solely through my faith.

Thanksgiving

*Do not be anxious about anything, but in every
situation, by prayer and petition, with thanksgiving,
present your requests to God.*
PHILIPPIANS 4:6 NIV

Everyone gets nervous or has anxious moments. And many have developed a game plan for when nerves strike. Some think happy thoughts, others attempt self-medication, still others immerse themselves in upbeat music. Here, Paul offers the best antianxiety plan ever with a more direct approach: prayer.

When your peace deserts you, turn to the Lord. Let Him accept your prayers and petitions and help alleviate your fears. But remember to turn to Him in thanksgiving and in gratitude too. A feeling of joy will bubble up within you when you consider everything for which you are grateful. When you turn your worries over to God and pray for a solution for what ails you, remember those many blessings He has given you.

Today, lean into one of the most upbeat verses ever written: "This is the day the LORD has made. We will rejoice and be glad in it" (Psalm 118:24 NLT). Then actually rejoice as you turn your troubles over to God, thanking Him for all and trusting Him to answer your prayers and petitions. What better antianxiety approach could there be?

*Dear Lord, as I come to You in prayer with my concerns,
I also come with a heart full of gratitude for
Your many blessings. In You I trust.*

Daily Deeds

And whatever you do, whether in word or
deed, do it all in the name of the Lord Jesus,
giving thanks to God the Father through him.
COLOSSIANS 3:17 NIV

O n any given day, you accomplish tons of tasks. After waking up, you might trudge off to work, interacting with many people along the way. You might be asked to do some mundane tasks or face unpleasant challenges. In the evening, you head home to face more tasks—cooking dinner, doing the dishes, walking the dog, etc.—all in the span of one day. It's easy to get lost in the monotony.

When you feel as if you're trudging through the tedium, keep in mind and take to heart today's verse. No matter what you do, do it in Jesus' name. And give praise to God through the course of your day.

While you may not love your job, other people would give anything to be employed. While you might not enjoy dealing with people, many sit in lonely isolation, wishing they had someone to simply talk to. Have to wash dirty dinner dishes? Many have no food to eat.

In each situation that comes your way, give thanks to God for there is much for which to be grateful!

Dear Lord, thank You for all You have given me.
And when I'm caught in the monotony, remind me
of the importance and value of my daily deeds.

Good Day

And as for you, brothers and sisters,
never tire of doing what is good.
2 Thessalonians 3:13 niv

I n the hustle and bustle of everyday life, it is sometimes easy to get burned out or to tire of playing by the book. Sometimes, you may be tempted to take shortcuts to achieve quicker results and lose sight along the way of what is right and good. You're not alone.

Remember your high school or college days? Studying for exams was most likely a bit rough. You studied hard, perhaps even pulling all-nighters, and did the best you could to learn the material. Yet something stopped you from taking shortcuts or from cheating (hopefully).

In your heart of hearts, you knew cheating was wrong. And even though you may have been burned out from studying and giving it your all, you continued to walk that narrow road. In doing so, you were fulfilling the words of this scripture, perhaps without even realizing it.

Though it is not always easy, never tire of doing what is right. In this way, you will not only please God but will become an example to others of how to live your life with God as your guide.

Dear Lord, help me to always do what is good
and right and pleasing in Your eyes.

Training Day

For physical training is of some value, but
godliness has value for all things, holding promise
for both the present life and the life to come.
1 TIMOTHY 4:8 NIV

I f you have ever trained for a physical competition, you know how much goes into preparation. You try to be the best you can possibly be in your field and in the best physical shape. However, as the years go by, you realize your physical state is starting to decline gradually. It's only natural.

Yet there is good news! Although your body may be on the decline, your spirit will go on and on not only in this life here on earth but in your heavenly life. So, it is even more important to make spiritual growth the true focus of your life training and to keep your spiritual health in tip-top shape by praying and living a godly life.

Although it is definitely important to stay physically healthy here on earth, be sure to set your sights on your heavenly goals as well. You can do that each day as you "set your minds on things above, not on earthly things" (Colossians 3:2).

Dear Lord, in all ways, help me train to be my best
possible self, to care not only for my earthly body but to
focus on my spiritual health as well so that I will be in
good shape for Your promised life to come.

Teacher's Guide

All Scripture is God-breathed and is useful for teaching,
rebuking, correcting and training in righteousness.
2 TIMOTHY 3:16 NIV

Sometimes a short passage of scripture carries a huge message. This is one of those times!

While scripture is the result of people putting pen to paper, their messages are inspired by the one true God. That's why the Bible is more than just a bestseller, taking up space on many bookshelves. The words that lie within it are "God-breathed." Although they may vary in style based on the author, take heart! The messages themselves come directly from God.

In Proverbs, we read that each word from God is perfect. What's more, it says that it is a shield for all who choose to take refuge in Him. What a wonderful parallel to today's scripture and an assurance of God's perfection! Since scripture comes directly from God, delivered through the hands and minds of those whom He has chosen, you can be certain that all of God's words have a message for you.

The phrase "God-breathed" tells us that God had His hand in every chapter, every verse of His holy book. And the answers to your questions are all contained within. God guarantees it.

Dear Lord, I thank You for Your Word and its
assurances. I pray You will help me keep in mind
that Your answers are but a short read away.

You Are Invited!

*Let us then approach God's throne of grace with
confidence, so that we may receive mercy and find
grace to help us in our time of need.*
HEBREWS 4:16 NIV

It's always exciting to receive an invitation, whether it's for a party or a wedding or a graduation. It's nice to be welcomed to a happy event or opportunity.

With that in mind, you will be delighted to learn that God has given you an open invitation to approach His throne of grace with confidence. And not just on good days but especially when times get tough! You do not have to be afraid, for God states clearly you will receive both mercy and grace in your time of need.

God's throne room is a reception hall like no other. There you receive His infinite mercy and grace not because of anything you did but because you are in need. And with this mercy and grace comes peace. "Grace and peace be yours in abundance through the knowledge of God and of Jesus our Lord" (2 Peter 1:2).

How comforting to know God's mercy, grace, and peace come hand in hand. How will you RSVP to God's invitation to approach His throne of grace?

*Dear Lord, I thank You for Your grace, which works
through me to regenerate and sanctify me and inspires
me to persevere during good times and in bad.*

Heavenly Haven

*Let us draw near to God with a sincere heart and with
the full assurance that faith brings, having our hearts
sprinkled to cleanse us from a guilty conscience and
having our bodies washed with pure water.*

HEBREWS 10:22 NIV

D id you ever sit on the beach and watch seafaring vessels be guided by the beacon of a lighthouse? If not for this light, they may not find the right course and instead find themselves stuck on a sandbar, floundering in the shallows, or shipwrecked upon the rocks.

Just as ships are drawn to lighthouses, people from all over the world are drawn to the light of God. It appeals to those who have a sincere heart and a strong faith and to those who are looking for direction, for the Way of life that will keep them from getting stuck, floundering, and wrecking.

As you draw near to Jesus, that "light of the world" (John 8:12), do so with a sincere heart and the confidence that when you accepted Him, God absolved you of all guilt. You have been cleansed *and* given a full pardon and a clear pathway to the Lord of Light!

So, stick with the Light, and you too will find your way to the heavenly haven you seek.

*Dear Lord, I am blessed beyond measure to be drawn to You,
to know I'm cleansed inside and out, free from sin and guilt.
Be my light and haven today and always.*

Have Faith

*Now faith is confidence in what we hope for
and assurance about what we do not see.*
HEBREWS 11:1 NIV

F aith is mentioned so many times in God's Word, but did you ever stop to think about exactly what the word *faith* means? You've only to read this verse to understand it. Faith is confidence. It is the firm belief that you can completely rely on someone or something that may not yet be in existence.

Faith is also described as the assurance of that which we cannot see. It is full trust that God, even in the darkness, will be holding our hand and leading us to the light. You may not fully understand what comes your way, but you can certainly have confidence He does. What a wonderful feeling, to have full assurance and confidence in God! This faith isn't blind but rather comes from the knowledge we have in the Word of God through His scriptures and the teachings through His Son, Jesus Christ.

So, woman of Christ, have confidence in your hopes. Have assurance and peace about what has not yet been made visible to you. Fully trust in God with all.

*Dear Lord, how wonderful it is to know that I can be completely
confident in You and Your promises, that I can live each day
in peace, knowing I can have assurance of those things I
cannot see but that You have declared to be true.*

Wisdom Explained

But the wisdom that comes from heaven is first of
all pure; then peace-loving, considerate, submissive,
full of mercy and good fruit, impartial and sincere.

JAMES 3:17 NIV

James tells us that in this world, there are two kinds of wisdom: earthly wisdom and Godly wisdom. While both are important, one is vital. You need earthly wisdom—knowledge you can learn from textbooks or that you gain from your experiences—to navigate day-to-day life on this planet, no doubt about it. But that's not the wisdom that is vital.

The wisdom that comes from above, God's wisdom, is the wisdom you truly need. The wisdom that is heaven-sent is pure. It brings peace and mercy to you and inspires you to do good works in His name. Heavenly wisdom teaches you humility and sincerity. In direct contrast to earthly wisdom, which can lead to envy and ambition, God's wisdom also encourages selfless good works.

Yet this heavenly wisdom is not acquired through textbooks but by faith in God and by respectfully yielding to His will and way. It's just that simple.

What kind of wisdom do *you* want to possess?

Dear Lord, I want to be wise in Your eyes, to gain
Your wisdom, and to help make this world a better
place through selfless good works and love for others.

True Beauty

Your beauty should not come from outward adornment, such as
elaborate hairstyles and the wearing of gold jewelry or fine clothes.
Rather, it should be that of your inner self, the unfading beauty of
a gentle and quiet spirit, which is of great worth in God's sight.

1 PETER 3:3–4 NIV

Chances are you are inundated by ads for beauty enhancement products and services. Expensive makeup items, hair products, diet aids, clothing, the list goes on and on. The message you get is that beauty is something you can purchase. Yet these material things only enhance your outward appearance. Although they may make you more attractive to yourself or others, Peter reminds you that true beauty cannot be bought but comes from within.

What God values more than anything is your inner self because *that* person is your true being. And having a quiet and gentle spirit is what pleases your Lord.

In Proverbs 31, you can read the description of a woman of noble character. Take particular note of verse 30, which says, "Charm is deceptive, and beauty is fleeting; but a woman who fears the LORD is to be praised." Today and every day, remember that outward beauty is indeed fleeting. But inward beauty never fades, never develops wrinkles, never declines in health. Where does your true beauty lie?

Dear Lord, help me be beautiful on the inside, to focus
my energy on the beauty that matters in Your eyes.

Heaven

*But in keeping with his promise we are looking forward to a
new heaven and a new earth, where righteousness dwells.*

2 PETER 3:13 NIV

W hat do you see when you think of heaven? Thanks to Hollywood, you may have an image of St. Peter waiting at the pearly gates, ready to check your name off a list. You are ushered down a long path surrounded by fluffy clouds, perhaps with angels busily scurrying around performing some heavenly task.

Yet Peter tells us to look forward to a *new* heaven and a *new* earth. He says righteousness will dwell there. The question is, Will this take place on our present earth? Will God cleanse the earth of evil and deliver it to the righteous? No one can know for sure the real meaning of Peter's words. But the question of "where" the new heaven and earth will be is not all that important. The knowledge of *what* is the thing that should resonate with you.

Remember that faith is the assurance of those things that we cannot see. So, when God promises you that you will dwell in righteousness, be confident He will indeed deliver. When the day arrives that you see heaven for yourself, you will most certainly understand.

*Dear Lord, I thank You for Your promise of a new
heaven and a new earth. I look forward to dwelling
with righteousness in Your holy kingdom to come.*

Help Is on the Way

*If anyone has material possessions and sees a
brother or sister in need but has no pity on them,
how can the love of God be in that person?*

1 JOHN 3:17 NIV

Walking through the city, you are bound to see homeless people living in the streets, wondering where their next meal will come from. Homelessness has even spread into the suburbs as more and more people find themselves in dire straits with no way out. They may be suffering from joblessness, addiction, or hunger.

How do you respond when you see someone in distress? John tells you that we should have pity on them. Sure, the sight of someone in distress tugs at our heartstrings. But what can we do? John answers: "Dear children, let us not love with words or speech but with actions and in truth" (1 John 3:18).

Helping is easier said than done many times. If you're not sure what to do for someone who's in distress, consider supporting an organization that offers help to him or her. Bring attention to the situation. Make some noise. Do something.

Remember, everyone is a child of God, no one more important than another.

*Dear Lord, open my eyes to the plight of the less fortunate.
Give me the courage to reach out with love and compassion
and to take whatever action You'd like me to take. I offer this
prayer to You who'd once had no place to lay His head.*

A Call to Love

And now, dear lady, I am not writing you a new
command but one we have had from the beginning.
I ask that we love one another.

2 JOHN 5 NIV

The Beatles' song called "All You Need Is Love" has a very simple message. Yet that message is one that is immensely important, as is the message from today's scripture.

The apostle John's message that we are to love one another transcends emotion. It reminds us of Jesus' order: "A new command I give you: Love one another. As I have loved you, so you must love one another" (John 13:34). Jesus was by far the greatest example of this selfless and all-consuming love.

Jesus' message was so important that John felt the need to repeat it more than once. And Paul himself put it even more beautifully in the often-used scripture from 1 Corinthians 13:13: "And now these three remain: faith, hope and love. But the greatest of these is love."

Today and every day, make a conscious decision to choose love. Love God. Love your neighbor. Love yourself. And love your neighbor as yourself. Just plain love.

> *Dear Lord, I thank You for Your reminder to love*
> *one another just as You love us, no matter what.*
> *May that be my calling each and every day.*

Knocking at the Door

Here I am! I stand at the door and knock. If anyone
hears my voice and opens the door, I will come in
and eat with that person, and they with me.

REVELATION 3:20 NIV

I magine you are sitting down to Christmas dinner and there's a knock at the door. When you open it, the person on the other side of the door is Jesus. What do you do? Do you invite Him in? Do you think about the ways that perhaps you have let Him down or not lived according to His teachings? Or do you close the door on Him?

In this letter Jesus dictates to John, He gives the rather apathetic and uncommitted Christians of Laodicea an open invitation to listen for His knock and His voice and allow Him entry. Jesus was extending a warm and sincere offer of love and forgiveness. In the same way that Jesus issued this invitation to the church of Laodicea, He offers it to *all* who read His words. If you let Him in, He will accept you and all past sins will be forgiven.

Jesus is at the door of your life, regardless of past actions, spiritual journey, or even unbelief. Just open the door to Him and He will come into your life.

Today, open that door. Invite Jesus in.

Dear Lord, I accept Your gracious invitation to eat
with me and to show me the way. Thank You
for Your incredibly generous invitation.

Hallelujah!

Angels, numbering thousands upon thousands, and ten thousand times ten thousand. . .encircled the throne and the living creatures and the elders. In a loud voice they were saying: "Worthy is the Lamb, who was slain, to receive power and wealth and wisdom and strength and honor and glory and praise!"

REVELATION 5:11–12 NIV

The words above are part of a heavenly song, sung by thousands upon thousands of angels praising Jesus, the Lamb of God, the Lamb that John the Baptist said "takes away the sin of the world!" (John 1:29).

Before Jesus arrived on the scene, lambs were sacrificed to honor God. They were a temporary atonement for the sins of God's people. But Jesus was sacrificed as a ransom for *all* of the sins of humankind forever. Through the killing of *this* Lamb, the ultimate price for our eternal life was paid.

Jesus is worthy of all heavenly wealth, wisdom, and strength. And He is worthy of our daily praise and honor. So today, raise your voice loudly, and joyfully sing the praise of the Lamb of God! How blessed we are that God sent His only Son to save us all. Rejoice! And sing: "Worthy is the Lamb, who was slain, to receive power and wealth and wisdom and strength and honor and glory and praise!"

Dear Lord, I praise You, I thank You for the Lamb of God. Hallelujah! Praise the Lamb of God!

Living Water

"For the Lamb at the center of the throne will be their
shepherd; 'he will lead them to springs of living water.
And God will wipe away every tear from their eyes.'"

REVELATION 7:17 NIV

The book of Revelation contains a lot of imagery, and the precise meaning of what John saw is debated by many. However, what is *not* debatable are the words of today's verse.

Jesus, the Lamb of God, is at the center of His heavenly throne. He is the shepherd of the survivors of the end days, the ones God deemed worthy. And as their shepherd, Jesus will lead believers to the springs of living water. And God will wipe away their tears and quell their fears.

Are you craving for Jesus to quench your thirst? If so, remember Jesus' words, "Whoever believes in me, as Scripture has said, rivers of living water will flow from within them" (John 7:38). And allow the Lord your shepherd to make you lie down in green meadows and to lead you beside the quiet waters (Psalm 23:1–2). Visualize the abundant water, flowing and calm, and the fact that God will truly wipe every tear from your eyes, bringing you the peace and comfort you're longing for.

Dear Lord, I pray there is a place for me at Your
springs of living water. Guide me and console me,
that I may live in Your kingdom forever.

The Messiah

The seventh angel sounded his trumpet, and there were loud voices in heaven, which said: "The kingdom of the world has become the kingdom of our Lord and of his Messiah, and he will reign for ever and ever."

REVELATION 11:15 NIV

You may think these words sound familiar to you, and indeed they should. They appear in George Frideric Handel's *Messiah*, which contains the famous "Hallelujah Chorus." This piece, a three-part oratorio, is performed often, especially around the holidays.

> *The kingdom of this world*
> *Is become the kingdom of our Lord,*
> *And of His Christ, and of His Christ;*
> *And He shall reign forever and ever.*

These joyous words are cause for celebration! Imagine a world of peace, of love, free from strife. That is God's kingdom, where He rules along with Jesus, the Messiah, and where there is no more suffering. No matter what life is bringing you now, you can be sure that one day, the kingdom of the Lord will be there for the taking. You have but to believe His words. And He will reign forever and ever.

> *Dear Lord, Hallelujah! I raise my voice in joyous song and praise toward heaven and look forward to a time when the kingdom of the world is replaced with Your heavenly realm. Blessed be Your eternal reign. Forever and ever.*

Heavenly Musicians

They held harps given them by God and sang the song
of God's servant Moses and of the Lamb: "Great and
marvelous are your deeds, Lord God Almighty. Just and
true are your ways, King of the nations."
REVELATION 15:2–3 NIV

~~~~~

Could there be any more heavenly sound than a choir of harps? This majestic instrument is divine in composition and pitch. And it's the one chosen by God to give to His followers, those who had won the battle over the beast, to accompany their songs of victory and praise.

The Lamb of God, Jesus Christ, also triumphed over evil, sacrificing Himself for our eternal life. His is the ultimate triumph and worthy of praise!

The tradition of raising voices in song goes back many years and is a wonderful way to express praise and joy and to pay tribute to God. "Come, let us sing for joy to the LORD; let us shout aloud to the Rock of our salvation" (Psalm 95:1). Singing can do more than just honor those you praise. As you sing, your spirit and mood cannot help but lift. Give it a try! Sing out loudly! Sing out God's praises. Sing to your Lord!

Dear Lord, I raise my voice in song to praise You as I marvel
at Your amazing deeds! Your victories have saved and sustained
humankind. For that and so much more, I thank You.

Glorious Wedding

Let us rejoice and be glad and give him glory! For the wedding of the Lamb has come, and his bride has made herself ready.
REVELATION 19:7 NIV

Weddings are happy occasions. Generally, those who are invited to witness the nuptials believe the union of two hearts is cause for celebration. And, oddly enough, when a couple appears truly happy, people will often say the match was "made in heaven."

Such is the pure love at the wedding of the Lamb where, at long last, Jesus is united in perfect harmony with His loyal followers. In the perfect world described in Revelation, Jesus and His people will live happily ever after in a world with no pain and no evil. What more could any newlyweds ask?

At weddings between human beings, the bride is radiant. Chances are she's spent an enormous amount of time preparing for this momentous occasion. Such is the case in the heavenly wedding. God's chosen people, the church, have spent a great deal of time in preparation—learning, praying, obeying, and repenting. At the appointed time, the bride, dressed in her gown of righteous deeds, is ready to take those vows.

Blessed will you be—now and forever—if you accept the invitation to this heavenly celebration! Your faith will not just get you through the door but will make you part of the beautiful bride (the Church)!

*Dear Lord, what a joyous occasion is this
ultimate union! Thank You for the invitation!*

No More Tears

" 'He will wipe every tear from their eyes. There will
be no more death' or mourning or crying or pain,
for the old order of things has passed away."

REVELATION 21:4 NIV

❧

Everyone experiences periods of sadness. Sometimes tears flow at the loss of a loved one, and the pain seems overwhelming. Yet death comes to us all, and we're powerless to stop it. Then there are the days when, for no apparent rhyme or reason, sadness just creeps in. Yet there is hope. And it's given to a believer by the God who loves her. He promises each of His daughters a world with no more tears.

In Revelation 21:4, God guarantees there will be no more sadness, mourning, pain, or death. You will no longer be separated from your loved ones. Worry and anguish will be things of the past. It will literally be a new world, a time of peace and joy!

If you are struggling with sadness, if your face is stained with tears, do not lose hope. Your current situation is temporary, and your God promises brighter days will come. The old order of things will pass away to be replaced with the blissful happiness found in dwelling in and with God.

Dear Lord, please wipe my tears away. Help me to trust
in Your words, to remember better times will come,
times when I'll feel no more pain, times when night will
disappear and You will be my only Light.

Contributors

Born in Paraguay, **Terry Alburger** lives in Bucks County, Pennsylvania. She has always had a passion for writing, which blossomed in her position at Brittany Pointe retirement community. Terry is a columnist for a local newspaper, is currently writing her twelfth play, and is the editor of Brittany Pointe's newsletter. Terry's devotions appear in the months of August and December.

Linda Hang is a freelancer from Ohio. She enjoys old movies, kayaking, and discovering each day what God has planned for her—like writing. Her unexpected writing projects include *3-Minute Prayers for Women* and *Unfinished: Devotions and Prayers for a Heart Under Construction.* Linda's devotions appear in the month of July.

Bestselling and award-winning author **Anita Higman** has fifty books published. She's been a Barnes & Noble "Author of the Month" for Houston and has a BA in the combined fields of speech communication, psychology, and art. A few of Anita's favorite things are fairy tale castles, steampunk clothes, traveling through Europe, exotic teas like orchid and heather, romantic movies, and laughing with her friends. Feel free to drop by Anita's website at anitahigman.com or connect with her on her Facebook Reader Page at https://www.facebook.com/AuthorAnitaHigman. She would love to hear from you! Anita's devotions appear in the month of June.

Donna K. Maltese is a freelance writer, editor, and writing coach. Mother of two adult children and grandmother of a little one, she resides in Bucks County, Pennsylvania, with her husband. When not playing with words, Donna is knitting, journaling, reading, or exploring mindscapes within and landscapes without. Donna's devotions appear in the months of May and November.

Carey Scott: Word nerd. Story teller. Life coach. Jesus girl. Raising two rock star kids. Author of *Untangled, Uncommon,* and *Unafraid.* Advocate for authenticity. Coffee lover. Pumpkin spice adorer. Deep-water wader. Texas born but Colorado dweller. Takes up space at CareyScott.org. Carey's devotions appear in the months of January and April.

Stacey Thureen is the author of *Daily Wisdom for the Mommy-to-Be: Everyday Encouragement During Your Pregnancy* and *3-Minute Devotions for Mommy and Me: Encouraging Readings for Parents and Kids ages 3-7* published by Barbour Books. Connect with her at www.StaceyThureen. com. Stacey's readings can be found in the months of February and October.

Janice Thompson is the author of more than one hundred books for the Christian market—including inspirational romances, cozy mysteries, and devotionals. She lives in Spring, Texas, with her three ornery pups and spends her days writing and baking up cakes and cookies. Her tagline "Love, Laughter, and Happily Ever Afters" sums up her take on life. Janice is strong in her faith and does her best to keep the Lord at the center of all she does. Janice's devotions appear in the months of March and September.

Read Thru the Bible in a Year Plan

1/1	Gen. 1-3	2/11	Lev. 21-23
1/2	Gen. 4:1-7:9	2/12	Lev. 24-25
1/3	Gen. 7:10-10:32	2/13	Lev. 26-27
1/4	Gen. 11-14	2/14	Num. 1-2
1/5	Gen. 15-18	2/15	Num. 3-4
1/6	Gen. 19-21	2/16	Num. 5-6
1/7	Gen. 22-24	2/17	Num. 7
1/8	Gen. 25-27	2/18	Num. 8-10
1/9	Gen. 28-29	2/19	Num. 11-12
1/10	Gen. 30-31	2/20	Num. 13-14
1/11	Gen. 32-34	2/21	Num. 15-16
1/12	Gen. 35-36	2/22	Num. 17-19
1/13	Gen. 37-39	2/23	Num. 20-21
1/14	Gen. 40-41	2/24	Num. 22-24
1/15	Gen. 42-43	2/25	Num. 25-27
1/16	Gen. 44-45	2/26	Num. 28-30
1/17	Gen. 46-48	2/27	Num. 31-32
1/18	Gen. 49-50	2/28	Num. 33-34
1/19	Exod. 1-3	3/1	Num. 35-36
1/20	Exod. 4-6	3/2	Deut. 1-2
1/21	Exod. 7-9	3/3	Deut. 3-4
1/22	Exod. 10-12	3/4	Deut. 5-7
1/23	Exod. 13-15	3/5	Deut. 8-11
1/24	Exod. 16-18	3/6	Deut. 12-14
1/25	Exod. 19-20	3/7	Deut. 15-17
1/26	Exod. 21-23	3/8	Deut. 18-20
1/27	Exod. 24-27	3/9	Deut. 21-23
1/28	Exod. 28-29	3/10	Deut. 24-26
1/29	Exod. 30-31	3/11	Deut. 27-28
1/30	Exod. 32-33	3/12	Deut. 29-31
1/31	Exod. 34-35	3/13	Deut. 32-34
2/1	Exod. 36-38	3/14	Josh. 1-2
2/2	Exod. 39-40	3/15	Josh. 3-5
2/3	Lev. 1-4	3/16	Josh. 6-8
2/4	Lev. 5-7	3/17	Josh. 9-10
2/5	Lev. 8-10	3/18	Josh. 11-13
2/6	Lev. 11-12	3/19	Josh. 14-16
2/7	Lev. 13:1-14:32	3/20	Josh. 17-19
2/8	Lev. 14:33-15:33	3/21	Josh. 20-22
2/9	Lev. 16-17	3/22	Josh. 23-24
2/10	Lev. 18-20	3/23	Judg. 1-3

Scripture Index